Praise for *Calling c*

"Offers beautiful, fresh language for Christians of all denominations, sure to deepen the reader's understanding of God and broaden the idea of community. These prayers can enrich our worship, transforming our hearts and—ultimately—strengthening our world."

—Rev. Canon Jan Naylor Cope,
vicar, Washington National Cathedral

"A powerful, prayerful, extremely useful worship aid [for] progressive congregations of many denominations and small base communities alike.... Browse the table of contents when you need just the right prayer for many occasions."

—Diann L. Neu, cofounder and codirector of the Women's
Alliance for Theology, Ethics and Ritual (WATER);
coeditor, *New Feminist Christianity: Many Voices, Many Views*

"Beautifully written, these prayers reflect the integrity of a remarkable worshiping community and come as an inspiring gift to all those who gather weekly to shape and sustain themselves as God's faithful people."

—Rev. Wesley Granberg-Michaelson,
general secretary emeritus,
Reformed Church in America

"In plain but powerful words, [this book] says exactly just what we all would want to say to God."

—Bishop Eugene Taylor Sutton,
Episcopal Diocese of Maryland

"Simply and beautifully conveys the rich tradition of communal prayer that is but one of the many gifts of Seekers Church to the broader Christian community. Rooted in scripture and reflecting that community's concern for peace, social justice, and environmental stewardship, it is sure to enrich the devotional life of both individuals and faith communities."

—William Dietrich, spiritual director; former executive
director, Shalem Institute for Spiritual Formation

"Stirring... A delightful, creative gift of nurture and inspiration for faith communities and personal meditation."

—Rev. Jann Aldredge-Clanton, PhD, author, *She Lives! Sophia Wisdom Works in the World* and *Inclusive Hymns for Liberating Christians*

"[A] rich collection.... Bring[s] human need before God in a poignant and compassionate way. Growing out of the life of one church, this book will bless many."

—Ruth Duck, ThD, professor of worship, Garrett-Evangelical Theological Seminary

"When our way becomes tangled, we search for words. When we are silenced, whether by delight or defeat, worry or wonder, words give shape to our longing. These prayers give us the right words to remember who we are, who God is, and the nature of the journey we are on together. Beautiful words, sacred words, they open us to the Divine and one another. They help us reconnect with what matters most."

—Kayla McClurg, author, *Passage by Passage: A Gospel Journey*; facilitator, *inward/outward*

"A rich treasury of biblically provoked invocations, thanksgivings and prayers of the people. [Readers] will find their imagination and vocabulary for giving thanks to God richly expanded by using these prayers, and all will find an invitation to congregational intercession that is at once comprehensive and concretely real."

—Rev. Taylor W. Burton-Edwards, director of worship resources, the General Board of Discipleship of the United Methodist Church

CALLING ON GOD

Inclusive Christian Prayers for Three Years of Sundays

Peter Bankson & Deborah Sokolove

Walking Together, Finding the Way®
SKYLIGHT PATHS®
PUBLISHING
Woodstock, Vermont

Calling on God:
Inclusive Christian Prayers for Three Years of Sundays

2014 Quality Paperback Edition, First Printing
© 2014 by Peter Bankson and Deborah Sokolove

For information regarding permission to reprint material from this book, please mail or fax your request in writing to SkyLight Paths Publishing, Permissions Department, at the address / fax number listed below, or email your request to permissions@skylightpaths.com.

Readings from the Revised Common Lectionary, © 1992 Consultation on Common Texts, administered by Augsburg Fortress, are reproduced by permission of Augsburg Fortress.

Library of Congress Cataloging-in-Publication Data
Bankson, Peter.
  Calling on God : inclusive Christian prayers for three years of Sundays / by Peter Bankson and Deborah Sokolove.
    pages cm
  Includes bibliographical references.
  ISBN 978-1-59473-568-4 (pbk.)—ISBN 978-1-59473-580-6 (ebook) 1. Prayers. 2. Church year—Prayers and devotions. I. Title.
  BV245.B3155 2014
  264'.13—dc23
                                2014020628
10 9 8 7 6 5 4 3 2 1

Manufactured in the United States of America
Cover design: Michael Myers
Cover art: Deborah Sokolove

SkyLight Paths Publishing is creating a place where people of different spiritual traditions come together for challenge and inspiration, a place where we can help each other understand the mystery that lies at the heart of our existence.
SkyLight Paths sees both believers and seekers as a community that increasingly transcends traditional boundaries of religion and denomination—people wanting to learn from each other, walking together, finding the way.

SkyLight Paths, "Walking Together, Finding the Way" and colophon are trademarks of LongHill Partners, Inc., registered in the U.S. Patent and Trademark Office.

Walking Together, Finding the Way
Published by SkyLight Paths Publishing
A Division of LongHill Partners, Inc.
Sunset Farm Offices, Route 4, P.O. Box 237
Woodstock, VT 05091
Tel: (802) 457-4000 Fax: (802) 457-4004
www.skylightpaths.com

Contents

Year C

Introduction

Prayer is at the heart of spiritual life. Prayer can be formal and public, or deeply personal, as simple as "thank you" or "help me," the immediate cry of the heart to the One who is infinitely beyond us yet as close as our breathing. Silence may also be a form of prayer, in which listening for God's leading is understood as more important than telling God about our needs, desires, and fears. The biblical psalms, composed by the Israelite people largely as prayers addressed to God, speak of anguish and of celebration, of delight in the created universe and of the desire to conquer enemies.

The prayers in this collection were originally written for the public worship of Seekers Church, a small, progressive congregation called to creative liturgical expression, inclusive language, and shared leadership. This shared leadership extends to the writing of texts for congregational prayer, which are created anew for each season of the liturgical year. We have collected these prayers because they are written afresh each week and have never been published elsewhere. The other parts of the service, which are used for an entire season, are available on the Seekers Church website (www.seekerschurch.org/worship/liturgies).

The members of Seekers Church have a strong commitment to the church as chosen family, sharing our lives deeply as we try to live out Christ's command to love one another. Although we meet often in smaller groupings, the center of our life together is Sunday worship, which begins with a gathering time for welcoming guests and making announcements, and ends with lively conversation over coffee for at least an hour after the benediction. In between, we sing and pray in silence and aloud, sharing laughter and tears, using a liturgy that grows out of our life in Christ and is grounded in the liturgical traditions of the Church Universal.

Everyone who prays sometimes struggles for words. This is especially true for those whose understanding of the Divine is both grounded in the biblical tradition and open to new ways to speak to and about God. Whether sitting in silence in a favorite chair, saying grace at the family table, or leading worship for a large congregation, people of faith often fall into habitual patterns of prayer. While the familiar formulas of prayers learned by heart are often a comfort to the soul, at other times we are called to name the extravagant wildness of God, the overflowing abundance of creation, and the deep aching need of a broken world in new words and images that speak to contemporary concerns.

The prayers in this volume fall into this second category. They are an invitation to pray boldly, to speak to God directly, giving thanks for everything from whales and microbes to mobile phones and supermarkets, and asking God to heal all the many instances of brokenness that we see around us. In addition to the texts that are repeated over several weeks, each Sunday the person leading worship composes an opening prayer and a set of "bidding prayers," inviting the prayers of the people. Each of us has a unique style, but schooled by our collective writing discipline we strive to make our bidding prayers poetic, evocative, and connected both to Scripture and to everyday life. In this book we offer some of those prayers, drawn from those Peter and Deborah have composed for leading worship in our beloved church. (Since they were composed over many years, and the liturgical seasons do not always line up with the meteorological seasons, do not be surprised if in some of them the references to the natural world may be celebrating the coming of spring, while the following week may be bemoaning an unnaturally long winter.) We hope that as you use them as inspiration for your own prayers, whether in community or for your private devotions, you will adapt them to your particular situation and adjust the imagery to fit with the world outside your windows.

Year A

ADVENT

FIRST SUNDAY OF ADVENT

Isaiah 2:1–5; Psalm 122; Romans 13:11–14; Matthew 24:36–44

Opening Prayer

Just and merciful Light of the world,
  you call us to be your people,
  to come into your holy presence
  that we may learn your ways
  and walk in the paths of peace.

You show us your goodness in every sunrise,
  opening our eyes to a world washed clean,
  inviting us to delight in fat sparrows feasting on suet,
  and to laugh at black squirrels racing up tree trunks
  and dogs leaping through drifts of brown, fallen leaves.

As we yearn for the days of your promised coming,
  hold us in the warm embrace of your holy Body,
  and teach us how to live not only for our own pleasure,
  but for the healing of the world. Amen.

Thanksgiving and Praise

Just and merciful Creator of life and love,
  every moment is a gift from you,
  a glimpse of the peace and plenty for all
  that you promised our ancestors in faith.

We give you thanks for sunlight so bright that it hurts our eyes,
  and for long, dark nights filled with sparkling stars.

We give you thanks for quick emails and long conversations,
for festive meals and quick snacks on the run,
for memories of years gone by
and hopes for new tomorrows,
for the comforts of home and the challenges of travel,
for nightly rest and days filled with work and play.

We give thanks, most of all,
for your promise that the day is coming
when every person and nation will walk in your holy light,
and your great love will rule every heart.

And for what else shall we give thanks this day?

Petition and Intercession

Just and merciful Judge of peoples and of hearts,
you tell us to beat our swords into plowshares,
and our spears into pruning hooks,
and promise that nation
shall not lift up sword against nation,
neither shall they learn war any more.

Yet we still hear of wars and rumors of wars,
of oppression and slavery and random killing,
of rage and hatred and every kind of evil.

And so we cry out, O God, and ask,
When will it end? When will your reign of peace begin?

Hear the cries of your people, O God,
as we pray for justice,
as we pray for healing,
as we pray for peace,
in words that are spoken aloud
and those held in the silence of our hearts.

SECOND SUNDAY OF ADVENT

Isaiah 11:1–10; Psalm 72:1–7, 18–19; Romans 15:4–13; Matthew 3:1–12

▬▬▬ Opening Prayer ▬▬▬

God of wisdom and understanding,
  God of steadfastness and encouragement,
  God of hope and peace,
  you fill us with awe and delight
  when we contemplate your love and grace.

You have created a world of beauty and wonder,
  where frozen forest pathways glitter like diamonds,
  where flocks of starlings draw elegant patterns
  on the darkening sky,
  where bare branches are already tipped
  with the promise of spring.

Long ago you came to live among us,
  and promised to come again,
  bringing a world of peace and plenty,
  where no one will hurt or destroy or oppress,
  where the mountains and hills and valleys and plains
  yield enough for all to share.

As you live in us and around us and through us now,
  teach us to become the living Body of Christ,
  on whom your Spirit rests,
  whose delight is to live in awe of you. Amen.

▬▬▬ Thanksgiving and Praise ▬▬▬

God of steadfastness and encouragement,
  God of hope and peace,
  God of wisdom and understanding,
  your creation breaks our hearts
  with its fragile yet enduring beauty,
  the everyday gifts of breath and life.

We give you thanks for the crunch of fallen leaves,
   announcing our passage with every footstep;
   we give you thanks for the soothing warmth of hearty soup,
   our frigid fingertips cupped around the bowl;
   we give you thanks for the silvery sheen of ice,
   transforming a dirty puddle into a fleeting vision of glory.

We give you thanks for your promises
   to deliver us from all that keeps us from you,
   for filling us with the joy and peace
   of believing in your Holy Child, Jesus,
   and showering us with the abundant hope of your Holy Spirit.
   And for what else shall we give thanks this day?

▬▬▬ Petition and Intercession ▬▬▬

God of hope and peace,
   God of wisdom and understanding,
   God of steadfastness and encouragement,
   our gratitude for your many gifts opens our hearts,
   and we plead for a world that is still broken and bereft.

Where is the ruler who will judge the poor with righteousness
   and decide with equity for the meek of the earth?

Where is the savior who will defend the cause of the poor,
   give deliverance to the needy, and crush the oppressor?

Where is the one who will bring an end to war and violence,
   wipe away every tear, and bring comfort to all who mourn?

You, O God, are that one, and it is to you that we cry out.

We pray that you will show us how to provide
   adequate homes for those who have none,
   good schools where all children can learn in safety,
   and neighborhoods where everyone
   can live and work in peace.

We pray that you will show us
   how to use the earth's resources wisely,
   without pollution and destruction,

to share what we produce, so that all will have enough,
to care for those who are unable to care for themselves.

We pray for justice and for peace,
for healing and for strength,
for ourselves, for those who are close to us,
and for those whom we have never met.

Aloud and in silence, we bring our prayers to you.

THIRD SUNDAY OF ADVENT

Isaiah 35:1–10; Luke 1:46b–55; James 5:7–10; Matthew 11:2–11

Opening Prayer

Holy Maker of heaven and earth,
of seas and rivers and valleys and plains,
we magnify and sanctify your holy name
and rejoice every day in you, our God, our Savior,
for you keep faith forever with all who seek you.

You have placed us in a world filled with wonders,
where new-fallen snow nestles like flowers
in the crooks of pine branches;
where ice crystals draw lacy shades on windowpanes;
where the sound of sleet falling on rooftops
becomes a rhythmic lullaby in the long, dark night.

As we wait for signs of your promised reign,
help us to stay awake,
to prepare the way for your coming,
to become the living Body of Christ,
who comes to us as Jesus, in whose name we pray. Amen.

Thanksgiving and Praise

Holy Giver of light and life,
of hope for the future and memory of all that has gone before,
we magnify and sanctify your holy name
and rejoice every day in you, our God, our Savior,

for you have made us and sustained us
and brought us to this day.
We give you thanks for the promise
to fill the hungry with good things,
to open the eyes of those who refuse to see,
to raise up those who are bowed down,
and to set the prisoners free.

We give you thanks for the promise hidden in bare branches,
that they will sprout forth new growth in spring
and shade in the summer.

We give you thanks for the simple pleasures of each day,
of hats and mittens and scarves,
of warm coats and warm rooms,
of friends that celebrate with us in our joys,
and comfort us when we are hurt.

We give you thanks for life itself,
for each new morning filled with promise,
for days filled with work and play,
for healing rest when we lie down to sleep.
And for what else shall we give thanks this day?

Petition and Intercession

Holy Comforter of all who are afflicted,
we magnify and sanctify your holy name
and rejoice in you, our God, our Savior,
for you look with favor on all who are in need of mercy.

You have promised a world in which all who are cast out
shall come to you with singing;
everlasting joy shall be upon their heads;
they shall obtain joy and gladness,
and sorrow and sighing shall flee away.

And yet we look at the world around us,
and see that these promises are not yet fulfilled,
and we cry out to you for justice, for peace, for healing.

We pray for immigrants and migrants,
  who hope for a better life for themselves and their children,
  but too often find only exploitation and misery.
We pray for all who are imprisoned,
  who hope for a better life when they are released,
  but too often are barred
  from work, from homes, from families.

We pray for all whose lives are marked by poverty and need,
  for those who are sick or in pain,
  for those who are broken in spirit or in mind,
  that you will keep your promise
  that the blind will receive their sight,
  the lame walk, the lepers be cleansed,
  the deaf hear, the dead be raised,
  and the poor have good news brought to them.

Holy Comforter of all who are afflicted,
  we bring to you our prayers of petition and intercession
  whether spoken aloud or hidden in the silence of our hearts.

FOURTH SUNDAY OF ADVENT

Isaiah 7:10–16; Psalm 80:1–7, 17–19; Romans 1:1–7; Matthew 1:18–25

 Opening Prayer

God of prophecy and promise,
  God of new beginnings,
  God of comfort and joy,
  you have promised to give us a sign,
  to restore our hope,
  to let your face shine on all your people.

Even as we wait for your coming, you show yourself to us
  in the glimmer of ice crystals
  frosting windowpanes and gateposts;
  in the drifts of dead, brown leaves
  that flutter in the blustery wind;

in the bright, full moon,
floating behind thin clouds just before dawn.

In these fragile moments of glory,
and in the ancient stories that we hear anew today,
the good news of your coming reign is made real,
not for us alone, but for the healing of the world.

Grant grace and peace to us
and to all who are called as your beloved,
that we may become the Body of Christ,
in whose name we pray. Amen.

Thanksgiving and Praise

God of new beginnings,
God of comfort and joy,
God of prophecy and promise,
we give you thanks for every moment of our lives.

We give you thanks for the wind and cold of winter,
for stars and planets and glowing moon,
for the earth we walk on,
for the food and water and air that sustain us.

We give you thanks for wrapping paper and bright ribbons,
for the cards and notes that remind us of distant friends,
for the carols of joy that fill our ears and open our hearts,
even as we wait for your promised coming.

Aloud and in the silence of our hearts,
we thank you for all your gifts to us and to the world.

Petition and Intercession

God of comfort and joy,
God of prophecy and promise,
God of new beginnings,
we trust in your promises of healing and salvation.

Still, as we wait for your coming to be among us,
we see the signs of brokenness,

of heartache,
of desolation and grief,
on every street corner
and hidden in every heart.
In this season of cold, short days and long, cold nights,
we pray that you will make a place
for every man and woman and child who searches,
like Mary and Joseph, for a place to call home,
who yearns in vain for a warm, familiar bed.

We pray that you will give strength and courage
to all who are about to give birth,
to all who yearn for children,
to all who have opened their hearts
to children they have not borne.

We pray that you will comfort all who are approaching death,
all who mourn or live with daily pain,
all who are broken in body or mind or spirit.

Above all, we pray that you will keep your promise
to live among us and fill all the earth with grace and peace.

And for what else shall we pray this day?

CHRISTMASTIDE

FIRST SUNDAY AFTER CHRISTMAS DAY

Isaiah 63:7–9; Psalm 148; Hebrews 2:10–18; Matthew 2:13–23

Opening Prayer

God of life and love,
  Holy Mystery of wildness and order,
  Prolific Creator of every thought and thing,

We come together here to celebrate
  the mystery of your gift of life,
  the wonder of your gift of consciousness,
  the great joy of your gift of Christ among us.

Draw our hearts together in one act of worship,
  as we have drawn ourselves together in this place,
  for we long to worship you in spirit and in truth. Amen.

Thanksgiving and Praise

God of life and love,
  like Mary and Joseph,
  who fled to Egypt when you warned them through a dream,
  we listen for your call.

We wait with praise and thanksgiving rising from within.
This cold morning at the end of a turbulent year,
  we raise our voices with the angels and the seas,
  the mountains and the flocks.

We marvel at how fast our world is changing,
  at all the signs of change, and hope, and new life.
We celebrate your coming among us as a child,
  the coming of a new year,
  the way you guide us so mysteriously out of danger.
God of all creation,
  hear our prayers of praise and thanks
  as we lift them in the silence of our hearts
  and share them aloud in the sacred silence of this place.

Petition and Intercession

God of life and love,
  Holy Mystery of wildness and order,
  Fertile Creator of everything,
  although we celebrate, the pain is never far away.
We know so many places of brokenness and separation;
  so much anger and distrust.
Like children, we want to know the reason why.
Why did Herod have to slay those baby boys in Bethlehem?
Why must there be death now on our streets?
Why must so many people have no work,
  no way to support themselves?
Why do we cut ourselves off from each other?
Why is there suffering and death?
Holy Mystery,
  who in your unfathomable wisdom
  has made us without full understanding,
  hear our prayers for those in pain and need.
We pray for discernment and acceptance
  as we wait on your call, and act in your name,
  through the enlivening power of our Savior,
  who is Jesus the Christ.

Second Sunday after Christmas Day

Jeremiah 31:7–14; Psalm 147:12–20; Ephesians 1:3–14;
John 1:(1–9), 10–18

▬▬▬ Opening Prayer ▬▬▬

Holy Maker of all,
  you strengthen our boundaries,
  set limits on our aspirations,
  and fill us with a kind of hope
  that may seem foolish, but shows us how to live.

Holy Mystery, incarnate in an infant,
  we pray that you reveal yourself among us
  as we gather to celebrate the coming of your Word
  as flesh and blood in our midst.

We gather here this morning,
  eager for the brightness of your presence deep within us.

Fill us with the fire of your love;
  bind us to each other in your body—
  for we come to worship in the name of your baby,
  our Savior, who is Jesus, the Christ. Amen.

▬▬▬ Thanksgiving and Praise ▬▬▬

All-powerful God of Creation,
  you started with the Word,
  and through that formed all life,
  and placed the light of love within us.

Your mighty power sends the snow like wool,
  scatters frost like ashes, and hurls down hail like crumbs.

Then in an instant, O holy Source of all being,
  you send out your Word
  to melt the frozen fear that is so common,
  to free the living water, bringing reconciliation.

O God, you take the future from our hands.
  No matter how much we want to be in control,

to know now how things will turn out,
  to shape the coming week, or year,
  your future is unknowable to us, so we must hope.

No matter how much we want to understand,
  to know the reasons for the pain and suffering we see,
  to have a theory for the way
  our lives have come to be the way they are,
  your wisdom is unknowable to us, so we must trust.

Yet we are called to celebrate your presence with us
  in this world you have created,
  your self-portrait, your autobiography.

Hear now our prayers of thanksgiving and praise,
  spoken out in the silence of this sanctuary
  and lifted up in the sanctuary of our hearts.

▬ **Petition and Intercession** ▬

Holy God of new life,
  even though you take the future from our hands,
  you give us a way to help, calling us to a kind of hope
  that goes beyond all understanding.
We hope for peace and reconciliation
  in places besieged by conflict,
  for justice in the face of tyranny,
  and for healing in body, mind, and spirit.
O God, your light has come to fill us with new life,
  to defend the cause of those who are poor,
  to deliver those who are needy,
  to help usher in days of righteousness and peace.
With love from you that fills our hearts with hope,
  we offer now our prayers for those in need,
  spoken into the silence
  and lifted up in the silence of our hearts.

THE EPIPHANY OF CHRIST

Isaiah 60:1–6; Psalm 72:1–7, 10–14; Ephesians 3:1–12;
Matthew 2:1–12

Opening Prayer

Holy Source of this fresh new year,
   give us opportunities to reflect on what has gone before,
   on what we may encounter on the road ahead.

You invite us to begin again.

Come open the gates of your city so we may enter in;
   fill us with the mysterious baptism of your love;
   bind us to each other in your body—
   for we are here to worship in the name of your chosen one,
   our Savior, who is Jesus, the Christ. Amen.

Thanksgiving and Praise

Holy Light of love,
   shining brightly in the dark corners of our lives,
   we wake up in your presence,
   startled by your gentle embrace.
This day we celebrate your recognition by wise leaders
   as they found you in a lowly state.
We celebrate the way your love flowed
   even in those early days, washing clear a path of simple truth,
   strong enough to shake the wilderness,
   a healing voice of sacrificial love.

We are amazed so often by the power of that love,
  and give you thanks for calling us to you.
We know the warmth of slow fireside conversations,
  the caring word that comes
  when we most need and least expect it,
  the comfort of relationships bound together by years of love.
Hear now our prayers of praise and thanks
  as they well up within us, and float out on the air we share.

▰▰▰ **Petition and Intercession** ▰▰▰

O God, you take the future out of our hands
  no matter how much we want to be in control,
  to know what's coming next,
  to shape the coming week, or year, of life.
We feel the pain of war in distant lands,
  the shame of greed, neglect, and strife across our nation,
  and the guilt of misunderstanding and disappointment
  right here in our midst.
We want to claim control,
  to take the future in our hands,
  to make it right,
  but often our way is not your Way, the way of love.
Loving God, even though you take the future from our hands,
  you do give us a way to help:
  you call us, as individuals and as a community,
  to love, to pray,
  to care for those whose needs we know about.
We bring our prayers to you,
  our prayers for those in need, and for ourselves,
  that we may understand in fresh, new ways,
  the call you have for each of us,
  and for this faith community you have called to life.
Hear now, O Lord of love, our prayers for those in need.

ORDINARY TIME

The Sundays after Epiphany

BAPTISM OF CHRIST
(FIRST SUNDAY AFTER EPIPHANY)

ORDINARY I

Isaiah 42:1–9; Psalm 29; Acts 10:34–43; Matthew 3:13–17

Opening Prayer

Holy Mystery, you came to walk among us,
  leading us toward the waters of baptism,
  inviting us to enter into your life as healer,
  as servant,
  as Light of the world.

Holy Maker of past and future,
  you bless children and elders,
  filling them with stories and love,
  showing us the promise of new things
  hidden in what has come before.

Holy Breather of life everlasting,
  reveal yourself among us as we celebrate
  your coming as flesh and blood in our midst,
  the beloved Child of God, our Savior, Jesus the Christ. Amen.

Thanksgiving and Praise

Blessed are you, Holy One, Creator of heaven and earth,
  Breather of life everlasting,
  Mystery beyond our knowing,
  for giving us life

and sustaining us
and bringing us to this day.

We give you thanks for the rich diversity of the universe
where each day you bring us into being.

We give thanks for the land,
lying quietly these cold, dark days,
getting ready to bring forth life again.

We give thanks for the creatures you have made in such variety,
seeking safe places to rest
as they get ready for what lies ahead.

We give thanks for the people
of many lands and languages and traditions
as we look forward to longer days
and new opportunities for caring and compassion.

We see your creative hand at play in so many ways,
and we give thanks for new beginnings.

Hear now our prayers of praise and thanksgiving,
spoken aloud and held in the silence of our hearts.

Petition and Intercession

God of past and future,
Light of the world,
Creative Spirit,
you are always calling us to righteousness,
to new possibilities for peace and justice.

But sometimes we lack the vision to see those possibilities,
the commitment to claim them as our own,
the strength to carry what seems like more than we can bear.

We see so many places where pain and need are piled deep,
like snowdrifts that block the way,
delivered by a blizzard of anger, fear, or hatred.

We know that your loving Holy Spirit
can melt the dark of doubt and fear,
and pray that we might be channels of your healing grace.

Hear now our prayers for those who are in pain,
  for those who are out in the cold,
  for those for whom we have promised to pray,
  and for our own needs
  as we seek to be channels of your grace
  for the healing of the world.

SECOND SUNDAY AFTER EPIPHANY

ORDINARY 2

Isaiah 49:1–7; Psalm 40:1–11; 1 Corinthians 1:1–9; John 1:29–42

Opening Prayer

Holy God of all creation,
  we gather here to worship you
  with praise and prayer and song.
We're here to celebrate the way your Spirit moves among us,
  to celebrate the way
  you draw us up from pits of desolation,
  to celebrate the way you put the solid rock of community
  here, beneath our feet.
Loving Maker of community, we gather in the name of Jesus,
  who is the Christ,
  the one who shows us how to hope,
  even when voices all around
  are warning us to be afraid. Amen.

Thanksgiving and Praise

God of constant creativity, even when we can't see anything
  that looks like signs or miracles,
  we know that you are bringing hope,
  and we give thanks.
Holy Maker of all this complex reality
  we welcome sisters and brothers in the family of faith,
  who come to share the hope you pour into their lives,
  to raise their voices in a call for peace and justice,

to help us know that you are present everywhere,
and we give thanks.

They're here to tell the good news of your presence,
to share with us the hope they have seen,
to wonder with us over what we long to see
and share the hope you send to all of us.
Hear now our prayers of praise and thanks,
for we would hold your healing light high overhead,
a light to comfort and encourage all.

▬▬ **Petition and Intercession** ▬▬

Holy Builder of the promise of tomorrow,
we live with so much turbulent uncertainty,
with such a sense that things are as they've never been
and will not be this way again, no matter how we try.

This constant change erodes our understanding,
gives pain and fear a firm foundation,
and threatens to keep hope on the run.
We watch as violence erupts
with anger, fear, and condemnation piling up.

We listen to the cries of those whose plans and dreams
are tossed aside by anger, violence, disease,
or by the callous disregard of others who might help.

We feel the strain of fighting illness,
the hollow grief of mourning death,
the paralyzing fear of facing powers
who have lost whatever vision
of just mercy they might once have had.

Holy Maker of the universe,
hear now our prayers for those in pain and need,
and for ourselves, for we would be your hopeful people.

THIRD SUNDAY AFTER EPIPHANY

ORDINARY 3

Isaiah 9:1–4; Psalm 27:1, 4–9; 1 Corinthians 1:10–18; Matthew 4:12–23

Opening Prayer

O wondrous Imagination, Creator of the universe,
  we gather again to be present to you in community,
  surrounded by our chosen family of faith.

We gather again to celebrate the power of your Holy Spirit,
  a steady source of hope
  in the midst of gray, dormant times
  before the coming of spring.

As you are filling the cold soil with shoots of green life,
  we pray that you will fill our hearts
  with swelling shouts of joy,
  for we gather in the name of your incarnate presence,
  our Savior, who is Jesus the Christ. Amen.

Thanksgiving and Praise

Holy God of earlier dawns and softening air,
  we give you thanks
  that life is more tenacious than ice.

We give you thanks
  that you have called us into community,
  and sent us out to work for justice and mercy
  in all the places where we live and work and love and play.

God of hope that will not go away,
  even in the face of haughty, self-promoting righteousness,
  we give you thanks that light still overcomes the darkness.

Hear now, O holy Lover of life,
  our prayers of praise and thanks.

Petition and Intercession

Holy Creator of the universe,
  you are our light and our salvation;
  whom shall we fear?

You are the stronghold of our lives;
  of whom shall we be afraid?

When faithful people are assailed by evildoers
  who utter slanders against them,
  these adversaries stumble and fall.

And we know it is your love that brings justice in the end,
  O God of all creation.

Isaiah prophesied that there will be no gloom
  in the land that was filled with anguish,
  for the people who walked in darkness have seen a great light;
  those who dwelt in a land of great shadows,
  on them has light shined.

O God of Abraham and Sarah,
  God of Jesus and Mary and Joseph, and all of the disciples,
  we claim that promise,
  for we are dwelling in a land filled with anguish.

We know so many places where war and poverty
  have forced people from their homes;
  where illness and despair grip the hearts
  of people who live without hope;
  where children lash out at those
  who seem to have stolen their future.

Holy Source of light in the darkness,
  hear now our prayers for those in pain and need,
  our prayers for one another and for ourselves,
  for we are fragile earthen vessels,
  cracked and yet still loved and called by you.

Fourth Sunday after Epiphany

Ordinary 4

Micah 6:1–8; Psalm 15; 1 Corinthians 1:18–31; Matthew 5:1–12

▭▭▭▭ Opening Prayer ▭▭▭▭

Holy God of all creation, we know that you are everything.
You call us into community, and bless us
 even when we are suffering and rejected by the world.

And so we come here,
 gathered in this place
 to give you thanks with our whole hearts,
 O Holy One.

Fill us with your love, we pray,
 for we know we are your people,
 gathered in the name of Christ. Amen.

▭▭▭▭ Thanksgiving and Praise ▭▭▭▭

God of bright, crisp winter skies,
 God of the goose, the squirrel, and the human too,
 holy God of all creation,
 we celebrate the mystery of your world,
 so full of hope and contradictions.

This week you brought the cherry trees to bloom;
 we hope those fragile blossoms make it through the frigid night.

We give you thanks that even when we feel poor in spirit
 you have promised us a place of honor in your realm.

We thank you for the comfort that flows from you
 to those who mourn,
 and for the peacemakers,
 who gather close around you
 like beloved children.

Although they may seem foolish
 to those wise in worldly ways,
 your blessings pour out in an ever-flowing stream,
 washing pain and desolation into quiet pools of healing love.

We thank you for your faithful love of all creation,
  for all the ways you open up our eyes
  to see the goodness in this living land,
  for teaching us that this creation
  is ours to care for, ours to love.
Hear now our prayers of praise and thanks,
  our songs of joy and hope.

Petition and Intercession

O loving, healing God,
  we've brought our burdens with us,
  our neatly bundled bags of hurt and disappointment,
  our righteous anger,
  our outrage over how injustice seems to have the upper hand.

We know so many places where anger dominates,
  so many faces twisted shut by pain and grief.
You've called us into this community
  so we can learn to love and serve,
  so we can take our place as cocreators.

But the weight of all those burdens
  is often more than we can bear alone.

As we pray for your forgiving presence,
  we ask for strength to bear the load,
  for wisdom in the face of violence and anger.

Hear now our prayers for those we know
  who carry anger, pain, and grief,
  and for ourselves,
  for we would empty ourselves as we serve one another here
  and leave to serve the wider world of your creation.

FIFTH SUNDAY AFTER EPIPHANY
ORDINARY 5
Isaiah 58:1–9a, (9b–12); Psalm 112:1–9, (10);
1 Corinthians 2:1–12, (13–16); Matthew 5:13–20

═══ Opening Prayer ═══

God of all creation, holy Maker of this universe,
  we come together here as one small band of your people,
  called to be salt of the earth, a necessary seasoning
  for this rich, complex concoction
  where you have called us into life.

We come because you call us to be your people;
  you call us forth from many places, many histories;
  you call us to become one body
  through the miracle of Christ.

O God of every hope of new life for the earth,
  we pray that you will fill us with your love,
  for we gather in the name of Jesus, who is the Christ. Amen.

═══ Thanksgiving and Praise ═══

God of winter waiting, we watch the earth emerge again
  from wet, gray blankets, like a child struggling with a fever.

We wonder if the warm, damp air
  has raised our hopes for new beginnings
  farther than the weather will allow.

In this between-time, we stop
  and watch for signs of you around us in the world.

God of hungry waiting, we now raise our voices
  to share the many ways
  we know that you are here.

May we be the ink, the pen,
  the blank pages of your journal of good news,
  for we would be the people of the risen Christ,
  in whose name we live our lives together.

Hear now our prayers of praise and thanks,
for the bounty and the promise of this life.

Petition and Intercession

God of hope in life begun again beyond our sight,
we know our understanding is so limited.

So many times, we transform an opportunity
for learning and compassion
into an opportunity for righteous indignation.
So many times, we lose the lesson in the pain.

Today, we bring to you the pain and suffering
we feel and see around us.
We pray for healing in a world
torn by violence in distant lands
and on our streets at home.
We pray for healing in our nation,
dragged through the mud of sin and accusation,
wrangling and defense.
We pray for healing in ourselves,
facing the pain of illness and diminishment and grief.

For we would stand with the prophet Isaiah,
who recognized that the sacrifice you call us to
means sharing bread with the hungry,
and bringing the homeless poor into our homes,
and covering the naked, rather than hiding ourselves.

Hear now our prayers for those in need.

SIXTH SUNDAY AFTER EPIPHANY
PROPER I, ORDINARY 6

Deuteronomy 30:15–20; Psalm 119:1–8; 1 Corinthians 3:1–9;
Matthew 5:21–37

Opening Prayer

God of all creation, maker of the snowflake and the iceberg,
holy Illustrator of infinite uniqueness,

we gather here this winter morning,
hungry to know that we are your people.

Blow your Holy Spirit into us
like one crisp, creative, cosmic wind.
Fill us with an understanding of what it really means
to be called by you.

Help us know your presence as that holy healing breath,
the *ruah* of redemption,
for we gather in the name of your child Jesus,
who is the Christ, the bearer of good news. Amen.

▬▬▬ Thanksgiving and Praise ▬▬▬

Loving, nurturing Maker of meaning,
this year the quince and cherry
had almost offered up their blossoms for the year
before the snow came, and the icy wind.

And now the blooms are waiting,
just the white and salmon promise
of a week of springtime splendor
peeking through the calyx wrap
that keeps the icy wind at bay.

We're thankful for the wisdom of the garden
in the face of this erratic coming of the spring,
with lazy, warming promises and sudden frigid threats
like heavy breathing of the land in labor.

We're thankful, too, that we are often given signs
that even though the path into the future seems so clear,
it may be right to wait
until the days are longer and the soil is a little warmer.

O master Gardener of community,
we bring our prayers of praise and thanks to you,
our thanks for guidance in tense transition times,
our praise for promises that wait beneath the snow.
And what else, O Holy One,
shall we raise up in thanks and praise?

Petition and Intercession

Loving Healer of the land,
  maker of the rain that fills the earth
  with wet promise of growth to come,
  we know how painful life can be.

We know so many whose pain has grown so big
  they cannot see around it.

We know so many who are suffering from illness or injustice,
  from fear or deep frustration, from shame or poverty.

We think of Jesus's guidance to work for reconciliation,
  and see so many places
  where righteous indignation seems to hold the higher ground.

We think that if it's going to be right
  it must be complicated.

We think that asking someone else to help
  is often more than we can bear.

And yet, O holy, loving Healer of creation,
  we know you call us to be loving healers too,
  even in our brokenness.

Hear now our prayers for those in need,
  and for ourselves,
  who feel more need than we can easily admit.

SEVENTH SUNDAY AFTER EPIPHANY
PROPER 2, ORDINARY 7

Leviticus 19:1–2, 9–18; Psalm 119:33–40; 1 Corinthians 3:10–11,
16–23; Matthew 5:38–48

Opening Prayer

O Holy One, we come into your presence
  as people drawn together by a distant light.

We come just as we are, with doubt and confusion
  blowing wildly through our hope.

But we know that this is a place that nurtures hope,
   and so we gather again to remind ourselves
   that we are your people.

Holy Mystery, we pray that you will fill this hour
   with the brightness of your presence,
   for we gather in the name of our Savior,
   who is Jesus the Christ.

Thanksgiving and Praise

Holy, loving Mystery of life,
   we see again that your epiphanies
   are all around us, waiting for us to recognize them.

Yesterday the sun rose strong,
   blown into every dark corner by a wind
   that bent the bare trees to their roots.

That bright light helps us see that once again
   the faithful crocus reaches up to celebrate,
   to call the neighborhood to foolish hope.

Epiphanies are where we find them.
Your law is always there to guide us,
   to show us what is good and just,
   to help us learn to love our enemies,
   to not defraud our neighbor.

You call us out to see that hope is still alive.
We're thankful for the brightness of the moon,
   reminding us, with cold, clear light,
   that if we will keep our eyes fixed on you,
   you will show us paths to hope.

A tiny glimmer out there between the trees,
   a shiny token of your holy, endless love that we can barely see,
   strikes some deep chord of recognition,
   shows us what we have only felt before.
   Our feet are on the ground,
   our hands are making something useful,

and there are others in our sight—
pilgrims whom we could only hear before,
your body in the flesh.

We give you thanks that meaning comes in unexpected ways,
and raise our prayers of thanks
for all the ways we know your presence with us.
Hear now those prayers of praise and thanks.

Petition and Intercession

God of mystery,
we pray that as you turn our hearts to your decrees,
and help us reach out in compassion
to those in pain and need,
that you will strengthen us to bear the pain we see,
around us and within,
and move ahead in foolish hope
that somewhere in the dark your candle glows.

Show us the light that leads,
renew our faith,
and help us find and walk the path we've never seen,
for we have come together here
to remember that we are your people,
the people of the living Christ,

Hear now our prayers, O loving God,
for all those who are suffering today.

Eighth Sunday after Epiphany
Proper 3, Ordinary 8
Isaiah 49:8–16a; Psalm 131; 1 Corinthians 4:1–5; Matthew 6:24–34

Opening Prayer

O holy, mysterious Maker of creation,
  surround us with your strong arms,
  spirit us away into the depths of your heart,
  show us signs of hope, we pray.

For we would learn to trust our lives to you,
  to see the lesson in the beauty of the lilies,
  to serve you as your faithful people,
  gathered here today to pray and learn,
  to sing and celebrate
  as you welcome us into the realm of righteousness,
  where Jesus is the bearer of good news, the Christ. Amen.

Thanksgiving and Praise

God of all creation, we bless you.
God of a past remembered and a future hidden from our eyes,
  we praise your holy name.
We come because you have called us to be your people.
We come, even though we cannot see where you are leading us.
We come as stewards of your holy mysteries,
  resting our hope on you, O Holy One.

We offer praise and thanks for new life,
  shown forth in emerging crocus and circling geese,
  in fresh dreams for a peaceful future,
  and the unformed shape of things to come;
  the hope of reconciliation,
  and your call to the work that gives our lives away in love.

Hear now our prayers of praise and thanks,
  for the hope that is within us,
  for the dreams you choose to give us,

and for the faith to move ahead
into a future we cannot anticipate.

Petition and Intercession

God of mercy and history,
  loving God of all that is and all that shall ever be,
  we know that throughout history
  you have come to those who needed healing,
  to those who were suffering from pain and poverty and grief.

We know that throughout history
  you have called your faithful people
  to be stewards of your mysteries,
  to trust you always,
  and pour out our hearts to you in prayer.

We know that Jesus came to help us understand
  that we are called to seek your realm today
  and let you hold the future in your loving embrace.

We bring to you the burdens of our lives:
  the pain and fear that burdens those we love;
  the pain and fear that burdens those
  we do not yet know well enough to love.
We bring the pain that we have caused
  and the pain we have suffered.

We pray that the gift of your healing
  may be poured on all those places
  where people rise up against oppression,
  where threat and violence cause fears to rise
  and hearts to close against the needs of others.

We pray for hope to see the mystery of your healing love
  poured out for the healing of war and violence and discord,
  and for the faith to offer what we have to those in need,
  even if we think we don't have much to give.

Hear now our prayers for those in need
  around the world,

across the land,

within this room,

and deep within our hearts.

NINTH SUNDAY AFTER EPIPHANY
PROPER 4, ORDINARY 9

Deuteronomy 11:18–21, 26–28; Psalm 31:1–5, 19–24;
Romans 1:16–17, 3:22b–28, (29–31); Matthew 7:21–29

Opening Prayer

Holy God of storm and sun,

we are pulled from darkness by the majesty of your dawn.

We gather in this place

to celebrate your love for us,

your presence with us,

your life flowing through us.

Come among us O holy Maker of the universe,

come fill us with the power of your presence,

for we gather in the spirit of our Savior, Jesus,

who is the Christ. Amen.

Thanksgiving and Praise

Persistent Originator of new life,

as days grow longer,

we see the fresh new growth

in rising shoots and budding stalks,

signs that there will be another harvest.

Holy Fount of every blessing,

you call us to obey your commandments.

We feel the urge

to help your teaching grow new buds and shoots,

sprouting in our hearts and souls,

inspiring teaching for the children

and conversation whether we are at home or on the way.

And when we fail to do
   the work you call us to, O God of love,
      you offer us forgiveness and reconciliation
      through the life and death and resurrection of Jesus.

Thanks be to you that we are saved by faith
   and called to work,
      to be your servants in these complicated times.

Today we bring our prayers of praise and thanks
   for commandments that will help us
   be your Body in the time and place,
   and for your loving forgiveness,
   that through our faith in Christ
   we can be restored to right relationship
   with you and within your Body.

And, O Holy One, for what else
   shall we offer prayers of praise and thanks?

Petition and Intercession

Amazing Mystery of healing faith,
   God of loving reconciliation,
   we know so many places
      where lives and reputations seem built on sand,
      unable to withstand the pressures of a world
      bent on self-satisfaction,
      a world that seems bereft of radical compassion.

Holy Fount of every blessing,
   we pray for those who suffer pain from illness, violence,
   and loss of loving support.

Hear now our prayers for those in need,
   the ones we've carried by ourselves
   as though by strength alone we could bring healing—
   our prayers for those we think we can't reach out to
   because our fear or anger
   keeps us from the depths of your unfailing love.

We share our prayers aloud into this faithful place,
and lift them in the silence of our hearts.

TRANSFIGURATION (LAST SUNDAY AFTER EPIPHANY)

Exodus 24:12–18; Psalm 2 or Psalm 99; 2 Peter 1:16–21;
Matthew 17:1–9

Opening Prayer

Eternal, incarnate, ever-dancing Lover of all,
  you hold us in the embrace of your mystery,
  inviting us to enter always more deeply
  into your gift of abundant life.

Through the blinding glint of sun on melting snow,
  through the moving of your Spirit within us,
  through the waters of baptism,
  you call us to become your people.

As you once spoke to your people from a pillar of cloud,
  speak to us, gathered here today,
  that we may more fully become
  the Body of Christ for the healing of the world. Amen.

Thanksgiving and Praise

Light of the world, Wisdom of God, Lover of all,
  the good news of your kindness
  fills our hearts with thanksgiving.

We give thanks for the subtle signs of coming spring,
  for waking again to sunshine,
  even as icy sidewalks still remind us
  to walk with care.

We give thanks for the generosity of strangers,
  for the greetings of travelers from distant lands,
  for the signs of new life
  within us and among us.

On this day of celebration and rejoicing,
  for what else shall we give thanks?

Petition and Intercession

Holy Wisdom, holy Lover, holy Breath,
  the seeds of your goodness
  are sometimes hidden
  beneath the snow of our despair.

Our hearts tremble when we hear of war and destruction,
  and break at the sight of those who have
  no place to live,
  no food to eat,
  no one left to love.

Our eyes fill with tears
  for those who live in pain,
  for those who mourn,
  and for our own losses and hurts.

As members of your broken, risen Body,
  aloud and in silence,
  we pray for the healing
  of this broken, hurting world.

LENT

FIRST SUNDAY IN LENT

Genesis 2:15–17, 3:1–7; Psalm 32; Romans 5:12–19; Matthew 4:1–11

Opening Prayer

Out of the depths, we cry to you, O Holy One!

God of ultimate compassion,
  we seek to know your living presence in our midst.

Holy Lover of this harsh reality,
  you carry us into the future
  even though we eat the apple of awareness time after time
  and fall into that painful place
  where choices and temptations seem to reign supreme.

We come to be reminded
  that you are a holy hiding place for us,
  a safe zone in the midst of trial and temptation;
  you preserve us from trouble
  and surround us with glad cries of deliverance.

Reveal yourself to us, for we gather
  in the name of the one who taught us what it means
  to love, to serve, and celebrate
  your holy child, our Savior, who is Jesus the Christ. Amen.

Thanksgiving and Praise

Holy Mystery, Wisdom without limit, loving Maker of all,
  you have created us to grow,
  and yet we long for things to stay the same.

The moving presence of your Spirit in community
  is clear, and yet invisible.
It's like the sense that spring is coming,
  even through the icy, windy nights.
The signs are there, though,
  if we just know how to look.

In the produce counter at the grocery store
  garlic bulbs are lifting bright green shoots out of the bin,
  sending out those fragile roots,
  looking for a bit of soil.

How do they know which way to turn?
The mystery of joy and pain that mingle in our lives
  is nearly always more than we can understand.

We try, and fail, and come into your presence
  bringing tattered pieces of our plans,
  shredded by the forces all around us.

But, Miracle of love, you've shown us time and time again
  that you can weave new fabric from the pieces
  we were ready to discard.

We praise you for the mysteries of life,
  for hope, for new beginnings,
  and for the love that flows from you.

Holy God, our hearts are full,
  full of prayers of praise and thanks.

  And for what else shall we pray?

Petition and Intercession

This early, cold beginning of the Lenten season
  reminds us what a challenge it can be
  to live a life of hope.

This week we are reminded of Jesus facing great temptation,
  the face of evil offered power and dominion
  over all that he could see

if only he would transfer his allegiance,
abandon God, and concentrate his caring on himself.

He made a hard choice, to live a life of hope,
even in the face of such temptation.

We celebrate the good news
that Jesus cared more for creation,
and for his relationship with you
than for his comfort or success.

We've come to open up our hearts to those in need;
to let compassion flow,
to stand with those who suffer illness, fear and grief.

Holy Wellspring of compassion, receive the prayers we offer now,
the groanings of our hearts.

SECOND SUNDAY IN LENT

Genesis 12:1–4a; Psalm 121; Romans 4:1–5, 13–17; John 3:1–17
or Matthew 17:1–9

Opening Prayer

Holy Source of crystal nights and icy sun,
we are pulled from darkness by the majesty of your dawn.

We gather in this place to celebrate your love for us,
your presence with us,
the way your life flows through us.

Holy Maker of the universe,
come fill us with the power of your presence,
for we gather in the spirit of our Savior, Jesus,
who is the Christ. Amen.

Thanksgiving and Praise

Holy God of joy and pain,
God of life and death and promise of new life again,
we have heard your call to be on the road.

Like Abraham, in our own way we take the road less traveled,
  seeking prophets in our own time,
  learning slowly what it means
  to have compassion for those we meet,
  and those whose lives are only tales we hear
  in newsy sound bites.

We bring our wonder for the richness of your whole creation,
  our hunger for the joy of life,
  our praise and thanks for all you have created,
  every thought and thing, every gift and grace,
  every wonder of this universe,
  transfigured by your presence.

Hear now our prayers of praise and thanks
  for all you are and everything you do.

Petition and Intercession

God of healing love and compassion,
  we bring our cares and pain to you as well.

We know that you are mystery,
  a mystery that we will never understand,
  and yet we know your healing presence
  in the care that we receive,
  often from the most unexpected sources.

We pray that you will lift our burdens from us,
  bring peace to those who grieve,
  health to those who are in pain,
  and blessed forgiveness to all who turn again to you.

We pray for all who labor,
  trying to earn food and shelter
  for themselves and those they love.

Holy God, as we consider
  just how great your mystery must be,
  we bring our prayers for others, and for ourselves.

Hear now the prayers of our hearts.

THIRD SUNDAY IN LENT

Exodus 17:1–7; Psalm 95; Romans 5:1–11; John 4:5–42

Opening Prayer

Compassionate Maker of all that is,
  you have called us to become your people.

When the Israelites were fearful
  that they would die of thirst in the desert,
  you brought water from the rock at Horeb,
  slaking their thirst and calming their fears.

When Jesus met the Samaritan woman at the well,
  he promised to become in us a spring of water
  gushing up to eternal life.

Today, we see your ever-flowing grace
  poured out in snow and sun,
  in the waxing and waning of the moon,
  in the first bright yellow daffodils
  braving the cold mornings as winter turns into spring.

In this season, and in every season,
  pour out your Spirit of love among us and through us,
  that we may truly be the Body of Christ,
  living water for a thirsty world. Amen.

Thanksgiving and Praise

Ever-flowing, overflowing Fount of living water,
  you fill our lives with so many abundant gifts
  that we hardly know how to begin to thank you.

We thank you for the gift of life and breath,
  for hearts that see more truly than eyes,
  for ears that hear song even in silence,
  for the bread of your life that sustains us
  even when our bodies hunger.

We give thanks for a hand outstretched in friendship
  where we expected only anger.

We give thanks for open acceptance
where we expected only closed doors.

We give thanks for the compassion of others,
and for the melting of our own hearts.
And for what else shall we give thanks?

Petition and Intercession

Although our lives overflow with good things,
we are often overwhelmed
by the mud and muck of a broken, dirty world.

Infinite Spring of compassion,
we pray for those who are mired in despair,
for those whose lives seem empty and without hope,
for those whose days are filled with pain.

We pray for those who never have enough to eat,
and for those who daily turn the bread of others into stones.

We pray for those who are oppressed,
and for those who abuse their power to oppress them.

We pray for those who thirst for God,
and we pray for the slaking of our own thirsts and hungers.
And for what else shall we pray?

FOURTH SUNDAY IN LENT

1 Samuel 16:1–13; Psalm 23; Ephesians 5:8–14; John 9:1–41

Opening Prayer

Holy Mist of hope,
opener of ears and eyes and hearts,
we come together here this morning
because we've heard your call.

We bring bright memories
of birdsong floating on the damp grey dawn,
of jonquils sneaking through the woods,
of laughing energy as children let us join them in their play.

We bring ourselves together here this morning,
   watching as the miracle of life comes softly blossoming.

We pray that you will open up our hearts
   to a reality that's bigger than we can understand,
   the way your love floods over all creation,
   rising to meet the morning sun.

Fill us with that special love of yours,
   Creator of the universe,
   for we gather as your people,
   to worship in the name of our Savior,
   who is Jesus the Christ. Amen.

Thanksgiving and Praise

Holy Coach of the Spring Team,
   the team of crocus and jonquil and budding
      rhododendron,
   the team of quiet frost and sudden hail and flood,
   the team of stone and story, diversity and dream,
   we celebrate the miracle of your March madness.

We marvel at the paradox of flowers in the mud,
   of sunsets pushing back the coming of the night
   to make room for violets in the lawn,
   of new dreams rising out of pain and love and hope.

O lover of this cold, wet earth and all the promise that it
      holds for us,
   we celebrate the hope that sprouts each week among us here,
   our hope for new life for your body in this familiar place,
   new life for us,
   together with our neighbors
   and those who come to share our space
   to celebrate their life in your creation.

O God of all creation,
   hear now our prayers of praise and thanks,
   our wonder and our gratitude.

▬▬ Petition and Intercession ▬▬

God of hope and healing,
  we feel the safety of this bright familiar space,
  the closeness of a chosen, open family,
  that we can come to know and trust and love.

Sometimes we forget, for just a moment,
  the fear and pain that fill the waking hours of so many.

We hear a story of the healing love of Jesus,
  and know that there are so many who are blind,
  or lame, or lost, or isolated,
  so many who must sit and beg for help
  because they are not strong enough right now
  to stand up and help themselves.

Our minds are flooded with images of unrest
  and violence in distant lands,
  as people fight to have their way,
  rebelling at the thought that others want something different.

Help us, O Creator and lover of all,
  help us find ways to care for all of your creation.

We know that you are calling us to lives of love and ministry,
  to be your eyes and hands and heart right here,
  where you have called us.

Hear now our prayers for all of those in pain and need.

FIFTH SUNDAY IN LENT

Ezekiel 37:1–14; Psalm 130; Romans 8:6–11; John 11:1–45

▬▬ Opening Prayer ▬▬

God of lingering snow and biting wind,
  we come.

God of golden daffodils of hope,
  we come.

God of the homeless and the hopeful,
  we bring our hunger for compassion,
  our cares for those in need
  and those who have the strength to help.

Fruitful, energizing Gardener of hope
  we gather here to celebrate your presence with us,
  to share our deepening awareness
  that we are bulb and blossom of your being,
  that you have planted us in fertile soil,
  and water us with love.

Come fertilize our longing,
  for we gather in the name of our Savior,
  Jesus the Christ. Amen.

Thanksgiving and Praise

Lord, the somber notes of Lent surround us.
The hidden patches of soiled snow remind us
  of the weight of sorrow, grief, and death.

Around us on the valley floor
  are littered hopes that died aborning,
  a mighty host of opportunities lying dormant in the dust.

How strange it is that these dark themes
  are punctuated by signs of hope.

Trees are showing signs of new green life,
  bright blades of green rise boldly on every sunny hillside,
  and there are faint suggestions that what is good and right
  shines defiant in the darkness of a warring world.

O God of life and hope restored by loving breath,
  we ask you for renewed wisdom
  to understand the wonder of the cross.

We ask for faith to see what we cannot understand:
  the mystery of life surrendered, life restored;
  the mystery that your redeeming transformation
  lies through the empty valley of the dead.

We raise our prayers of thanks and praise,
    shared aloud, and lifted in the silence of our hearts.

Petition and Intercession

Out of the depths we cry to you,
    O God: hear our voice.
    Let your ears be attentive to the voice of our supplications!
    If you, O God, should mark iniquities,
    who could stand?
    For all of us are living in the flesh.
    We're filled with schemes and hungers
    that isolate us from your love.

This separation from your love, this sin, is hard to see.
    Because we work so hard to be your hands and feet,
    part of your body in this time and place,
    it's easy to forget that all forgiveness is a gift from you.

This morning, as we watch your love fill those needy places,
    as we wait, hungrier than those who wait for the morning,
    we bring our broken, human selves to you.

Hear now, O Fount of steadfast love,
    the burdens that we bring,
    hear now and offer us your power to redeem.

O God of resurrection
    growing somewhere just beyond our sight,
    nourished by the penetrating damp,
    we give our hopes and fears and pains to you.

PALM/PASSION SUNDAY (SIXTH SUNDAY IN LENT)

Liturgy of the Palms: Matthew 21:1–11; Psalm 118:1–2, 19–29
Liturgy of the Passion: Isaiah 50:4–9a; Psalm 31:9–16;
Philippians 2:5–11; Matthew 26:14–27:66 or Matthew 27:11–54

Opening Prayer

O God of all,
  we gather here to celebrate your presence with us,
  our deepening awareness
  of the promise of new and resurrected life,
  calling from beyond the passion of the days ahead.
Come, holy God of mystery, come fill our hunger,
  for we gather in the name of our Savior,
  Jesus the Christ. Amen.

Thanksgiving and Praise

Holy God of new life stirring barely out of sight,
  we give you praise and thanks
  for all the gorgeous mystery of life.

We thank you for those purple crocus massed in silent chorus
  in the leaves of last year's productivity
  just outside the door.

And yesterday we smiled at the frisky deer,
  the pesky geese,
  the cardinal crying for a mate.

Holy Jeweler, who set that emerald moss
  in silver ripples in the tiny meadow brook,
  we come to celebrate the life that is your body in this place.

We thank you for bright smiles, stained fingers,
  and eggs transformed by children of many ages.

We thank you for time to share a day
  with others in our family of faith.

We thank you for almost hidden signs of hope
  in lands where war and violence rule the streets.

Holy Wellspring of compassion,
  we welcome you with quiet thanks
  and boisterous shouts of acclamation.

Hear now our prayers of thanks and praise
  as we offer them aloud
  and lift them up in the silence of our hearts.

▬▬ **Petition and Intercession** ▬▬

Be gracious to us, O Most Holy God,
  for even though our hearts know praise and thanks,
  we wallow in distress.

We watch as war and famine claim the lives of thousands.
We offer all the compassion we can muster
  toward those within our reach,
  whose days are dominated by pain and suffering.

We look within ourselves
  and see the sorrow that fills those inner places of despair.

Come, holy Lover of creation, our times are in your hand.
Let your radiance shine upon us;
  save us with your steadfast love,
  for we would be your servants in this time and place,
  the bearers of your unstoppable compassion.

Hear now our prayers for those in pain and need,
  for all those whose strength fails because of misery,
  the prayers we can find words for,
  and those that rise up through the silence within.

THE RESURRECTION OF CHRIST

Easter Sunday

Acts 10:34–43; Psalm 118:1–2, 14–24; Colossians 3:1–4; John 20:1–18

Opening Prayer

Before dawn this very morning,
  the great Seder celebration finished,
  the agony three days cold in the tomb,
  the empty cross awaiting death's next meal—
  into the darkness of that lifeless body
  the finger of God's Spirit moves slowly in a spiral
  as once it moved upon the face
  of waters about to be pregnant with creation.

From that primordial new beginning
  Christ comes forth,
  exploding from the tomb with radiant light and love!

Radiant, risen Christ, we gather in your presence
  to dance and sing and celebrate!

Come fill us with your joy,
  your power and your promise,
  for we have gathered as your resurrection people,
  beneath this empty cross,
  your sign of hope. Amen.

Thanksgiving and Praise

O God, the chorus of creation cries out:
  "Christ is risen! Alleluia!"

"Christ is risen! Alleluia!" sing the supple winds of spring.
Ring out rhododendron chorus,
  ring out in silent splendor: "Christ is risen! Alleluia!"

This is the feast of feasts,
  our festival of hope,
  the mother of all Sundays,
  lush with billowing clouds of azalea and redbud,
  radiant in the rising of the sun.

This morning, Easter dances on the rooftop,
  plays, childlike, in the cradle of our caring.

O God of constant new beginnings,
  hear our prayers of praise and thanks for all that you provide,
  but most deeply this morning, for the life and love of Christ.

▬▬▬ Petition and Intercession ▬▬▬

Artful, joyful Carpenter of deepest love,
  we find the roots of hope in your victory over death.

We hope that, being one with Christ,
  we will receive our own Easter mornings,
  full of astonishing new possibilities.

We pray for freedom for those who are imprisoned,
  for nourishment in the face of hunger,
  for comfort in the face of grief and sorrow.

We pray as well for those who are threatened by violence
  in war-torn nations and communities,
  for those who are the agents of this violence,
  and for those leaders whose decisions affect us all.

Hear now, O God of healing love,
  our prayers for those who suffer on this day of celebration.

THE GREAT
FIFTY DAYS

The Easter Season

SECOND SUNDAY OF EASTER

Acts 2:14a, 22–32; Psalm 16; 1 Peter 1:3–9; John 20:19–31

Opening Prayer

Ever-renewing Planter of cherry blossoms and daffodils,
  we gather this morning
  to see the new things you are doing among us
  and in the world outside our windows.

In this new light of resurrection,
  we learn again of your gift of love,
  given in Jesus, your own Word made flesh,
  your own Body given for the healing of the world.

As we celebrate the newness of this Easter season,
  fill our hearts with gladness,
  and teach us to see your Spirit among us,
  bringing new light into a broken world. Amen.

Thanksgiving and Praise

Giver of new visions, Bringer of delight,
  you fill each day with new beginnings,
  each night with mysterious splendor.

You open our hearts to love
  with the nail marks in your hands and feet,
  your gracious response to all our doubts.

You give us a vision of hope
  in the familiar faces of those we love,
  in the smiles of strangers on the street,
  in the warmth and sunshine of spring
  breaking forth from the grey skies of winter.

You send us news of resurrection
  in every human language,
  in the celebration of your scattered churches,
  and millions of pilgrims from around the world
  greeting one another with signs of peace.

For all this, and so much more,
  let us give our thanks and praise,
  for Christ is risen. Alleluia!

Petition and Intercession

Christ is risen. Alleluia!
  And yet the world still aches with brokenness,
  and Christ is still being crucified
  wherever there is war and oppression,
  greed and selfishness, rage and violence.

Our bodies, too, are prone to sickness and pain;
  the deaths of those we love leave us grieving and lonely.

We hear of floods and earthquakes,
  of divorces and bankruptcies,
  of people left homeless and hungry
  in nearby streets and distant lands.

Holy Mender of broken dreams,
  your children cry out in distress and anguish.
  Hear our prayers for the healing of the world.

Third Sunday of Easter

Acts 2:14a, 36–41; Psalm 116:1–4, 12–19; 1 Peter 1:17–23;
Luke 24:13–35

Opening Prayer

Great Giver of all rich, blossoming life,
  we lift the cup of salvation
  and call upon your holy name.

Loving Mystery, we have come
  to be with each other in your presence.

We have come because you call us.

Fill us with your love, O God of mystery,
  for we gather in the name of our Savior,
  who is Jesus the Christ. Amen.

Thanksgiving and Praise

O Spirit of life,
  not all that long ago, the trees were empty twig brooms
  sweeping snow from a cold, wet sky.

Today new life is everywhere around us.
This is a time of new energy and hope.
We marvel at the rich variety
  of tulips, daffodils, azaleas, hyacinths, and more!

We celebrate this time of rebirth in the world around us,
  as a rich reminder of the resurrection,
  and remind ourselves that Christ is with us.

We sing alleluias,
  and give thanks for your presence with us,
  and for the consciousness to know and appreciate
  all that you have done.

Hear now our prayers of praise and thanks,
  for every gift you are bestowing in this moment.

Petition and Intercession

God of new life,
  no matter how hard we work,
  and no matter how much we worry,
  the world does not seem like a perfect place.

The pain and suffering are still there.
The homeless fill our streets;
  young children abandon hope in the future;
  every day people die
  from violence, disease, and starvation;
  and there are those inner torments
  of anger, loneliness, and grief as well.

O God, we know that your love is our reality,
  but it is so easy to lose our focus.

Like those on the road to Emmaus,
  we fail to see you until you come to us as a stranger.

Let us give you the burdens of our hearts!
Hear now our prayers for those in need,
  for others
  and for ourselves.

FOURTH SUNDAY OF EASTER

Acts 2:42–47; Psalm 23; 1 Peter 2:19–25; John 10:1–10

Opening Prayer

Holy God, Creator of the world and everything that's in it,
  holy Maker of starry dogwood and nesting geese,
  creator of mirth and mercy,
  we have gathered here again to remind ourselves
  that you are God of all,
  and that we are your people.

Fill us with your Spirit
  as you filled those faithful sisters and brothers

who have gone before us,
for we gather here this morning
to celebrate and pray in the name of our Savior,
who is Jesus the Christ. Amen.

▬▬▬ **Thanksgiving and Praise** ▬▬▬

Bright blossoming God of Easter hope,
  holy Maker of sailing maple seed
  and pale pink bleeding heart,
  God of long-anticipated sprouts and new beginnings,
  we find our inner landscape
  buffeted by the winds of change.

Today we stop to wonder how it was
  for those who knew Jesus as their teacher,
  who felt his vital presence after he'd been crucified,
  received the blessing from his wounded hands
  and heard him promise that although he'd go away,
  they would not be alone—
  then watched him leave.
  Again.

Fountain of eternal hope,
  we thank you that we've known that mystery
  well enough to ask for more.

Today we look around and see
  the energetic sprouts of change,
  the signs of new, compassionate relationships,
  the opportunity to help each other
  when we find ourselves with unexpected needs,
  the tiny, evanescent signs of hope
  fluttering through the war-torn nations of your world.

Your loving presence is a joyful mystery!
For gentle signs of hope,
  for opportunities to help,
  for mysteries of presence in the Spirit,

for these and so much more,
we offer you our prayers of praise and thanks.

Hear now our thankful offerings as we share them aloud
and lift them in the joyful silence of our hearts.

Petition and Intercession

Holy Comforter of the fearful and the heavy-laden,
God of hope that springs from nothing
like some fiery plume of galaxies in labor,
giving birth to stars and so much more;
holy Mystery of the Spirit that sustains us
even in the midst of fear and pain,
we've brought our pain and fear into this room today.

We hurt from illness and the fear it generates.

We ache for those caught up in war and violence.

We can't let go of fears that those we love will suffer even more.

And there is often not much we can think to do.

At times our hearts are full of grateful thanks
for all the wonder of this life,
and then we learn that someone else we love is stricken,
or the violence has flared again,
or flood and famine are rampaging,
battering what little hope is left for those caught in the path.

We've learned that times like these
are very difficult to face alone.

And so we've come together, like sheep who need a shepherd,
and together turn to you to ask for comfort, help, and healing.
Hear now our prayers, O God of Easter hope,
for those in pain and need, and for ourselves,
for we have come to know that we won't make it
on our own.

Fifth Sunday of Easter

Acts 7:55–60; Psalm 31:1–5, 15–16; 1 Peter 2:2–10; John 14:1–14

Opening Prayer

Holy Giver of resurrection power,
   you fill the world with your glory,
      shining through the countless petals of primrose and petunia,
      the heady scent of honeysuckle and lavender,
      the ongoing chorus of robin and cardinal and wren.

In this world of overwhelming abundance
   and overwhelming need,
      you have called us to feel your life flowing through us,
      and around us, and within us,
      to be transformed into the living resurrected Body of Christ.

In our songs and stories, in our tears and laughter,
   in our prayers and in our silence,
      help us to feel the presence of your Spirit,
      to know your power and your love,
      so that we might learn to do your work in all that we say or
         do. Amen.

Thanksgiving and Praise

Astonishing Giver of life,
   from white dogwood flowers
      that dazzle our eyes against a clear, blue sky,
      to the yellow buttercups
      that dot the dark green, grassy meadows,
      you fill the world with overflowing abundance.

The breathtaking colors of spring overwhelm our senses,
   reminding us that every good thing comes from you,
      that every breath is an opportunity
      to know your Holy Spirit more deeply.

We give thanks for the warm days and cool evenings
   of this long-awaited spring,

for friendship and conversation,
  for shared meals and shared hopes,
  and shared stories from the past,
  for calling us to be your holy Body.

Like Stephen, who saw the heavens open before him,
  revealing your glory,
  we give thanks that you give us the courage
  to do your work in the world.

In words spoken aloud and in the silence for our hearts,
  for what else shall we give thanks this day?

═══ Petition and Intercession ═══

Righteous Protector of the persecuted and the oppressed,
  the abundance of your gifts leads us to wonder
  why some are rich and others poor,
  why some seem untouched by the sorrows of the world,
  while others suffer more than anyone should have to bear.

We pray for a world
  in which no child ever goes hungry or unloved,
  in which every person
  is treated with dignity and compassion,
  and all who are in need receive whatever will bring them joy.

We pray for a world where justice and peace
  are as ordinary as sunshine,
  where love and respect are as common as grass,
  where your Holy Spirit shines forth
  in every gesture and word.

We ask you to comfort all who mourn,
  to bring healing to all who are in sickness or in pain,
  to guide the hands and hearts and minds
  of all who do your work.

We pray for all who have asked us to pray,
  we pray for our own needs,
  and we pray for those who cannot pray for themselves.

Aloud and in silence,
we bring our prayers of petition and intercession.

SIXTH SUNDAY OF EASTER

Acts 17:22–31; Psalm 66:8–20; 1 Peter 3:13–22; John 14:15–21

Opening Prayer

God of all Creation, bright, greening fountain of blossoms,
we come together this damp morning
to celebrate the love that pours from you
through us and out into the world.

Fill us with the good news of the risen Christ,
fill us until your love pours out
in ways we could never imagine.
Open us to the mystery of death and resurrection
as we gather in the spirit of the risen Christ. Amen.

Thanksgiving and Praise

Holy, wondrous God, Creator of the universe,
God of quiet promises of new life springing into sight,
God of mighty rivers and terrifying storms,
we've come today to celebrate your presence
in this time and place.

We see your holy, growing power and investment in the future,
our gardens are alive with blossom,
birds labor from dawn to dusk
to make a home for their next generation,
singing as they work.

The dandelion army is already on the march,
claiming new territory for the future.
This is the time for new beginnings,
not only in the world around us,
but in the world within,
and we give thanks for the good news in Christ,

good news that promises that we, too,
are each invited to a new beginning.

We bring our prayers of praise and thanks
for hope and healing in our troubled world.

Petition and Intercession

God of healing and forgiveness, we come today with burdens, too.

We know that pain and violence are also growing fast this season.

There is the pain of those we love,
who suffer from disease and isolation.

There is the pain of those in Palestine and Israel and Afghanistan
who suffer from the violence of terror and counterterror
performed while the name of peace is invoked.

We share with so many the fear that comes
when people rise up in angry violence
and kill to get the attention they feel they have been denied.

We come, O God of healing love,
to raise our prayers for those in need.

Hear now our prayers for them, and for ourselves,
for we would be dandelions of hope
in the face of violence and fear.

SEVENTH SUNDAY OF EASTER

Acts 1:6–14; Psalm 68:1–10, 32–35; 1 Peter 4:12–14, 5:6–11;
John 17:1–11

Opening Prayer

Holy God, we come into this sanctuary
to sing praises to your holy name,
for we would name ourselves an Easter people,
part of the Body of Christ.

We come to worship you in spirit and in truth,
amazed and comforted by the presence of your Holy Spirit,

we come to sing praise and await renewal of your blessing,
gathered in the name of the Messiah, Jesus the Christ. Amen.

▬▬ Thanksgiving and Praise ▬▬

Bright, blossoming God of Easter hope,
  holy Maker of pollen and petal,
  God of new beginnings,
  we find our inner landscape pummeled
  by the winds of change.

Life is so quick,
  we have to help each other stay alert
  or we will not see you in the blur around us.

We watch the wind tear fragile flowers from the stem
  before the bees have left the scene,
  but know that there was time enough
  to guarantee new life for both.

We catch quick glimpses of your presence,
  O holy Spring of living water,
  as we hurry through this season of celebration
  faster than we'd like.

God of the world and everything that is in it,
  we shout our thanks and praise
  into the howl of your creativity,
  and claim your promise that the Holy Spirit is on the way.

Hear now, O God of Easter hope,
  our prayers of praise and thanks
  for your protecting presence.

▬▬ Petition and Intercession ▬▬

God of all grace,
  our joy this Easter season is often beaten to the ground
  like some drowned tulip,
  naked stamen standing in a puddle,
  mud-stained petals twisting in the tiny current
  heading for the sea.

When we would take the time
  to understand and savor the richness of your gift of life,
  we find it bound together with the pain of war and violence,
  and cannot feel a way to grasp it.

O raging Torrent of holy passion,
  we come half hoping not to find you here,
  half wanting just the quiet of the morning
  and not the clamor of the life you keep creating.

The pains of life, the anguish of death and separation,
  the slow, grinding ache of neglect and poverty,
  the sharp knife of recognition that comes from greed,
  or disregard, or blindness chosen,
  these pains seem to move with us,
  lingering in our bodies
  even as the joy you offer us so freely slips out of sight.

O God of all this creation,
  holy Maker of our lives in this community,
  we lift up our hearts in joy and pain.

Hear now the prayers we can pluck
  from the life that rushes past.

Help us to know your healing presence
  as deeply as did those disciples gathered in the upper room.

Fill us with your healing Holy Spirit
  as we offer you our prayers for those in pain and need.

PENTECOST

Acts 2:1–21; Psalm 104:24–34, 35b; 1 Corinthians 12:3b–13; John 20:19–23

Opening Prayer

Holy, burning, breathing Spirit,
  you call us to lives more amazing
  than any of us can imagine.

In tongues of fire, in rushing wind,
  you came to those first disciples,
  teaching them to speak
  as they had never spoken before.

In those ancient times,
  you promised prophesy and vision,
  dreams and portents,
  pouring your own self
  into those who would hear your call.

And still, today, you pour out your Spirit like a rushing river,
  filling our thirsty souls with living water,
  teaching us to pray and praise your holy name. Amen.

Thanksgiving and Praise

Holy, burning, breathing Spirit,
  you sweep through us and among us,
  giving gifts too numerous to count,
  surprising us with every breath.

We give thanks for the ever-surprising abundance of spring,
   for massive clumps of pink and red azaleas,
   for clouds of white dogwood,
   for rose bushes that blossom both red and yellow,
   for the intense blue of irises just bursting from green sheaths.

We give thanks for warm days and cool nights,
   for sunshine and rain,
   for the sea and stars,
   for living things, both small and great,
   that fill the world you have created.

And we give thanks for our human lives,
   for work and for play,
   for silence and for speech,
   for company and for solitude.
   And for what else shall we give thanks?

Petition and Intercession

As our gratitude is greater than we can ever express,
   so, too, is our awareness of the broken places in our world.

Too many people live in daily pain,
   too many wars spread hatred and fear,
   too many rivers carry pollution to the sea.

Holy, burning, breathing Spirit,
   pour out your love among us and through us,
   as we pray aloud and in silence
   for the healing of the world.

ORDINARY TIME

The Sundays after Pentecost

TRINITY SUNDAY (FIRST SUNDAY AFTER PENTECOST)

Genesis 1:1–2:4a; Psalm 8; 2 Corinthians 13:11–13; Matthew 28:16–20

Opening Prayer

Holy Maker of day and night, sky and water, moon and stars,
  you have formed us in your image
  and called us to be your people.

Holy Spirit of beauty and truth,
  you invite us to delight in rainstorms and sunshine;
  in the bright, orange trumpets of day lilies;
  the tender, yellow threads of honeysuckle blossoms;
  and the deep, crimson cascades of tea roses
  pouring over fences and arbors and sun-kissed walls.

Holy Teacher of love and sacrifice,
  you have called us to be your disciples,
  to baptize those who would follow you
  in the name of the Holy Trinity,
  whose nameless name fills all the earth.

Holy, mighty, immortal One,
  fill us with your love
  and make us live as your own, true Body,
  pouring out our lives for the healing of the world.

Thanksgiving and Praise

Holy, mighty, immortal One,
  you make yourself known to us

as soaring Spirit,
nourishing Body,
unknowable Mystery.

From moment to moment, you sustain us,
filling our lives with gifts of glory and honor
that we only dimly perceive.

We give you thanks for friends and family and colleagues,
for flowers and ferns and mosses and ivy,
for deer and cattle and elephants and songbirds,
for warm, sunny days and dark, starry nights.

We give you thanks for your Body, the church,
which offers a place where each of us can feel at home,
and sends us out to do your will.

For all these gifts,
and even more than we can imagine or desire,
we give our thanks and praise,
aloud and in the silence of our hearts.

Petition and Intercession

Holy, mighty, immortal One,
our gratitude for your gifts of life and love
opens our hearts to the sorrows of the world.

We pray for the invisible hands
of those who work while others sleep,
for the strength and courage of those who do dangerous jobs
so that others may live in comfort,
for the minds and hearts of all
who struggle for justice and peace.

We pray that you will comfort
all who sit in darkened rooms,
listening to the labored breath of loved ones in pain.

We pray that you will protect all who live in fear of violence,
and lead those who would do them harm
into the paths of peace.

Aloud and in silence,
> we pray for all whose needs are known to us
> for those who do not know they are in need,
> and for our own needs and deepest desires.

Sunday between May 22 and May 28 inclusive (if after Trinity Sunday)
Proper 3, Ordinary 8

Isaiah 49:8–16a; Psalm 131; 1 Corinthians 4:1–5; Matthew 6:24–34

Opening Prayer

Holy, mysterious Maker of creation,
> surround us with your strong arms,
> spirit us away into the depths of your heart,
> show us signs of hope, we pray.

We come to learn more deeply of your resurrection power,
> to know the Holy Spirit flowing through community,
> to learn to serve you as your faithful people.

We gather here today to pray and sing and celebrate
> as you welcome us into the realm of righteousness,
> where Jesus is the bearer of good news, the Christ. Amen.

Thanksgiving and Praise

God of all creation, we bless you.
God of a past remembered and a future hidden from our eyes,
> we praise your holy name.

We come because you have called us to be your people.

We come, even though we cannot see where you are leading us.

We come as stewards of your Holy Spirit,
> guided by your hope, empowered by your love.

Holy Three-in-One,
> we offer praise and thanks for new life,
> shown forth in flocks of lilies and circling geese,
> in fresh dreams for a peaceful future,

and the unformed shape of things to come;
the hope of reconciliation,
and your call to the work that gives our lives away in love.

Hear now our prayers of praise and thanks,
for the hope that is within us,
for the dreams you choose to give us,
and for the faith to move ahead
into a future we cannot anticipate.

▬▬ Petition and Intercession ▬▬

God of mercy and history,
loving God of all that is and all that shall ever be,
we know that throughout history
you have come to those who needed healing,
to those who were suffering
from pain and poverty and grief.

We know that throughout history
you have called your faithful people
to be stewards of your Triune mysteries,
to trust you always,
and pour out our hearts to you in prayer.

We know that Jesus came to help us understand
that we are called to seek your realm today
and let you hold the future in your loving embrace.

We know your presence as the Holy Spirit,
that empowering breath
that fills our sails and moves us
into fresh opportunities to serve.

We bring to you the burdens of our lives:
the pain and fear that burdens those we love;
the pain and fear that burdens those
we do not yet know well enough to love.

We bring the pain that we have caused
and the pain we have suffered.

We pray that the gift of your healing
  may be poured on all those places
  where people rise up against oppression,
  where threat and violence cause fears to rise
  and hearts to close against the needs of others.

We pray for hope to see the mystery of your healing love
  poured out for the ending of war and violence and discord,
  and for the faith to offer what we have to those in need,
  even if we think we don't have much to give.

Hear now our prayers for those in need
  around the world,
  across the land,
  within this room,
  and deep within our hearts.

Sunday between May 29 and June 4 inclusive (if after Trinity Sunday)

Proper 4, Ordinary 9

Genesis 6:9–22, 7:24, 8:14–19; Psalm 46;
Romans 1:16–17; 3:22b–28, (29–31); Matthew 7:21–29

Opening Prayer

O God of all creation, here we are.
We've come because you call us to receive your love,
  and pass it on to those around us,
  even to the ones we think we might not like.

We know that you are in the midst of community,
  calling forth the faithful to love and service.

We take our place among the throngs
  who listen for your Word,
  and build our house of faith upon that solid rock.

Fill us with your love this morning as we gather here,
  for we gather in the name of Jesus, who is the Christ.

Amen.

Thanksgiving and Praise

O Mystery of life,
   maker of that mockingbird that sounds like an alarm clock,
   waking us to celebrate these bright, cool days,
   we marvel at the rich variety of life
   that leaps forth from the earth on every side.

We think of Noah, watching in amazement
   as two of every living thing gathered at his gangplank
   hungry to be saved.

This week a scarlet cardinal was calling everyone
   to claim the joy that you have scattered all around,
   like clouds of maple seeds whirling on the winds of change.

It was a joy to watch,
   as one by one your seeds of hope appeared.

And here, we watch each other as we grow,
   like seeds of hope,
   into the opportunities before us—
   opportunities to serve a world hungry for your call.

O holy Maker of this place we call our home,
   we bring our prayers of praise and thanks,
   for all the rich variety of life, and love, and hope
   that flows from you,
   the prayers of thanks that you have planted in our hearts.

O God of all that is,
   receive our words, our thoughts,
   our wordless feelings of thanksgiving.

Petition and Intercession

O Mystery of life,
   holy Lover of the universe,
   we've come here worn with worries for so many things.

We watch the violence continue in so many places,
   and feel so helpless here in this protected place.

How can we help?
We hear of those who can't make sense of their lives,
  who mourn such terrible loss
  from floods and fires, earthquakes and tornadoes,
  whose children plead for food their parents cannot afford.

At some deep level, O holy Creator,
  we know that they are part of our community.
We hunger for the joy you promise,
  to feed our empty souls
  and share with those we serve.

We thirst for grace,
  and turn to you with throats burned dry and souls that cry
  for justice, peace, and Sabbath for all of your creation.

Liberator of those bound by chains of hunger, fear, and grief,
  You are our refuge and our strength,
  a very present help in trouble.

Holy God of Sabbath rest and healing,
  hear now our prayers for those who hunger and thirst,
  and hear the rattle of our own parched throats
  as we raise our prayers to you.

SUNDAY BETWEEN JUNE 5 AND JUNE 11 INCLUSIVE (IF AFTER TRINITY SUNDAY)

PROPER 5, ORDINARY 10

Genesis 12:1–9; Psalm 33:1–12; Romans 4:13–25;
Matthew 9:9–13, 18–26

Opening Prayer

Radiant, transcendent Keeper of promises,
  gentle, willing Healer of all that is broken,
  bright, soaring Song of joy,
  every day you call us anew,
  saying, "Follow me," and showering us with blessings.

Long ago you called our ancestors, Abraham and Sarah,
  to leave their country and kindred,
  the home they had always known,
  to set out on a journey to find new life in you.

Today, you invite us to leave our old ways
  and become a new people,
  to sing a new song
  and learn the ways of kindness and of faith.

You fill the world with creatures
  more numerous than the stars,
  awakening our eyes to the tall stalks of lilies,
  proudly opening their red and purple and yellow blossoms
  to drink in the warm rain of early summer.

You open our ears to the cheery whistle of robins,
  hidden within branches heavy with bright, green leaves,
  reminding us that everything comes into being by your Word,
  sustained in every moment by your steadfast love.

Hear us, now, as we praise and greet you.
  Teach us how to become your people,
  the living Body of Christ on earth,
  in whom all the families of earth shall be blessed. Amen.

Thanksgiving and Praise

Bright, soaring Song of joy,
  by your holy Word the heavens were made,
  the moon and the stars by the breath of your mouth;
  you gathered the waters of the sea as in a bottle,
  put the deeps into storehouses,
  and filled them with creatures too numerous to count.

We praise you with song, with music, with laughter;
  we give you thanks for every astonishing moment of grace.

For rain that waters forests and fields,
  for sunshine that warms our bodies

and opens our hearts to life,
　we give you thanks.

For the wild exhilaration of riding a backyard zip line,
　for the quiet comfort of deep conversation with friends,
　we give you thanks.

For gardens and swamps,
　for bike paths and highways,
　for solitary suppers and raucous celebrations,
　we give you thanks.

For all that we can say and all that forever remains unsaid,
　we give you thanks in the words of our mouths,
　and in the silence of our hearts.

Petition and Intercession

Gentle, willing Healer of all that is broken,
　you came to heal the sick,
　to ease the suffering of those in pain.

And yet the world remains a broken place,
　where too many cannot reach the hem of your garment,
　where too many do not feel
　the healing touch of your hand.

And so we cry out to you, who gives life to the dead:
　have mercy on those who suffer,
　protect those who live in fear of violence,
　bring peace to all who grieve.

We pray for those who yearn for children,
　and for those who struggle to provide
　for the children in their care.

We pray for the needs of those we love,
　and even for those who hate us.
　Aloud and in silence, we pray for the healing of the world.

SUNDAY BETWEEN JUNE 12 AND JUNE 18 INCLUSIVE (IF AFTER TRINITY SUNDAY)

PROPER 6, ORDINARY II

Genesis 18:1–15, (21:1–7); Psalm 116:1–2, 12–19; Romans 5:1–8;
Matthew 9:35–10:8, (9–23)

Opening Prayer

Luminous Source of wisdom and joy,
  boundless Ocean of mystery and peace,
  comforting Healer of all our sorrows,
  you appear suddenly in our midst
  like the messengers who came to Abraham,
  bringing laughter to Sarah near the oaks of Mamre.

You show us your glory in bright rays of sunshine,
  turning the edges of storm clouds to gold
  in the late afternoon.

You delight us with the extravagance of your creation:
  seas filled with tuna and shark and whale,
  forests abounding with deer and fox and owl,
  the very soil alive with earthworms and cicadas
  and creatures too small for us to see.

Give us the words to proclaim
  the good news of your coming,
  that the realm of God is near at hand,
  for you are good, and your steadfast love endures forever.
    Amen.

Thanksgiving and Praise

Boundless Ocean of mystery and peace,
  we give you thanks for the evidence of your great love,
  that even while we were still sinners, Christ died for us.

We give you thanks for the early dawn light,
  golden glints of sunshine enlivening the deep, blue sky.

We give you thanks for the sliver of new moon,
  sailing between banks of dark clouds at the end of a storm.

We give you thanks for honey and honeysuckle,
   for bowls of ripe blueberries and succulent peaches,
   for food for the body and food for the soul.

We give you thanks for all the things that make us laugh,
   and even for those that make us cry.

Holy One, we bring to you our prayers of thanksgiving and praise,
   aloud and in the silence of our hearts.

Petition and Intercession

Comforting Healer of all our sorrows,
   you told your disciples to cure the sick, to raise the dead,
   to cleanse the lepers, and to cast out demons.
But though we give up our lives for the sake of others,
   the wounds of a broken world are greater than we can bear,
   and so we cry out to you.

We pray for those who have no homes,
   and those whose homes are empty and silent.

We pray for all who care for elderly parents,
   and for those who have no parents to care for.

We pray for all whose loneliness is more than they can bear,
   and for all who ache for even a few moments of solitude.

Aloud and in silence, we bring our petitions for our own needs,
   and our prayers of intercession for the healing of the world,
   in the name of Jesus, who is the Christ.

SUNDAY BETWEEN JUNE 19 AND JUNE 25 INCLUSIVE (IF AFTER TRINITY SUNDAY)

PROPER 7, ORDINARY 12

Genesis 21:8–21; Psalm 86:1–10, 16–17; Romans 6:1b–11;
Matthew 10:24–39

Opening Prayer

Joyful, embracing Creator of new beginnings,
   wild, boundless Spirit of the cosmos,

tender, loving Wellspring of compassion,
you notice every fledgling leaping courageously from its nest,
still fuzzy with down
yet trusting its as-yet-untested wings.

You see every new leaf as it uncurls from its stem,
stretching to catch the sun and rain that you provide;
You count the very hairs on our heads,
reminding each one of us
that we are all your beloved children.

As you once saved Hagar and Ishmael
from dying of thirst in the desert,
hold us now in your infinite embrace
and fill our hearts with gladness,
as we walk with Christ into the newness of life. Amen.

Thanksgiving and Praise

Wild, boundless Spirit of the cosmos,
you cause water to spring up in the desert,
and fill us with new life when we give up our lives
for you.

We give you thanks for the shrieking cries of gulls
swooping behind a boat as it crosses the bay;
for the gleeful play of dolphins,
arching their bodies above the waves;
for the unexpected clop of horses' hoofs on a city street,
for all the creatures of air and land and sea.

We give you thanks for rays of golden light
lining the glowing edges of dark thunderclouds
piling up against a deep, blue sky;
for cool mornings and warm afternoons
as spring turns suddenly into summer;
for long walks and unhurried meals,
for deep conversation
and the comfortable silences of old friends.

For all that we have noticed,
  and all the gifts that have no names,
  aloud and in silence, we give our thanks to you.

Petition and Intercession

Tender, loving Wellspring of compassion,
  like Hagar, we lift up our voices and weep,
  unwilling to look on the suffering
  that surrounds us on every side.

We weep for those whose only home is a doorway,
  for those who are battered by rain
  or swelter in the summer heat,
  never knowing when or what they might eat again,
  fearing that each night may be their last.

We weep for those whose bodies are filled with pain,
  with lungs that cannot expand enough
  to take a deep breath,
  with hearts that cannot keep in rhythm,
  or knees that cannot bend to walk down stairs.

We weep for the children of poverty, of war, of violence;
  for those whose parents are in prison,
  and for those whose parents have died of AIDS.

Incline your ear, Holy One, to these, our prayers.
Aloud and in silence we bring our pleas for ourselves,
  for those who are close to us,
  and for those who are known only to you.

SUNDAY BETWEEN JUNE 26 AND JULY 2 INCLUSIVE
PROPER 8, ORDINARY 13

Genesis 22:1–14; Psalm 13; Romans 6:12–23; Matthew 10:40–42

Opening Prayer

Constant, welcoming Creator of abundant life,
  steadfast, merciful Teacher of righteousness,

generous, surprising Spirit of grace,
when Abraham and Isaac climbed the mountain together,
you, yourself, provided the sacrifice in the form of a ram.
When the disciples set out
to heal disease and sickness in your name,
you said that welcoming them would be welcoming you.

Today, you greet us with open arms,
pouring out your endless love like sunshine,
and strewing our paths with blue-eyed periwinkles,
yellow-petaled daisies, and carpets of wild strawberry.

Today, and every day,
you welcome all who want to be freed from sin,
inviting us into eternal life
as members of the risen Body of Christ. Amen.

Thanksgiving and Praise

Generous, surprising Spirit of grace,
you give light to our eyes,
and our hearts trust in your salvation.

We give you thanks for fireflies,
flickering across the lawn at dusk;
and for lightening,
arcing across a darkening sky.

We give you thanks for ice cream
and ice water on a sweltering afternoon;
for bicycles and swimming pools
and hikes in the woods;
for dreams of languid summer days
filled with gentle breezes.

In every thing, in every season,
for all your goodness, we give you thanks,
aloud and in the silence of our hearts.

Petition and Intercession

Steadfast, merciful Teacher of righteousness,
  when we look at the heartache in your broken world,
  our souls ache with sorrow and we cry out with the
    psalmist,
  How long, Holy One?
  Will you forget these little ones forever?
  How long will you hide your face from your hurting people?

Trusting in your steadfast love, your constant compassion,
  we pray for those whose faith is tested:
  for children who work in sweatshops and factories,
  and for those who stay home from school
  to care for those still younger;
  for parents who work long hours at dangerous jobs,
  and for those who have no jobs at all.

We pray for those who live in so much pain
  that they wish for death,
  for those who have no hope for the future,
  for those who have no memory of the past.

We pray for caregivers and doctors and nurses,
  for those who sit by bedsides,
  for those who wait by telephones,
  for those who wait for good news that never comes.

Aloud and in silence, we pray for all who are in need,
  for a time when all can say,
  "Our hearts rejoice in your salvation."

SUNDAY BETWEEN JULY 3 AND JULY 9 INCLUSIVE
PROPER 9, ORDINARY 14

Genesis 24:34–38, 42–49, 58–67; Psalm 45:10–17; Romans 7:15–25a;
Matthew 11:16–19, 25–30

Opening Prayer

Burning, breathing Spirit of compassion,
  you have called us, once again,
    to gather together and become your people.

You call to us in wind and fire,
  in thunder and rain,
    in midnight darkness and in the morning sun.

You call to us in the stories of our ancestors in faith
  who struggled to know you
    and to put into words what they had learned
    so that we, their children, might know you, too.

Today, as we practice one more time to be your holy Body,
  give us breath to sing and praise you,
  give us ears to hear your Word,
  give us eyes to see the living Christ
    in the faces of everyone we meet. Amen.

Thanksgiving and Praise

Ground of our being,
  God, our refuge and strength,
    we give you thanks for the gifts of compassion and love
    that fill our hearts with sweetness,
    our days with grace and peace.

We give thanks that you give us rest
  from the heavy burdens of our lives:
    that you help us to do what we cannot do alone;
    that you give us the strength and courage
    to serve a world that continually breaks your heart.

We give thanks for the gifts of beauty and wonder,
  for thunderstorms and sunsets,

for laughter and conversation,
for flavors and textures and colors
that nourish our souls and delight our senses.

Burning, breathing Spirit of compassion,
we give thanks for the everyday miracles
of breathing and eating, of sleeping and rising,
of knowing that in every moment,
you are continually creating our world anew.
And for what else shall we give thanks?

Petition and Intercession

God of Abraham and Ishmael and Isaac,
God of Sarah and Hagar and Rebecca,
you come to us like fire,
like the fierce burning of desire,
or like a yearning for justice,
for the peace that only you can provide.

You come like a hot wind from the desert,
bringing tears to our eyes
as we turn towards the sorrows of the world;
or like a cooling breeze
flowing down from high mountain passes,
soothing our souls as we cry out in sorrow and pain.

Holy, burning, breathing Spirit of compassion,
hear our prayers for healing, for justice, for peace.

SUNDAY BETWEEN JULY 10 AND JULY 16 INCLUSIVE
PROPER 10, ORDINARY 15

Genesis 25:19–34; Psalm 119:105–112; Romans 8:1–11;
Matthew 13:1–9

Opening Prayer

Holy One, sustainer of all our days,
you hold us in your embrace,

nourishing our souls
as the soil nourishes newly-sown seeds.

As the heat of summer slows our steps
and invites us into a different rhythm,
help us to see that truth may dance to a different tune
than the ones we are used to.

Like the brothers that struggled in Rebecca's womb,
so unlike one another in every way,
yet swimming in the same dark sea,
help us to hear your one, great heartbeat,
calling us into new life
as members of a fragile, earthen vessel
that is also your universal, grace-filled, holy Body. Amen.

Thanksgiving and Praise

Jesus assures us that we can walk on water,
if only we believe that we are already swimming
in the infinite grace of God.

We float in a sea of blessings:
the beating of our hearts
is the undercurrent of every thought;
the rhythm of our breath connects us
to all that swims in the earthly ocean of air.

We give thanks for the simple pleasures of ice cream,
melting in our mouths on a hot, summer night;
for the sweet tartness of ripe, juicy blueberries;
for the flashing signals of lightning bugs,
beaming "Here I am!" across a darkening field.

We give thanks for a funny story,
making us smile in the midst of a difficult day;
for an unexpected call from a faraway friend,
when we are drowning in waves of loneliness;
for the endless love of God,

who holds us all in a sea of un-earned grace.

And for what else shall we give thanks?

Petition and Intercession

With our gratitude as boundless as the infinite grace of God,
   our hearts go on breaking with the anguish of a broken world.

The news is filled with pain and terror every morning:
   we hear of bombs and terrorist attacks,
      the pain of war and genocide that claim new lives every day.

Closer to home, our friends are diagnosed with cancer,
   anger and distrust turn loved ones into enemies,
      the city streets are awash in fear and pain.

For comfort and for healing,
   for ourselves and for the world,
   we cry out in silence and aloud
   to you, O Holy One, sustainer of all our days.

SUNDAY BETWEEN JULY 17 AND JULY 23 INCLUSIVE
PROPER 11, ORDINARY 16

Genesis 28:10–19a; Psalm 139:1–12, 23–24; Romans 8:12–25;
Matthew 13:24–30, 36–43

Opening Prayer

Holy, burning Wind of all creation,
   maker of shouting cicada and flaming impatiens,
   lover of all that pours forth
   when energy slows down enough
   to make something matter,
   we gather in your presence.

God of ripening fruit and grain, swelling toward the harvest,
   we come together to celebrate your presence
   in this world you are creating.

We come together to make prayer and song together,
   to praise your presence and sit in awe before your mystery.

We come to celebrate the good news of the risen Christ,
  alive and leading us to something new
  and hidden still from us.

Holy, loving God,
  we pray that we will know your presence here this morning,
  for we gather in the name of the one
  you filled with your good news,
  our Savior, who is Jesus the Christ. Amen.

Thanksgiving and Praise

Constant, dancing Champion of new beginnings,
  we celebrate the power of your Spirit,
  pouring forth the promise of your inheritance,
  the firm assurance that in our faithful commitment to your call
  you have made us part of your creation family,
  true joint heirs with Christ.

We are so thankful that you have searched us and know us,
  and that you love us and lead us in the everlasting Way.

We bring our thanks, O glorious, forgiving Gardener of life,
  our thanks for health and opportunities to care,
  our thanks for food and shelter, health and hope,
  our thanks for dreams and sweet corn and time to start again.

Hear now, O Holy One,
  our prayers of praise and thanksgiving,
  spoken aloud and lifted in the silence of our hearts.

Petition and Intercession

Gentle, embracing Redeemer of the broken,
  we know how quickly the fierce heat of summer
  can boil away our patience.

We know, too, how hard it is to start something new
  when all the world seems bent on hiding from the sun.

Your promises of love, and healing, and forgiveness
  are harder to believe when we have run the course
  and come to where the trail begins again.

We've tried to be faithful to your call to us
  to be one small part of your body in this place,
  to work for justice in the places where we labor.

Some of us are tired, God, of looking for new opportunities.
We go to sleep,
  hoping you will bring us some fresh vision in a dream,
  some ladder of hope like the one you offered to Jacob.

We've come again to this small clearing in the forest,
  where we can see the paths we've walked before
  and know those paths will not take us
  to the new place you are preparing for us.

Our patience has worn thin.

Show us the way, God;
  give us a pillar of cloud by day,
  a pillar of fire by night, so we will know the path before us
  is one you've called us to.

We pray that you will fill us with your healing power.
We want our witness to your presence
  to give hope to others, and to ourselves.

O wondrous Healer of all pain and sorrow,
  we lift up in your presence, aloud and in silence,
  the needs of those we know and love,
  the needs of those who suffer in this fiery season of growth,
  and our own needs as well.

SUNDAY BETWEEN JULY 24 AND JULY 30 INCLUSIVE
PROPER 12, ORDINARY 17

Genesis 29:15–28; Psalm 105:1–11, 45b; Romans 8:26–39;
Matthew 13:31–33, 44–52

Opening Prayer

Holy Spring of living water,
  we come together on this Sabbath morning
  to celebrate your presence in our time and place.

We come together to remind ourselves
   that we really are your people,
   one small part of the Body of the risen Christ.

We come together to celebrate the mystery of community,
   the healing power of love,
   the covenant that you have made to never leave us.

Come, Fountain of every blessing,
   come fill us with your Holy Spirit,
   call us to your service,
   and let us know that you are here among us,

For we gather in the name of Jesus, who is the Christ. Amen.

Thanksgiving and Praise

Holy, loving Gardener of hope,
   maker of the wisdom hidden in the mustard seed,
   you whose life-giving energy flows from the smallest sources,
   we come to you in joyful celebration.

We see those little signs that mark your holy presence:
   the leaping basil, feet firmly planted in rich, wet soil,
   laughing at the drought;
   the smiles of gratitude from those whose lives we touch;
   the eager brightness of a child's curiosity.

We know the joy of slower summer schedules,
   the kiss of twilight breezes,
   the welcome wink of fireflies
   that hold the night at bay until the stars arrive,
   then stay to celebrate their kinship
   with these distant mysteries.

We bring our joys, our prayers of praise and thanks
   for all the good news that rises up like steamy dawn
   to fuel our hopes and lift our spirits.

Hear now our prayers of praise and thanks,
   O holy Maker of this summer reality.

▬▬ Petition and Intercession ▬▬

God of all creation,
  holy Maker of that pearl of such great value
  hidden in a bucket of muddy shells,
  God of mystery and hidden treasure waiting to be found,
  we come to you with burdens on our hearts.

We see the pain of those
  who cannot find the work they need to do;
  we hear the cries of those whose pain
  is narrowing their vision until nothing else seems real;
  we feel the tug of fear as unknowns cloud our future.

Holy God of faithful service,
  you who gave Jacob that extra measure of commitment
  to labor for his love
  even when he'd paid the price and been deceived,
  we bring to you the images we carry of the rocky road ahead.

Help us, we pray, to carry what we can
  and leave the rest to you.

Help us to do the work you call us to,
  even when we're tired and discouraged
  and long to leave the bigger pieces
  for the mystery of your healing love.

O holy Maker of the long-awaited rain
  hear now our prayers for those in pain and need,
  and for ourselves,
  as we are bold to share with you
  the burdens we've been keeping to ourselves.

SUNDAY BETWEEN JULY 31 AND AUGUST 6 INCLUSIVE
PROPER 13, ORDINARY 18

Genesis 32:22–31; Psalm 17:1–7, 15; Romans 9:1–5;
Matthew 14:13–21

Opening Prayer

O holy Creator of the universe,
  God of the thirsty forest and the saturated shore,
  God of city street and mountain path,
   of stalking cats and leaping squirrels and mocking birds,
  we gather together in this holy moment as your people.

We gather here in this sacred space, eager to know your
    presence;
  we gather together as your body,
  called by your grace to feed the multitudes.

O God of all salvation, in this hour of celebration
  fill us with your Spirit,
  for we gather in the name of our Savior,
  who is Jesus the Christ. Amen.

Thanksgiving and Praise

God of new hope, holy Lover of creation,
  we come together as your people,
  moved by your call to care for every part of your creation.

We praise you for the flavor of this rich reality,
  for the variety of the creatures you have placed here,
  and particularly for the variety of our sisters and brothers,
  the human ones whom you have made so like your holy Self.

We celebrate the mysteries of truth we do not yet understand,
  and give thanks for the power of questions
  which can call us to new levels of understanding.

We pause to claim the gentle, healing power of Sabbath,
  the manna of empty silence that keeps us going
  even in the face of work and worry.

Hear now, O holy Giver of the wine of hope,
  our prayers of praise and thanksgiving
  for all the richness of your beautiful creation.

═══ Petition and Intercession ═══

Holy Maker of miracles,
  we know that there are so many people
  who hunger and thirst for more than food can satisfy;
  for love and acceptance,
  for hope and healing,
  for peace with justice.

We see those hungers in the eyes that dim from loss of hope;
  we hear it in the cries of the forgotten and oppressed;
  we feel it in the push of prophets
  urging us to give ourselves away,
  to spread the hope that feeds a longing
  bread can never satisfy.

O you who set a table in our midst
  and spread a banquet from the scraps
  that we've forgotten in our pockets,
  we sift in silence through the painful places in our hearts
  and raise to you our prayers for those in need,
  for those who hunger and thirst for bread—
  and so much more.

O loving Creator of the universe, open our eyes and ears
  so that we may know the work of peace with justice
  you have called us to,
  and find the strength
  to step out in faith with you along the Way.

We offer now our prayers of petition and intercession,
  aloud and in the silence of our hearts.

Sunday between August 7 and August 13 inclusive

Proper 14, Ordinary 19

Genesis 37:1–4, 12–28; Psalm 105:1–6, 16–22, 45b; Romans 10:5–15;
Matthew 14:22–33

Opening Prayer

O holy Maker of this mysterious reality,
  God of damp parking lot, dense forest and bright seashore,
  God of crowded city street and empty mountain path,
  God of the joyful and the angry,
  we gather together in this holy moment as your people.

We gather together to know your presence,
  flowing within us as your Body,
  called by your grace to step out of the boat in faith and trust,
  welcoming new realities
  even when we do not understand them.

Fill us with the breath of your Holy Spirit,
  O God of all salvation,
  for we gather in the name of our Savior,
  who is Jesus the Christ. Amen.

Thanksgiving and Praise

Holy, loving, inclusive Mystery,
  we give you thanks for calling all of us to be your people,
  for coming among us as a Savior,
  and for filling us with the power of your Spirit.

We praise you for lively forests and meadows,
  for realms of grass and blossom, birds and butterflies,
  each one unique.

We give you thanks for the creativity of community,
  and for your gift of loving compassion
  that calls us to work for peace and justice
  as we reach out to one another.

Hear now our prayers of praise and thanks,
  for all the richness of your beautiful creation.

Petition and Intercession

Holy Maker of miracles, sometimes we feel like Joseph,
   trying to do the will of his father,
   but sold into slavery by his brothers.

We want to do your will,
   to step out of the boat in faith,
   but our fears and the fears of others get in the way.

We hunger for the assurance
   that your justice and your righteousness will triumph.

We long to see the poor defended,
   the needy delivered from their want,
   and those who would oppress others
   stayed from evil and brought, themselves, to justice.

O God, you came among us as Jesus of Nazareth,
   the redeemer of creation,
   to show us just how love can heal,
   even when it does not own the power to overthrow.

Fill us with that love, we pray,
   for we would be your healing people.

Hear now our prayers for those in need,
   O God who calls us to step out of the boat in faith
   and claim our relationship with you.

Sunday between August 14 and August 20 inclusive

Proper 15, Ordinary 20

Genesis 45:1–15; Psalm 133; Romans 11:1–2a, 29–32;
Matthew 15:(10–20), 21–28

Opening Prayer

Holy Wellspring of welcome,
   you show the way to safety when famine threatens.

You open the way to unexpected welcome
  for one we have abandoned.

You open the gates to safety in times of deepest need.
O God, we come into this quiet sanctuary
  and know again how deeply we belong to you.

O God of all creation, fill us with your Holy Spirit,
  help us to recognize our sisters and brothers in the faith
  as we worship together
  in the name of our Savior, who is Jesus the Christ. Amen.

Thanksgiving and Praise

O God of miraculous love,
  how wonderfully you nourish your people!

How great is your love for those who call upon your name,
  for those who live according to your law of love!

Like Joseph's family, we wrestle with a certain sense of
    famine,
  and search in distant lands to find fresh food.

And when we come to one of those unfamiliar places
  and find that you have called a sister there to welcome us,
  we are amazed that you have been at work
  so far outside the box that we could never guess
  from which direction your good news will next appear.

Loving God, we would be filled by the crumbs
  that drop from your table,
  but you have set a place for us instead, a place of honor;
  for you have made us children, children with Christ,
  and heirs to your realm.

Holy God of all creation,
  we give thanks that you have opened yourself to us
  and called us to be your own.

Hear now our prayers of praise and thanks
  as we share them in the safety of this sanctuary,
  and ponder them in the silence of our hearts.

▬▬▬ Petition and Intercession ▬▬▬

God of healing love, you sent Paul the tent maker
  to spread the good news
  among those who did not think it had been sent for them.

And many heard that news and celebrate today
  because they know the healing presence of your Holy Spirit.

But still, we look around and see the people who seem all
    alone,
  so many tired and hungry,
  so many wounded and broken by war and hatred,
  so many children who see no hope for the future,
  so many who do not know the love and safety of community.

And we are also faced with hungers others carry,
  hungers that seem to force themselves
  into our own search for Sabbath.

Their need for faster roads and bigger homes
  in greener forests that belong to them alone,
  hungers that would clear the forests
  and pave the meadows to create a faster way
  to get from forest home to shopping mall.

Lover and redeemer, Holy Spirit of grace,
  we lift up in the light of your healing presence
  all those in pain and sorrow,
  those who are without friends or family,
  those without homes or hopes,
  and those whose needs for space and speed
  would take away all Sabbath silence.

O God of all creation, we bring our prayers to you,
  our words, our thoughts, our selves.

Hear now our prayers for those in need,
  O God of love and healing,
  as we lift them up in this sacred place,
  and in the silence of our hearts.

SUNDAY BETWEEN AUGUST 21 AND AUGUST 27 INCLUSIVE

PROPER 16, ORDINARY 21

Exodus 1:8–2:10; Psalm 124; Romans 12:1–8; Matthew 16:13–20

Opening Prayer

O Holy One, we come together here today
  to call upon your holy name,
  to offer you our thanks and praise,
  to spread the Word about mighty acts.

We gather in this place
  where we experience your presence, ready to rejoice.

For the depths of the earth are in your hand
  O Architect of sea and sky.

Your loving hands formed the dry land
  and all the rich variety of life that blossoms everywhere.

O come, let us worship and bow down,
  let us kneel before God, who is our Maker! Amen.

Thanksgiving and Praise

Holy Mystery, creator of the universe, maker of wind and water,
  though our world may seem burdened by hatred and violence,
  we know that you are with us.

You create each individual unique,
  then call us to join together in one compassionate body,
  combining all the rich variety of your creativity
  into communities equipped to do your will.

We thank you for gifts that differ wonderfully,
  according to your grace.

How unsearchable are your judgments
  and how inscrutable are your ways,
  O God of all creation.

With the disciple Peter,
  we claim your presence with us,
  and give you thanks and praise for the mystery of your love.

Hear now our prayers of praise and thanks,
   for living water in the deserts of our lives.

Petition and Intercession

O holy, loving God,
   we know that we will never fully understand
   the mystery of your creative ways.

You call us to be your servant people,
   to bind up the brokenhearted,
   to heal the sick,
   to visit those in prison, blocked from their full creativity
   by stone walls, or closed minds.

We know that your healing love can come,
   flowing from the heart of loving community
   to soothe, and heal,
   restore, enlighten, and empower.

Hear now our prayers for those in need:
   in need of healing, freedom, safety, and the power to create;
   in need of food, community, and love;
   in need of justice and peace.

Empower us to be your body in this place,
   O holy Creator of all,
   for we pray through Jesus who is our good news.

SUNDAY BETWEEN AUGUST 28 AND SEPTEMBER 3 INCLUSIVE

PROPER 17, ORDINARY 22

Exodus 3:1–15; Psalm 105:1–6, 23–26, 45b; Romans 12:9–21; Matthew 16:21–28

Opening Prayer

O come, people of faith, let us worship and bow down,
   let us make a joyful noise to the Mystery of all creation!

Let us come into God's presence filled with awe and wonder;
   let us raise our songs of praise to God!

For God is in the depths of the earth;
   God is in the heights of the mountains.

The storm-tossed sea is filled with God, who made it,
   calm and wild.

O holy Maker of this complicated mystery we know as life,
   we come to worship and bow down,
   to open our hearts to you, the maker of all! Amen.

Thanksgiving and Praise

Holy Mystery, Creator of the universe,
   mover of wind and water, Life of life,
   we come with growing understanding
   of the limits of our understanding.

We think we know the way things are,
   and then we come upon a bush that burns
   and burns, and burns.

And then we realize
   that there is more to you
   than books and theories can explain.

We think we know the way things ought to be,
   and then your grace breaks through
   the outward signs of poverty
   to show us what it means to live a life of faith.

We celebrate the power of your presence
   in every bit of this creation,
   and wait for the unfolding mystery of your love.

Hear now our prayers of praise and thanks,
   O holy Wellspring of life,
   for the mystery of your love,
   for living water in the deserts of our lives.

▬▬ Petition and Intercession ▬▬

Holy, loving Cascade of compassion,
   like Moses we hide our faces
   from the bright glory of your presence.

And, when we see so many needs around us,
   like Moses we doubt that we are up to the call.

We cry aloud, "Who am I, that I should stand up,
   advocate, ameliorate, lay down my life?"

Holy God of deepest healing,
   we know you call us to be your hands and feet,
   to offer healing help to those in need,
   to work for justice and inclusion for all.

We know so many places where your healing love is needed,
   where pain and grief
   have swept away the signs of hope and healing.

O holy Healer, give us the strength to feed our enemies,
   to leave all thoughts of vengeance to you,
   to overcome evil with good.

Hear now our prayers for those in pain and need,
   and for ourselves as well,
   for we pray that our love will be genuine
   as we hold fast to what is good.

We share our prayers of petition and intercession aloud,
   and lift them in the silence of our hearts.

SUNDAY BETWEEN SEPTEMBER 4 AND SEPTEMBER 10 INCLUSIVE

PROPER 18, ORDINARY 23

Exodus 12:1–14; Psalm 149; Romans 13:8–14; Matthew 18:15–20

Opening Prayer

Holy Maker of every thought and thing,
  God of blazing summer sun and drenching rain,
  God of loving forgiveness,
  we've gathered here in this place of quiet blessing.

We've come to pray and praise your presence
  in every part of our reality.

Holy God,
  we pray that you will help us know your presence,
  here and now, in every bone of our bodies,
  as we come together to know ourselves
  as one small part of the Body of the risen Christ. Amen.

Thanksgiving and Praise

God of loving forgiveness,
  holy Wellspring of hope and healing,
  we are reminded by the rain that,
  as important as it is to make our plans and follow through,
  it's also part of your plan for us
  to stay ready for the unexpected,
  ready to be called forth
  from the known into something new.

We're thankful when unexpected storms leave us
  still able to reach out to help each other
  and those around us.

We're thankful, too, that we can gather here today,
  lifting up those places
  where your wrath has passed over us,
  those times when we have known forgiveness,

and your gift of new and forgiving ways
  to love one another.

Holy One, in this time of prayer,
  silent and spoken aloud in your presence,
  show us those other places where we're called to gratitude.

Petition and Intercession

Holy Source of forgiveness and reconciliation,
  we feel the burden of so many cares and needs,
  the pain of war,
  the tide of violence and anger
  that seems to flow from unmet desires.

We carry grief for those whose lives have ended suddenly,
  and those whose sense of self has gone
  while life goes on.

We see so clearly all around us how easy it can be
  to welcome those who come dressed for the party,
  and ignore those who come wearing only what they have.

We pray that you will give us courage
  to love our neighbor as ourselves,
  even when those loving acts
  look foolish to the other neighbors,
  or others in the family.

Lord, help us learn to offer food and clothes
  to meet the needs of others
  before we hear ourselves say
  "Go in peace; keep warm and eat your fill."

Help us to share with you the burdens that we carry
  as we offer now our prayers for those in pain and need,
  and for ourselves,
  for we know how hard it is to learn to love.

SUNDAY BETWEEN SEPTEMBER 11 AND SEPTEMBER 17 INCLUSIVE

PROPER 19, ORDINARY 24

Exodus 14:19–31; Psalm 114; Romans 14:1–12; Matthew 18:21–35

Opening Prayer

Holy, mysterious Lover of all you have made,
  you call us to become your people:
  to remember ancient stories,
  to love our neighbors,
  to sing and praise your name.

In our prayers and in our silence,
  in our songs and in our laughter,
  in our tears and in our wonder,
  help us to know
  that you are always with us and among us.

As we remember the terror of the past,
  as we face the horror of today's disasters,
  give us the commitment and the courage
  to live in the name of Jesus, who is the Christ. Amen.

Thanksgiving and Praise

God of forgiveness and comfort,
  God of hope and renewal,
  we give you thanks for keeping us in your love.

We give thanks in large things and in small—
  for waking up to bright, crisp mornings;
  for being able to choose when to eat and when to fast;
  for the forgiveness of those we have wronged;
  for the love of family and friends.

We give thanks, also, for the challenges that come our way,
  for the opportunities we have to help others,
  for the moments when you ask us to be

the hands and feet of Christ,
bringing good news to the world.

And for what else shall we give thanks?

▬▬ **Petition and Intercession** ▬▬

Holy Mystery, as the Israelites in the wilderness
recognized your presence
in the pillar of fire by night
and the pillar of cloud by day,
we hear your voice in the cries
of the wounded and distressed.

Even as we give thanks
for the many blessings that fill our lives,
we hear the cries of those who have nothing,
of those who mourn,
of those who grieve for all that they have lost
or never had.

We pray that you will help the helpless,
bring comfort to the comfortless,
and heal the pain of the wounded and the ill.

For ourselves, we pray
for the courage and the commitment
to be the Body of Christ,
broken for the healing of the world.
And for what else shall we pray?

SUNDAY BETWEEN SEPTEMBER 18 AND SEPTEMBER 24 INCLUSIVE

PROPER 20, ORDINARY 25

Exodus 16:2–15; Psalm 105:1–6, 37–45; Philippians 1:21–30;
Matthew 20:1–16

Opening Prayer

Holy God of all creation, we gather in this place
  to remind ourselves that we are your people
  and you are our God.

We celebrate the good news
  that you are able to receive us as we are—
  the good news that you care enough to live among us,
  to dwell within us.

Holy Sustainer of this surprising mystery we call life,
  we bring ourselves together
  to help each other know just how much you care.
Fill us with your love,
  for we would be part of your web of healing and forgiveness,
  gathered to celebrate the risen Christ. Amen.

Thanksgiving and Praise

God of loving care,
  this week reminds us that the year is heading for its end:
  the sky washed clean by long, persistent storms;
  the first cold night and crisp Sunday morning;
  the first small acorns on the roof,
  all signs that what we've known before,
  we will know again.

O God of centuries and seasons,
  we give thanks that you are still with us
  even in the midst of war and rancor,
  through fire and flood you are close enough to touch our lives.

We give thanks that you have fed your people
  even in times of fear and scarcity,

sometimes offering just enough to sustain the faithful
  for one day at a time.

Thanks be to you, O Holy One,
  for all the ways you teach and guide:
  for parables and dark sayings;
  covenants and commandments;
  for prophets and teachers, lovers and leaders.

Your love flows to us through them all.

Hear our prayers O holy Lover of all,
  our thanks for what we have to share with those around us.

We share our prayers of praise and thanks aloud,
  and raise them up to you in the silence of our hearts.

Petition and Intercession

O mysterious Giver of life and light,
  you call us to stand firm in the Spirit,
  to offer hope and perseverance
  in a world where pain and hunger seem to dominate.

You give so much,
  yet in the presence of these wondrous gifts we find such pain.

We watch the battles rage in distant lands,
  see images of homes destroyed by raging fire,
  and cower as nations and communities are battered
  by the struggle between need and greed.

How can we bring your law of love
  to those who've closed their ears
  if we can't hear your still, small voice
  among the angry voices in our heads?

How can we serve you in these places filled with pain and fear
  if we are filled with pain and fear ourselves?

Call us forth, O Holy One, to be your hands and feet;
  fill us with a vision of your truth;
  move us into a fresh commitment to be your servants,
  your disciples here and now.

Hear now our prayers for those in need,
and for ourselves, for we would be your body in this place.

We raise our prayers aloud in this sacred space,
and ponder them in the silence of our hearts.

SUNDAY BETWEEN SEPTEMBER 25 AND OCTOBER 1 INCLUSIVE

PROPER 21, ORDINARY 26

Exodus 17:1–7; Psalm 78:1–4, 12–16; Philippians 2:1–13;
Matthew 21:23–32

Opening Prayer

Great Lover of unique variety,
Creator of light,
God of hope and work as well as failure and forgiveness,
we come today to know ourselves
as a community of your faithful people,
a band of pilgrims listening for the prophets,
a tiny part of the body of Christ.

O Holy One, we pray that you will fill us with your Spirit
as we worship in the name of Jesus, who is the Christ. Amen.

Thanksgiving and Praise

Amazing Lover of the hostas that bloom just now
in bold defiance of the season,
we gather at the foot of your holy mountain.

We hear the thunder and see the lightning,
and know that you are present with us.

Again and again,
you have brought your people into new lands,
filled their hearts with gladness,
lifted them above the flood,
and offered them life-giving water, flowing from dry stones.

When simple water is not enough,
  you bring us living water,
  the good news of your saving grace.

We know in our hearts
  the covenant you have made
  with faithful people of all ages,
  and know that we are freed to do your will.

We praise you for the brightness of this season,
  this time of harvest when many things are ending,
  and a time of rest is drawing near.

We praise you for signs of change
  in our own lives as well.

We thank you for the mystery of love,
  the power of compassion that spends life energy
  for others and not for self.

Hear now our prayers of praise and thanks,
  O holy Host of autumn harvest.

Petition and Intercession

Compassionate, creating God,
  forgiver of the angry whose pain slips out of sight
  when the light turns green,
  lover of the dedicated souls
  too busy with good works to help a stranger
  who is out of reach beyond the windshield,
  you made a new commitment to us
  through the life and death and resurrection of Jesus.

By your covenant, you have freed us to be your people.
Your call moves us to claim our heritage.
Holy Source of living water,
  we open our hearts to those in need.

Hear now our prayers for those whose lives are pain,
  for those whose hopes are ashes,

for those whose joy has fallen from the tree of life
before the harvest is complete.

And what other needs, O Holy One,
are you raising up in our hearts?

SUNDAY BETWEEN OCTOBER 2 AND OCTOBER 8 INCLUSIVE

PROPER 22, ORDINARY 27

Exodus 20:1–4, 7–9, 12–20; Psalm 19; Philippians 3:4b–14;
Matthew 21:33–46

Opening Prayer

Holy Maker of all that is,
the heavens tell your glory,
the sky proclaims that you are God.
Your holy Word is more than any words can say,
more than all the voices of humankind,
greater even than the sounds of all creation.

You set everything in its rightful place,
connecting us to stars and planets
to microbes and earthworms,
to fish and birds and horses and cattle
with laws of biology and gravity and energy.

You have given us commandments of steadfast love,
of respect for one another
and for the earth itself,
teaching us how to live according to your will.

In our songs and in our silence,
in our stories and in our prayers,
fill us with your Holy Spirit
and lead us ever more deeply
into the life of your Holy Child, Jesus. Amen.

▬▬▬ **Thanksgiving and Praise** ▬▬▬

Holy Lover of all that is,
  we see your face in every flower,
  your hands in every tree reaching upward to the sky.

We hear your voice in thunder and in gentle rain,
  in the gurgle of bubbling streams,
  and in the sigh of wind blowing across a sandy beach.

We give you thanks for all the sounds and sights
  that surround us,
  for bright, blue sky and heavy, dark clouds;
  for grasslands and forest,
  for deserts and glaciers,
  for oceans and rivers and waterfalls,
  and muddy puddles on busy city streets.

We give you thanks for the simple rules
  that help us live with one another—
  do not lie, do not steal, do not kill—
  and for your steadfast love which is beyond all rules.

We give you thanks for parents and children,
  for friends and neighbors and strangers,
  for all that is and all that we hope will be.
  Aloud and in silence, we give you our thanks and praise.

▬▬▬ **Petition and Intercession** ▬▬▬

Holy Healer of every hurt,
  you hold all things together in love.

Still, we often feel lost and alone,
  yearning for your love,
  looking for you even in the broken places of our lives.
  Even in our deepest wounds and heartache,
  we pray for healing, for wholeness,
  for the strength to forgive.

As you open our hearts to the pain of others,
  we pray for all who suffer from want and fear,

and for all who offer them comfort and shelter;
we pray for all who live with grief and regret,
and for all who offer them solace and understanding;
we pray for all whose minds or bodies are broken,
and for all who bind up their wounds.

We pray for an end to violence,
for an end to poverty,
for an end to all that stands in the way of your love.
And for what else shall we pray this day?

SUNDAY BETWEEN OCTOBER 9 AND OCTOBER 15 INCLUSIVE

PROPER 23, ORDINARY 28

Exodus 32:1–14; Psalm 106:1–6, 19–23; Philippians 4:1–9;
Matthew 22:1–14

Opening Prayer

Holy God of loving forgiveness,
we gather here this fall morning
remembering that your steadfast love endures forever.

We come because you call us to be your people,
to gather together in community,
to sing and celebrate the mystery
of your love for all creation.

We gather here to celebrate the joy of being in your presence,
for we gather in the name of your true child, Jesus,
who is the Christ, the Messiah,
the one whose coming reaches out to us
through the isolation of our sin,
to bring us into full community. Amen.

Thanksgiving and Praise

Eternal, nurturing Fountain of love,
your greatness is beyond the best description we can offer,

your love pours forth in streams of living water,
the earth is filled to overflowing with your love.

Our lives are held so tightly in your loving embrace
that every thought and thing we have belongs to you.

We remember that your steadfast love endures forever,
embracing and forgiving all who turn to you.

In days of chaos and competition,
we recognize how easy it can be
to let the interests of those who are bigger, louder
or more self-assured
crowd out the needs of those
who struggle for a place to simply live.

And yet, O loving Mother of forgiveness,
we feel the power of your love
in so many examples of caring, compassion and healing.

Hear now, O Holy One,
the love and thanks that we feel welling up within us.

Hear us as we speak,
and as our hearts are opened
to share our inmost thankful selves with you.

▬▬ Petition and Intercession ▬▬

Holy God of loving forgiveness
today we wonder at the pain
of your children in the wilderness:
wanting a clear sign of your presence in their midst,
hungry for assurance,
willing to turn an image of you into an idol.

We know our own hungers for certainty,
particularly in troubling times
when what we've been gathering into barns
for winter seasons of our lives
seems to have been attacked by rats.

We feel fear creeping into us
  from every anxious news update,
   and long for the assurance that you are in control.

We know so many places where need and insecurity
  have pushed their way past principle and policy,
   butting into line ahead of other, older, deeper needs.

O God of unfathomable complexity,
  we raise our prayers to you today
  knowing there is more to your creation
  than we will ever understand.

O holy Mystery, hear now our prayers for those in need,
  for all of us whose lives seem to have gone off-track,
  whose nights are filled with worry, pain, anxiety, and grief.

SUNDAY BETWEEN OCTOBER 16 AND OCTOBER 22 INCLUSIVE

PROPER 24, ORDINARY 29

Exodus 33:12–23; Psalm 99; 1 Thessalonians 1:1–10;
Matthew 22:15–22

Opening Prayer

Holy God of re-creation,
  we gather once again to celebrate
  the covenant that binds us to you and to each other,
  here in this time and place.

God of the open future,
  like Moses, we call out to you:
  "If we have found favor in your sight, show us your ways."

Show us your glory, we pray, today and in the days to come,
  for we gather as a people committed to your Way,
  the way of Christ, who is our Savior. Amen.

═══ Thanksgiving and Praise ═══

God of birth, and death, and resurrection,
  we are bound together
  by the knowledge of your love for us.

We see it as we work for justice
  in the places where you call us,
    the homes and offices and street corners
    where we reach out to those in need.

We see it in the way we care for one another,
  the love and caring that flows within the family of faith.

Lover of justice and compassion,
  you have established equity
  as a standard for your chosen people,
  and we give thanks.

Hear now the prayers of praise and thanks we lift to you,
  for all the power of your presence in the world.

═══ Petition and Intercession ═══

God of love and hope,
  we know how much it means to us
  to have a home, a home in faith,
  a place where we can celebrate the good news
  of your presence in our lives.

And yet we know so many places
  that seem cut off from the joy of that good news.

The strident tension of those who struggle
  to win a place as leaders
  shines a lurid light on all of us,
  and makes it hard to see
  how this might really be
  one nation under you.

We cry out for the plight of those who do not have the means
  to guarantee safety, opportunity and justice
  for themselves and their communities.

God of justice and compassion,
  hear now our prayers for those in distant lands who suffer,
  for this great nation,
  whose founders said it would be guided by your law,
  for those who suffer pain or loss,
  and for ourselves,
  for we long to be more responsive to your call.

Hear now, O Holy One,
  our prayers of petition and intercession,
  the ones we share aloud
  and those we whisper in the silence of our hearts.

SUNDAY BETWEEN OCTOBER 23 AND OCTOBER 29 INCLUSIVE

PROPER 25, ORDINARY 30

Deuteronomy 34:1–12; Psalm 90:1–6, 13–17; 1 Thessalonians 2:1–8;
Matthew 22:34–46

Opening Prayer

Holy God, it is so hard for us
  to claim the voice of prophets in our midst,
  who call us to move forward
  into the promised but unknown land,
  trusting that we will not be swept away by raging waters.

And yet, we know that
  even when we seem to have little or no control
  over the circumstances of our lives,
  you promise that you will be with us.

We pray that this community
  might be gathered up into your bosom
  as we worship here
  knowing we are cradled in the warmth your embrace,
  for we gather in the name of our Savior,
  who is Jesus the Christ. Amen.

Thanksgiving and Praise

God of harvests and the end of summer growth,
we celebrate the cooler nights
and rains that nourish seeds of next year's new beginnings.

We marvel at the beauty of your wild creatures,
barred owls that hunt the fields by night;
timid field mice nurturing their young
in hidden nests of twigs and moss
and young deer curious about our presence
in the woods they call their home.

We give you thanks for time to gather in community,
to celebrate and wonder together
about who you are calling us to be.

What is the treasure you have gathered
in this harvest time?

What seeds of mission have you scattered
on the wet soil of our life together here?

We marvel at the power of your creative love.

We celebrate the beauty of your created world.

We thank you for the warmth of community gathered.

Hear now our prayers of praise and thanks,
for we know we are your people,
and we long to know the miracle of your creation.

Petition and Intercession

God of love and healing,
you hold the universe so gently in your cosmic hand
that sometimes we must wait in stillness
for some sign that you are there.

In contrast, it is easier to see the pain and suffering
that marks our troubled times.

It is so hard to ignore the violence of war and storm,
but harder still to find the news
of healing hands upon the fevered brows

of those whose lives will end today from flood or quake,
from violence, or lack of food.

O God, we know that we can never heal the world,
and yet we also know that we are called to give ourselves
to stewardship of that small part of your creation
where you are calling us.

We pray for faith to go where you are sending us,
to spend our lives in service
even when there seems to be no hope.

Holy God, teach us to be obedient to the great
commandments,
to love you so completely that there's time for nothing else,
and then to love our neighbors,
even those we do not know or like.

Hear now, O Lord, our prayers
for those who can't escape the pain,
for those who grieve and mourn,
for those whose burdens seem to them impossible to bear,
and for ourselves.

Hear our prayers for all who are in need.

SUNDAY BETWEEN OCTOBER 30 AND NOVEMBER 5 INCLUSIVE

PROPER 26, ORDINARY 31

Joshua 3:7–17; Psalm 107:1–7, 33–37; 1 Thessalonians 2:9–13;
Matthew 23:1–12

Opening Prayer

Holy Mystery,
you turn rivers into deserts,
springs of water into thirsty ground,
a fruitful land into a salty waste.

You turn deserts into pools of water,
a parched land into springs of water,

making a place for hungry people
  to live and plant and grow.
You satisfy the thirsty,
  and the hungry you fill with good things.
You have taught as that the greatest among us
  should be but servants,
    that all who exalt themselves will be humbled,
    and all who humble themselves will be exalted.
Help us to live in daily awareness of your holy presence.
  Make of us your holy Body,
    the hands and feet and heart of Christ
    making your eternal realm real to a broken world. Amen.

Thanksgiving and Praise

Holy Hearer of all our stories,
  you ask us to live into love in every moment,
  to give thanks in all things.
We give you thanks for prophets and poets,
  for all who witness to your steadfast love,
  for all whose lives are poured out
  in service to your calling.
We give you thanks for bright, clear skies
  and grey clouds filled with rain;
  for chrysanthemums and pumpkins,
  for feasting and fasting,
  for memories and anticipation of happy times.
We give thanks for all these things,
  and all that we never notice.
  And for what else shall we give thanks this day?

Petition and Intercession

Holy Healer of all our wounds,
  you ask us to take in the pain of the world
  and return only compassion.

We pray for politicians and protesters,
 for those who keep the peace
 and those who trouble our dreams.

We pray for all whose lives are filled with pain,
 for those who live without shelter,
 for those who live without food for the body
 or food for the soul,
 for those who live without love.

In the words we speak out loud
 and in the silences between them,
 we pray for those we love
 and those we have never met;
 we pray for our own needs,
 and for those who cannot pray for themselves.

SUNDAY BETWEEN NOVEMBER 6 AND NOVEMBER 12 INCLUSIVE

PROPER 27, ORDINARY 32

Joshua 24:1–3a, 14–25; Psalm 78:1–7; 1 Thessalonians 4:13–18;
Matthew 25:1–13

Opening Prayer

Holy God of waiting and searching,
 God of shorn fields and full barns,
 God of cold concrete and wet cardboard blankets,
 we bring ourselves to you.

We come to learn again that we are part of your one Body,
 part of your emerging mystery,
 part of the good news you bring in Christ.

Holy lover of seed and bulb,
 we look around and know that we are home,
 that we are growing in your body,
 that you have given us the good news of salvation.

Help us know that you are here among us,
  for we gather in the name of Christ,
  who is the good news for this day
  and for the days to come. Amen.

Thanksgiving and Praise

Amazing, invigorating Breath of community,
  we come here, huddled against the gathering cold,
  hoping for a comforting word,
  hungry for the warmth of your abiding love.

The trees of state,
  so deeply notched by months of loud campaigning,
  have fallen before the gentle wind of ballots cast.

The forest floor is littered with the trunks and limbs
  of those who would have led, but were rejected,
  of those who tried to lead and are exhausted.

But, buried under all that litter of posture and politics,
  the hopeful roots of what is growing for next season
  are gathering strength from these cold rains and mild days.

O gracious, healing Gardener of the future,
  we raise our prayers of praise and thanks,
  for all that you've provided.

Petition and Intercession

Holy, rejuvenating Maker of change,
  we watch the pain that builds from years of isolation
  grow stronger in the face of arrogant self-satisfaction.

We know so many people who cannot see hope
  because their pain is more than they can bear alone.

We struggle with the hard reality of poverty and violence,
  and children left alone to find their own paths to the future.

Gracious, healing leader of the hopeless,
  help us learn and share the power of your promises:
  that those who weep now are blessed

because in the future they will laugh,

that those who are hungry now will be filled,

that the realm of God belongs to the poor.

Holy One, we bring our prayers to you,

our prayers for those who mourn,

for those who are alone,

for those who do not know the comfort of community.

We raise our prayers in faith that we are in you as you are
in us,

your eyes and ears and hands and feet,

some small part of the presence of the risen Savior,

Jesus, in whose name we pray.

Sunday between November 13 and November 19 inclusive

Proper 28, Ordinary 33

Judges 4:1–7; Psalm 123; 1 Thessalonians 5:1–11; Matthew 25:14–30

Opening Prayer

God of song and silence,

God of life and breath,

God of yesterday, today, and tomorrow,

you fill our eyes with the beauty of your creation,

our ears with the sounds of all that you have made.

You know us in every time and every season,

filling our hearts and minds with love,

filling our days and nights with hope,

filling our lives with the light of your presence.

Pour out your Holy Spirit on your holy Body gathered here

for the sake of all your creation. Amen.

Thanksgiving and Praise

God of life and breath,

God of yesterday, today, and tomorrow,

God of song and silence,
we give thanks for the signs of your presence
in the bright, red leaves of a maple tree
glowing against a deep, blue sky;
in the rushing waters of a clear, mountain stream;
in an intricate, silken web strung across a forest path.

We give you thanks for long years of friendship
making light of heavy work;
for the light banter of a homeless stranger,
hoping for a handout on a city street;
for the hopes and dreams of peace
that remind us that all things come from you.

We give thanks for stories of ancient victories,
for clear-eyed visions of what is broken in our world,
for your promises of better days to come.
And for what else shall we give thanks this day?

Petition and Intercession

God of yesterday, today, and tomorrow,
God of song and silence,
God of life and breath,
as the Israelite people came to you in their distress,
so do we come to you now,
pleading for an end to violence of every kind.

We pray for all who make the laws,
and all who act as judges and juries.

We pray for all who keep the peace,
and all who are compelled to make war.

We pray for all who are oppressed,
and pray that all who hurt or oppress others
will learn your ways of love.

Aloud and in silence, we beg you to have mercy on us
and on all your creation,
for all are in need of your grace.

THE REIGN OF CHRIST

SUNDAY BETWEEN NOVEMBER 20 AND NOVEMBER 26 INCLUSIVE

PROPER 29, ORDINARY 34

Ezekiel 34:11–16, 20–24; Psalm 100; Ephesians 1:15–23;
Matthew 25:31–46

Opening Prayer

O holy, loving Shepherd,
  searching for us in the scattered crowd,
  we come to offer you our heartfelt thanks,
  rejoicing as you lead us home,
  through the gates of your realm.

Holy Ruler of all reality,
  we celebrate the good news
  that your realm is all around us, close at hand.

You set before us a feast of justice
  to nourish us in these trying times.

We come together now,
  to worship you,
  O Holy One from whom all creation flows.

We come to find your healing and empowering presence,
  here and now in this community.
Reveal yourself to us, we pray,
  for we gather in the name of our Savior,
  who is Jesus the Christ. Amen.

Thanksgiving and Praise

God of love and laughter,
  God of quiet companionship,
  God of deep unknowable mystery—
  Holy God, we gather here to be your people,
  part of your Body, the sheep of your flock.

We come, bearing thanks for the harvests of our lives.
For the bounty of family and friendships,
  we give you thanks.

For rest in green pastures and nourishment in surprising places,
  we give you thanks.

For unexpected possibilities, new hopes,
  new calls to service and love,
  we give you thanks.

Hear now our prayers of praise and thanks
  for all the rich harvest of our lives.

Petition and Intercession

Holy God, we know that with the harvest comes the winter.
We know how hard life can be
  when there is not enough to go around;
  when food runs out,
  when sickness lays us low,
  when violence threatens to take away
  every meager comfort and hope.

We know of many who huddle outside the fold,
  longing for rest and healing,
  hungry for the nourishment that only you can bring.

Holy God, Good Shepherd,
  you who will search out the little ones
  and make sure they have a place at the table,
  hear now our prayers for those who have no comfort,
  no green pasture of safety,
  no nourishment in the presence of their enemies.

O God of love, we lift our prayers to you
  for those in pain and need,
  for those we know, and those we only know about,
  and for ourselves,
  for we so often know just how it is to wake up lost and lonely.

Year B

ADVENT

First Sunday of Advent

Isaiah 64:1–9; Psalm 80:1–7, 17–19; 1 Corinthians 1:3–9;
Mark 13:24–37

Opening Prayer

Mysterious, holy Promise of new beginnings,
  we thank you for the good news of the coming Christ,
    calling us into an unknowable future.
Give ear, O holy Shepherd of Israel,
  you who lead your people like a flock.

Let your face shine, that we may be saved.
Let your presence fill us with your Holy Spirit,
  for we gather as your church, the people of your flock,
    the body of the risen Christ,
      in whose name we worship and wait. Amen.

Thanksgiving and Praise

Mysterious, holy Promise of new beginnings,
  we gather on this cold, gray morning,
    a tiny band of people called to follow where you lead us,
      into an unknowable future.

We gather to remind ourselves
  that your way is not the way of many.
We realize that your peace is not the peace
  that this world fights to win.

This week we celebrate again
   the mystery of your incarnation among us.

We tell ourselves again the story
   of how you come
   to share the joys and pains of this creation;
   of how you enter our reality as a child,
   small and helpless
   in the face of greed and hatred, war and poverty.

Holy Giver of hope,
   we've gathered here to celebrate and give thanks
   for all the wonder of this world you have created.

Hear now our prayers of praise,
   for the marvelous surprises of this creation,
   our prayers of thanks for all the richness of your presence
   in this late harvest time.

Petition and Intercession

God of judgment and forgiveness,
   these days are dark and cold.

The hopes of easy victory are buried under heavy earth,
   soaked by the rains that wash bright summer from the trees
   and drive all creatures to search for shelter.

We've come again to wait,
   drawn together by the promise of your coming.

We've come to find the courage
   to let go of what has passed away.

We've come to gather strength for new beginnings
   promised, but not yet seen.

We lift our prayers for those who wait but have no hope.
We lift our prayers for those who suffer,
   for those in pain,
   for those whose anger binds them
   in some dungeon of despair.

Hear now our prayers for those in pain and need,
and for ourselves, for often we feel cold and wet
and bound in prisons of our own.

SECOND SUNDAY OF ADVENT

Isaiah 40:1–11; Psalm 85:1–2, 8–23; 2 Peter 3:8–15a; Mark 1:1–8

Opening Prayer

Holy One, you send your messengers to bring us good news,
to bring us words of comfort in the season of Christ's coming.

Last summer's leaves still cling to dark, brown branches,
reminding us, even as winter approaches,
that you are always with us.

The icy wind and scudding clouds
bring promises of deeper cold,
and the puffs of our breath, steaming in the bright, clear air,
tell us that your Holy Spirit lives in us and through us.

The sounds of a Christmas that is yet to come
fill our ears as we work and shop and drive,
letting us know that all the world
yearns for your boundless joy and peace.

Here, in this place, we look for signs of your presence,
and listen for the sound of your voice
in our prayers and songs and silences.

We wait for the coming of the one who saves us.
We yearn for you to tear open the heavens,
to create in us a new heaven and a new earth
where righteousness is at home. Amen.

Thanksgiving and Praise

Blessed are you, Holy One,
maker of heaven and earth,
savior of all that is broken,
spirit of all that is beautiful.

We come to your table filled with thanksgiving,
   overflowing with gratitude for the life
   that flows around us and through us.

We give thanks for the ordinary things that fill our days:
   for busses and trains and cars that get us where we need to go;
   for fast food and fine restaurants and home-cooked meals;
   for computers and telephones and paper and pens
   that keep us connected with family and friends far away;
   for cheerful sales clerks and friendly coworkers
   and loving friends who help us remember
   that we are always in your presence.

And we give thanks, most of all, for making us one in Christ,
   who bears the promise of new life,
   of love and peace.
   And for what else shall we give thanks?

Petition and Intercession

Holy One, you greet us with good news,
   with words of comfort in the season of Christ's coming.

And yet, every day we hear news of sickness and death,
   of disaster and loss,
   of leaders disgraced,
   of hope defeated.

Our breaking hearts cry out to you,
   great River of compassion,
   begging you to heal the hurts
   that divide our world, our nation,
   our personal relationships,
   and ourselves.

We pray for those who mourn,
   for those who have no place to live,
   for those whose bodies are a source of unrelenting pain,
   for those who feel no love in this season of good cheer.

We pray, also, for those who have all they need,
  for those who live in comfort and safety,
  for those who make laws and rules that others must follow,
  for those who do not even know
  that they, too, need our prayers.

Great Comforter of the broken-hearted,
  aloud and in silence we pray
  that you will bring healing to all that is broken.

THIRD SUNDAY OF ADVENT

Isaiah 61:1–4, 8–11; Psalm 126; 1 Thessalonians 5:16–24;
John 1:6–8, 19–28

Opening Prayer

O God of peace and justice,
  since the days of the prophet Isaiah
  you have sent your wise messengers
  to bring a vision of your realm, already close at hand.

And so we wait with growing expectation,
  yearning for your coming in this time and place.

God of all salvation, we pray that you will fill our hearts,
  open our eyes, clean out our ears, and loosen our tongues,
  for we gather in the Spirit of the very one for whom we wait,
  the redeemer of creation, who is Jesus the Christ. Amen.

Thanksgiving and Praise

Holy God of all creation,
  we marvel at the power of your promise to Isaiah
  to bring good news to the oppressed,
  to bind up the brokenhearted,
  to proclaim liberty to the captives and release to the prisoners,
  to proclaim the year of your favor.

We come with thanks
   that we are one small part of your tribe,
      the Body of the Christ for whom we wait.

How glorious are the fruits of your creation,
   the trees and fields at rest;
      the deer, and cats more wild than we think,
      the children, wise beyond their own experience.

How clearly they can hear the good news you proclaim!
We marvel at the power of your presence in our time,
   give thanks for all we have received,
      and for this time to wait in growing anticipation
      for your coming once again into our world.

Hear now our prayers of praise and thanks
   for all the bounty of your creation,
      the words of thanks we share aloud,
      and grateful thoughts we raise up in our hearts.

Petition and Intercession

O God of Advent waiting,
   we know in ways beyond the words our tongues can speak,
      that you are present to all the irony and agony of life.

We wonder why it is so difficult to live together in community,
   and why we struggle over what it means to do good,
      and how to do it here and now.

How can we be your vessel
   to bring good news to each other
      and to those around us who are in need?

We claim the promise of Isaiah, our gift from you:
   comfort for those who mourn, a garland instead of ashes.

We yearn to know your coming in this time and place.
You are here among us: come quickly, Lord Jesus!
We watch with deep concern
   as fear and fighting seem to hold the upper hand
      in so many places.

We long to know that you are present,
  even though we have trouble seeing you in the suffering.

We want the heavens torn open now, and ask:
  What can we do to help?

You are here among us: come quickly Lord Jesus!
Hear now our prayers for those in sorrow and in need,
  for we would know your presence with us, even as we wait.

We raise our prayers for your healing presence
  in all the pain and need we see.

Receive the prayers of your hearts,
  the ones we speak,
  and those that pulsate deep in the silence of our hearts.

FOURTH SUNDAY OF ADVENT

2 Samuel 7:1–11, 16; Luke 1:46b–55; Romans 16:25–27; Luke 1:26–38

Opening Prayer

God of hopeful waiting,
  God of children and revolutionaries,
  God of the unknowable future,
  today we come with growing anticipation,
  hungry for the rebirth of your Good News among us.

Fill us with your love, we pray.

Show us how we can more completely be
  the Body of the Christ we worship,
  whose birth we celebrate this week.

Fill us with your Holy Spirit
  as we gather in the name of our Savior Jesus, the Christ.

Amen.

Thanksgiving and Praise

God of new birth,
  amazing God who holds this universe in gentle love,

holy Giver of the most precious gift, Jesus the Messiah—
the Good News that you are coming among us
stirs us like a child hungering to be born.

Today, we celebrate the immanence of your new reality.
What joyful expectation!
We give you thanks and praise
for the rich complexity of this time in history,
and for your presence in the midst of so much global pain.

We want so much to be born anew
as your body in this time and place.

We hunger for a deeper knowing
of why you birthed us as your church,
how you nurtured us to life
as this particular family of faith,
and where you call us
into the ministries of love and reconciliation.

This Sabbath day
before we celebrate the birth of Jesus among us,
we lift our hearts and voices in praise and thanks
for all that you are doing at this time in history.

Petition and Intercession

Loving God, our hope is real, but there is fear on every side.
So many hungry, homeless, losing jobs; such violence;
such stubborn problems pushing in from every side;
so much confusion and so little sense of what we ought to do.

How can we be Christ's Body in this time and place?
Can we be born again in a garage?
And are we willing to work hard in one community
for years and years while our faith deepens?

When we are called into ministry, can we be radically inclusive?
Are we ready to choose a death with faith and love
over the comfortable life we think of as our birthright?

God help us to live like your children this week,
  hoping and expectant,
  knowing that what is coming is just as deeply revolutionary
  as it is good.

Help us to know this really is your world,
  the world where you call us to be your hands and feet,
  your eyes and ears,
  the very heart of your compassion.

Hear now, O Holy One, our prayers for those in need,
  and for ourselves,
  for we must count on you for what it takes
  to be part of the Body of the risen Christ.
  Aloud and in silence, we offer you the prayers of our hearts.

CHRISTMASTIDE

FIRST SUNDAY AFTER CHRISTMAS DAY

Isaiah 61:10–62:3; Psalm 148; Galatians 4:4–7; Luke 2:22–40

Opening Prayer

Holy Maker of all that is,
  you clothe us with the garments of salvation,
  with festive jewels of celebration.

At the turning of the year,
  you festoon the whole world
  with shimmering light;
  you hang the trees with garlands of glory,
  reminding us once more
  that you have come to live among us.

As we gather in this place of beauty,
  fill us with the spirit of the One
  who is eternally newborn among us,
  bringing words of peace and hope
  to all your creatures. Amen.

Thanksgiving and Praise

Bright Seed of new beginnings,
  you fill the earth with energy and light.
  Fire and hail, snow and frost, and stormy wind
  are in your hands,
  as welcome light begins to beckon
  from the southern sky.

We give thanks for bright stars,
  for moonlit nights,
  for a sparkle of sunshine through rain-fogged windows.
We give thanks for those who see your face
  in the puckered grimace of a newborn child;
  in the wizened grin of an old woman
  wheeling her cart along the street;
  in the laughter and the tears that bind us to one another.

Most of all, we are grateful for the life, death, and resurrection
  of the one who calls us into new life,
  and daily renews us as members
  of the risen Body of Christ.

Petition and Intercession

Mysterious Spirit of compassion,
  even as we celebrate the new birth of hope in our midst,
  we remember all those
  for whom hope is just a four-letter word.

We pray for those who know the darkness of depression,
  for those who lie wakeful through the long hours of night,
  for those whose bodies or minds are gripped in pain.

We pray for those who watch for morning,
  for those who live in fear,
  for those whose bellies are never full.

We pray for those who have too much,
  for those who have power over others,
  for those who do not think that they need anyone's prayers.
And we pray for ourselves,
  that we may become the Body of Christ for the world.

SECOND SUNDAY AFTER CHRISTMAS DAY

Jeremiah 31:7–14; Psalm 147:12–20; Ephesians 1:3–14;
John 1:(1–9), 10–18

Opening Prayer

O Holy One,
 you guide us through the challenges of reconciliation,
 giving us safe places for healing and growth.
Holy Wellspring of new life, you bless our children,
 and through them, the future of your creation.

As this new year begins,
 we pray that you will reveal yourself among us
 as we gather to celebrate the coming of your Word
 as flesh and blood in our midst,
 your coming as the Creator of reconciliation,
 the Prince of Peace, our Savior, Jesus the Christ. Amen.

Thanksgiving and Praise

Holy Maker of all that is new,
 God of every thought and thing,
 your wisdom is the root of all reality;
 your commitment is the source of all strength;
 your compassion is the fount of every blessing.

We give you thanks
 for all the richness of our life together in this time and place.
O God, we rejoice that you bring salvation into this reality,
 opening the way for healing, hope, and reconciliation
 here among us and in the wider world
 that seems so full of anger, greed, and arrogance.

Thanks be to you for the coming of Christ into our midst.
God of all creation,
 we ask your blessing on the time
 that this new year offers each of us.

May we be good stewards,
  and faith-full celebrants of time with you.

We raise our praise
  into the shining brightness of the sun and moon,
  the planets and the mysteries of life persistent.

Hear now, O patient Builder of reality,
  our prayers of praise and thanks,
  for life, for joy, for growth, for hope in the year just past,
  and for the faith to claim the new that only comes from you.

Petition and Intercession

Holy God of options yet undreamed by mortal imagination,
  we've carried life this far along the way.

Some days we celebrate the joy of that experience,
  and other days we'd just as soon
  be able to set our burdens down
  and call for help from backs much stronger than ours.

We hold up into your creating light
  the needs and hungers of this day,
  the blind and lame,
  those with child and those in labor,
  those who suffer from the violence of war and terror,
  the ill and those who are abandoned and alone.

We pray to see more clearly that the light of Christ,
  the healing light of all people,
  is shining in the darkness all around.

Hear now, O holy Source of healing and forgiveness,
  our prayers for those in need,
  and for ourselves,
  as we acknowledge just how much our future depends on you.

THE EPIPHANY OF CHRIST

Isaiah 60:1–6; Psalm 72:1–7, 10–14; Ephesians 3:1–12;
Matthew 2:1–12

Opening Prayer

Holy, loving Source of all creation,
  maker of this day and all that is a part of it,
  holy Lover of life and growth,
  we celebrate the light and life that you keep making.

Wonderful, groaning Mystery of love,
  we come to you with fresh awareness,
  open to your love in unexpected ways,
  like newborns reaching for a bright new smile.

Fill us with a knowledge of the holy
  that draws us into new beginnings,
  for we would be your living people,
  gathered in the name of Jesus of Nazareth,
  who is our guide and our redeemer. Amen.

Thanksgiving and Praise

Wonderful, nurturing Sower of new seed
  we gather here this morning,
  filled with such a mix of thoughts and feelings,
  such a smorgasbord of hopes and fears,
  such a stew of joys and pains.

We want the coming of this new year
  to bring an end to war and pain and illness and injustice,
  and yet we know that you have given life to us
  in such a form that we can never know the end before its time.
The quince that blooms beside the path
  may well know more about the winter still ahead
  than we can guess.

That bush, so nearly hidden by the ivy growing in the corner,
  is living out its call:
  to give itself to blossom every time it gets the chance,
  without a thought to whether there will be the opportunity
  for fruit this year.

The unexpected testimony of those brilliant blossoms
  lifts up the image of the Magi offering their unexpected gifts,
  their homage to a hope-filled future they did not expect.

O Fountain of life and hope,
  we give you thanks for this unexpected golden testimony.

Hear now our other prayers of praise and thanks,
  for all the wonders of this time,
  the ones we choose to share aloud,
  and those we cherish in the silence of our hearts.

▬▬ Petition and Intercession ▬▬

Holy Giver of light and hope,
  this turning of the year
  has brought us unexpected pain and grief:
  death and illness;
  the threat of ending opportunities for work and service;
  the fear of chronic pain and disability.

We know you give the future to us just one day at a time,
  and so we carry our concerns,
  our hopes for those we love and those we serve,
  like backpacks that are too heavy

to put down and pick up again,
so we rest standing up.

Holy Giver of healing and hope,
hear us as we share with you the burdens we are carrying,
and help us find a way to help each other
set down and leave with you
whatever we do not have strength to carry by ourselves.

Hear now our prayers for those in need and for ourselves,
for we would be strengthened by the Holy Spirit
that sets free the saints, and comforts the faithful in every age.

ORDINARY TIME

The Sundays after Epiphany

BAPTISM OF CHRIST
(FIRST SUNDAY AFTER EPIPHANY)

ORDINARY I

Genesis 1:1–5; Psalm 29; Acts 19:1–7; Mark 1:4–11

Opening Prayer

Unpredictable, enlivening Spirit of creation,
  you bring order out of chaos,
  joy out of suffering,
  life out of death.

You separate light from darkness,
  day from night,
  water from dry land.

Like Jesus in the Jordan,
  you call us to enter the waters of baptism,
  that we might know ourselves
  as your beloved children.

As we celebrate your life among us,
  help us to hear your voice
  in the sounds of birdcall and rainfall,
  in music and laughter,
  in our own words and in silence. Amen.

Thanksgiving and Praise

Holy Spirit, holy Lover, holy Child of God,
  the waters of your forgiveness

pour over us like a flood,
  washing away our tears of regret
    in a river of gratitude.

We give thanks for sunshine and moonlight,
  for clouds and rain,
    for raucous wind and bright, burning stars.

We give thanks for a cup of coffee shared with a friend,
  for a soft caress brushing our cheek with love,
    for the first sweet breath of a newborn baby,
    for the sharp, clean scent of pine trees on a cold, winter day.

In the silence of our hearts
  and in the words of our mouths,
    we give thanks for the gift of life and love.

Petition and Intercession

Holy One, Holy Spirit, holy Maker of all,
  our gratitude overflows like a river in flood,
    bringing with it reminders of pain and grief.

We remember the people who live in fear and pain,
  whose sufferings drown out hope and joy,
    whose lives are awash with misery.

We beg you to heal those who are broken in body or mind,
  to pour out your peace on those who are at war,
    to comfort those who cry out in distress.

We who have much, and we who have little,
  we who are hungry, and we who are fed,
    we pray for others, and we pray for ourselves,
    aloud and in the silence of our hearts.

Second Sunday after Epiphany
Ordinary 2

1 Samuel 3:1–10, (11–20); Psalm 139:1–6, 13–18;
1 Corinthians 6:12–20; John 1:43–51

Opening Prayer

Boundless, breathing Teacher of patience,
  you call to us as you called young Samuel,
  as you called Philip and Nathaniel and Simon and Peter,
  as you called Mary and Martha and Hannah and Miriam,
  and all the countless others who have heard your voice.

You call us to practice loving-kindness,
  to practice justice and mercy,
  to practice daily the ways of your unending peace.

In our words and in our silence,
  in our song and in our laughter,
  when we sit and when we rise,
  help us to know that you are always with us,
  breathing in and breathing out. Amen.

Thanksgiving and Praise

Boundless Breath, patient Parent, tender Teacher,
  you search us and know us,
  and love us in ways that are beyond our understanding.

We thank you for becoming flesh,
  for living among us, and dying and rising again,
  that we might practice becoming your holy Body,
  living in peace with all your other creatures.

We give thanks for the warmth
  of hot soup on a cold afternoon,
  for the smell of bread hot from the oven,
  for a cool glass of water when we are tired and thirsty.

We give thanks for visitors from far away,
  for friendly greetings from next-door neighbors,
  for long conversations with dear friends.

Aloud and in silence, we patiently practice
   giving thanks to you.

Petition and Intercession

Boundless, patient Breath of compassion
   you search us and know us.
   You know when we sit down and when we rise up;
   you discern our every thought and
   are acquainted with all our ways.
   Even before we speak, you know our prayers.

And still, we need to speak the words that fill our hearts
   when our grief is more than we can bear.

Our breaking hearts cry out to you,
   and we plead for those whose lives
   are filled with pain.

We pray for the children in refugee camps,
   for the wounded and dying in places at war,
   for the hungry and homeless people in our own city.

We pray for warriors and peacemakers,
   for those in prison and for those who guard them,
   for those who make laws and for those who obey.

Aloud and in silence, we patiently practice
   praying for the healing of the world.

THIRD SUNDAY AFTER EPIPHANY
ORDINARY 3
Jonah 3:1–5, 10; Psalm 62:5–12; 1 Corinthians 7:29–31; Mark 1:14–20

Opening Prayer

Constant, giving Source of grace,
   you pour out your blessings on all the earth,
   raining sun-drenched life onto frozen ground,
   breathing the promise of light into the longest nights.

Long ago, you sent Jonah to the people of Nineveh,
  telling them that their world would change,
  and their only hope was in seeking you.

Today we, too, live in a changing world,
  in which both calamity and miracles
  greet us with our morning coffee.

As Jesus turned the Galileans
  into fishers of souls,
  turn our practice of prayer and praise
  into the Good News of your eternal realm.

Breath your spirit into us, this day and every day,
  for you, alone, are our salvation. Amen.

Thanksgiving and Praise

Source of grace and light,
  Unending Sea of love and blessing,
  you fill us with the miracle of living
  with every breath, every heartbeat.

We give thanks for the blood that fills our veins,
  for the invisible workings of the cells of our bodies,
  for the energy that pulses from atom to atom,
  for the gravitational power that keeps planets and stars
  moving along their appointed courses.

We give thanks for the ancient stories
  that tell us of your steadfast love,
  for the women and men of every time and place
  who fish for the meaning of your call
  in the deep ocean of their daily practice of living.

And we give thanks for the life, death, and resurrection of
    Jesus,
  who told the disciples news that is still good today:
  the news that the realm of God is near at hand.

In the silent depth of our own hearts,
  and in the joyful sounding of our own words,

we each give thanks for breathing in
and breathing out.

Petition and Intercession

Boundless Sea of mercy and hope,
  like the people of Nineveh,
    putting on sackcloth and praying for kindness,
  we look to you for solace and for comfort
  when life is too much.

We pray for the people who have lost their homes
  to poverty or earthquake, storm or fire,
    and now sleep on the sidewalks and beg in the street.

We pray for all whose lives we cannot fix,
  for those who suffer from illness and pain,
  for those who suffer from heartache and grief,
  for those whose needs we don't even know.

And we pray for all those who try to help,
  and even for those who seem to make the problems worse.

We pray for our enemies,
  and we pray for our friends,
    and we pray for those who do not know how to pray.
  What other prayers are in our hearts?

FOURTH SUNDAY AFTER EPIPHANY
ORDINARY 4

Deuteronomy 18:15–20; Psalm 111; 1 Corinthians 8:1–13;
Mark 1:21–28

Opening Prayer

Surprising, sustaining Giver of grace,
  the ancient stories tell us that long ago
  you spoke through your prophets,
  revealing your love through powerful signs,
  showing a glimpse of your glory to all who would see.

You allow us to see shadows of your astonishing beauty
  in the deep, bright blue of the winter sky.
  Your frosty breath leaves sheets of shimmering ice
  on our windshields and doorsteps,
  and you make our words write trails of steam
  in the crisp morning air.

In every moment of every day,
  you call to us as you called to our ancestors in faith,
  inviting us into breathing in and breathing out
  of your Holy Spirit,
  inviting us into awareness of your loving presence,
  inviting us into knowing that, together,
  we are your very Body,
  risen for the healing of the world. Amen.

Thanksgiving and Praise

Sustaining, forgiving Lover of humankind,
  you loved us before we knew how to love,
  patiently waiting for us to turn towards you.

Our simple words of thanks are not enough for this great gift,
  or for the numberless other gifts that you pour out on us
  with every breath of our bodies,
  every beat of our hearts.

Yet we practice our gratitude, our praise, and our thanks,
  thanking you for millions of stars,
  for oceans and rivers and uncountable raindrops,
  for stark, bare branches scratching out wordless songs,
  for a startled deer
  turning its head at the crackle of last year's leaves.

We give thanks for birthdays and anniversaries,
  for feasting and fasting,
  for noisy parties and silent celebration,
  for lively conversation and comfortable solitude.

In silence or in speech, we give thanks
  that we are able to give thanks,
  to practice gratitude and praise,
  since everything within us and around us comes from you.

Petition and Intercession

Loving, sustaining Spirit of hope,
  our cup of gladness cannot be full
  until all of our brothers and sisters
  can rejoice with us in a whole and perfect world.

We ask that you send healing to all those with broken hearts,
  that you mend all broken relationships,
  broken bodies, and broken minds.

Give wisdom and patience
  to those who make laws,
  and to those who enforce and interpret them.

Bring peace to those at war,
  comfort those who mourn,
  give strength to the weary,
  and guide the steps of those who do not know
  where to find you.

And for ourselves, we ask,
  help us to be the risen Body of Christ,
  patiently practicing your holy love for all creation,
  in every thought and word and action.
Sisters and brothers, for what else shall we pray?

Fifth Sunday after Epiphany
Ordinary 5
Isaiah 40:21–31; Psalm 147:1–11, 20c; 1 Corinthians 9:16–23;
Mark 1:29–39

Opening Prayer

As it has been told from the beginning,
  you, Holy One, stretch out the heavens like a curtain,
  and spread them like a tent to live in.
  You determine the number of the stars,
  and give to all of them their names.
  To whom shall we compare you?
  Who is your equal?

And yet as you told us when you walked among us in Galilee,
  you are always among us and within us,
  in every breath,
  in every heartbeat,
  in every moment.

Greater than creation, alive within us all,
  you beckon to us from every drop of rain,
  from sunshine and from shadow,
  from crocus and from blackbird,
  from every person that we meet.

As we come to know ourselves
  as members of your holy, ever-broken, ever-risen Body,
  help us to remember that you are the everlasting God,
  calling us to gather in your name. Amen.

Thanksgiving and Praise

Everlasting God, we sing to you with thanksgiving
  for all your countless gifts.
  You cover the heavens with clouds,
  prepare rain for the earth,
  make grass grow on the hillsides.
  You give the animals their food,

and gather up the outcasts in your loving arms.

We give you thanks for the simple pleasures of daily life:
    for dinner with someone we love,
    for a caring phone call from a friend,
    for a comfortable bed and a soft pillow at the end of the day.

Holy Giver of life, Spirit of love, Lover of all,
    we give you thanks and praise for giving us this life,
    for sustaining us through each day and each night,
    for bringing us to this moment,
    in which we are able to simply give our thanks,
    aloud and in the silence of our hearts.

Petition and Intercession

Everlasting God, our gratitude for your countless gifts
    does not blot out our awareness
    of the suffering of your people.

You have promised that those who wait for you
    shall renew their strength,
    but in this broken world, too many still are weary,
    too many still faint and fall exhausted.

We pray for those who are willing to do any job,
    no matter how boring or menial,
    yet still find no work.

We pray for those who go to bed hungry,
    for those who are grateful for just a handful of rice,
    who watch their children's bellies swell from malnutrition.

We pray for those whose bodies ache from sickness,
    for those whose minds are filled with nameless dread,
    for those whose spirits are filled with rage.

We pray for those who make speeches,
    and for those who listen;
    for soldiers of every country,
    and for those who live in danger of war.

We pray for those who mourn,
  we pray for those who cannot pray,
  and we pray for ourselves.

For what else shall we pray?

SIXTH SUNDAY AFTER EPIPHANY
PROPER 1, ORDINARY 6

2 Kings 5:1–14; Psalm 30; 1 Corinthians 9:24–27; Mark 1:40–45

Opening Prayer

Luminous Singer of breath and hope,
  the ancient stories tell of prophets and warriors,
  of lepers and healers,
  of commanders and captives,
  of human bodies and living waters.

The morning paper tells of soldiers and athletes,
  of scientists and skaters,
  of politicians and prisoners,
  of human actions and the movements of stars.

In all these stories, old and new,
  in all the world around us,
  we hear the song of your creation,
  reminding us that you are present
  in every atom and every seed,
  in every crocus and every flake of snow.

As the echo of your voice
  moves among us and through us this day,
  make us into an instrument of your holy song.
  Help us to keep time
  with the beating heart of your child, Jesus,
  in whose name we pray. Amen.

═══ Thanksgiving and Praise ═══

Generous Giver of strength and grace,
　we celebrate days of radiant health,
　　the joyful ache of muscles pushed to the limit,
　　the solid sleep that refreshes the soul
　　as well as the body.

We delight in the beauty of newly fallen snow,
　in the glint of sunshine on a late winter afternoon,
　in the glimmer of starlight on a black, velvet night.

We rejoice to hear that a friend has found a job,
　that another has found love,
　　that another has been healed.

We give you thanks for all that makes our hearts sing,
　for all the moments that take our breath away,
　for all the wonders of your creation.

Aloud and in silence, we give our thanks and praise.

═══ Petition and Intercession ═══

Gentle Healer of every hurt,
　we beg for release from sickness and from pain,
　　from churning thoughts that give us no rest,
　　from mornings when we face the day with dread.

We ache for those who have no shelter from the cold,
　no place to hide from wind and rain,
　　no comfortable bed for the empty, lonely night.

We plead for those whose children waste from hunger,
　for those whose loneliness is more than they can bear,
　for those whose bodies are broken beyond repair.

We pray for those whose lives are shattered by war,
　for those who bear the weight of power,
　for those who have never known your love.

For all the hurts that we can name,
　and all the hurts that are known only to you,
　we cry out for your healing touch.

Seventh Sunday after Epiphany

Proper 2, Ordinary 7

Isaiah 43:18–25; Psalm 41; 2 Corinthians 1:18–22; Mark 2:1–12

Opening Prayer

Ever-surprising Renewer of all you have made,
  every moment of each day is filled with miracles.

The purple crocus springs up from frozen ground,
  proclaiming that you are the source of all beauty;

The tiny, sharp, green blades of daylilies poke through mud,
  promising bouquets of summer glory;

The changing weather—snow and biting winds one day,
  warm, soft breezes the next—
  remind us that every thought and thing belongs to you.

Blessing the fruit of patient practice,
  you have promised to do a new thing,
  to show us the way through difficult times,
  to guide us into your grace-filled realm of peace,
  if only we remember that you are God.

You, who make a way in the wilderness for all who are lost,
  and rivers to flow in the desert for those who thirst,
  form us anew into your own people,
  that we might declare your praise. Amen.

Thanksgiving and Praise

Faithful fulfiller of every promise,
  you have established us in Christ,
  put your seal upon us,
  and given us your Spirit,
  to fill our hearts with joy.

We give thanks that you forgive our sins,
  that your love sustains us in every moment.

We give thanks for the little things that remind us of that love:
  for a handful of deep red roses,

brightening a windowless room;
  for the pungent smell of garlic browning in butter,
  for a gentle word from a friend at the end of a difficult day.

We give thanks for walking and sitting,
  for sleeping and waking,
  for conversation and solitude,
  for feasting and fasting.

We give thanks for all your gifts,
  aloud and in the silence of our hearts.

Petition and Intercession

Ever-surprising Renewer of all you have made,
  every moment of each day is filled with miracles.

But everyday miracles are not enough:
  we pray for a world filled with people who have no homes,
  for parents who have nothing to feed their children,
  for men and women
  who own nothing but the clothes that they wear.

Like the friends of the paralyzed man,
  we want to break down the roof,
  to beg you to heal the brokenness of the world.

We pray for the people who have lost homes
  and lives and loved ones to natural disasters.

We pray for those who live in fear of war and violence,
  for those whose lives are twisted by selfishness and greed,
  for those whose bodies or minds are filled with pain,
  for those who mourn,
  and for those who cannot pray for themselves.

We pray for ourselves,
  that our hearts may be filled with compassion.
  And for what else shall we pray?

EIGHTH SUNDAY AFTER EPIPHANY
PROPER 3, ORDINARY 8

Hosea 2:14–20; Psalm 103:1–13, 22; 2 Corinthians 3:1–6;
Mark 2:13–22

Opening Prayer

O steadfast, forgiving Redeemer of the fallen,
  we gather here to share the joy
  of being part of your living body here and now,
  the Body of Christ.

O Holy One, we pray that you will fill us
  with that overflowing sense of your alluring presence,
  that you will sharpen our awareness
  of your presence in our lives,
  that you will show us what it means
  to be a living testimony to your love for all creation.

Wake us up to the power of your love flowing through us,
  for we gather in the name of our Savior,
  who is Jesus the Christ. Amen.

Thanksgiving and Praise

God of compassion and mercy,
  your love endures forever.

Patient, empowering Healer of the brokenhearted,
  we know that you are the power that forgives our iniquity,
  the physician that heals our disease,
  the overwhelming power that crowns us
  with steadfast love and mercy.

Holy One, we are so deeply thankful
  that you are merciful and gracious,
  slow to anger and abiding in steadfast love.

Our thanks overflows,
  for the surprising ways you lead us to places
  where pain and sorrow seem to have the upper hand,

then show us how to be the channels of your holy love
by simply being present.

Holy God of healing love,
   receive our prayers of praise and thanks,
   our gratitude for the empowering comfort
   of your presence in our lives.

We offer you our thankful exclamations
   and our silent, praise-filled meditations.

Petition and Intercession

Patient, empowering Healer of the brokenhearted,
   we know, deep down within,
   that we are living in the midst of pain
   we are not able to understand, or heal.

We know so many painful places in the world these days:
   places where the best efforts of caring people
   are not enough.

We know how hard so many have labored
   to solve the challenges of poverty, disease,
   and lack of opportunity.

Holy, steadfast, forgiving Redeemer of the fallen,
   we bring to you the heavy needs for hope and healing,
   the burdens we have been carrying
   for those we know and love,
   and for so many others,
   whose pain and suffering we only hear about.

Holy God of compassion and mercy,
   we lift aloud our prayers for those in pain and need,
   and honor them in the silence of our hearts,
   bringing them into the healing harmony
   of your holy presence,
   O Maker of all that has ever been.

NINTH SUNDAY AFTER EPIPHANY
PROPER 4, ORDINARY 9
Deuteronomy 5:12–15; Psalm 81:1–10; 2 Corinthians 4:5–12;
Mark 2:23–3:6

Opening Prayer

Holy God of Sabbath rest,
  loving Source of healing and renewal,
  you have called us to be your people,
  part of your holy Body,
  sisters and brothers of Jesus.

This mid-spring day we come like children,
  drawing near to your exciting presence,
  hungry for healing, loving guidance, and empowerment.

We come to raise our songs of praise,
  our shouts of joy,
  our tales of healing and renewal.

Be here within us, O God of all creation,
  for we gather in the name of your beloved firstborn,
  who is Jesus the Christ. Amen.

Thanksgiving and Praise

God of loving creativity,
  we marvel at the way
  your Holy Spirit holds us together.

Although we are often afflicted and perplexed,
  you do not let us be crushed or driven to despair.

Holy Potter of this fragile vessel of hope
  that we know as community,
  we raise a song of gladness
  for the healing power of your presence.

We know deep down
  that this extraordinary power belongs to you.

We celebrate the wonder of your love
as you relieve us of the burdens
that so often weigh us down.

Holy Mystery,
we look around, and see your healing hand at work,
and we are filled with thanks for all your gifts of life.

Hear now our prayers of praise and thanks,
for all the richness of your bountiful creation.

Petition and Intercession

Healing Holy Spirit, you who cause the light of hope
to shine brightly in the dark nights of despair,
you stand ready to shine through us
as we stand witness
to the pain and persecution of this time.

Holy God of Sabbath healing,
we gather in a city filled with strife,
with echoes of the hatred, violence, and war
that fill our world.

We see the children slain,
the elders left alone to die,
the able crippled by fear and hatred.

We long for peace in these turbulent times,
when greed and violence threaten in so many, many ways.

God of healing, we carry the burden of the sick,
of those with wounded bodies, shattered minds
and broken spirits.

We long for unexpected healing touch,
for nourishment provided on the way
like ripe grain standing tall,
not only for ourselves,
but for the whole of your beloved creation.

God of Sabbath healing, we lift our prayers to you
for all those who suffer in this time, and for ourselves,

for we know all too well just how fragile we are,
and yet we long to share your treasure
with this hurting world.

TRANSFIGURATION
(LAST SUNDAY AFTER EPIPHANY)

2 Kings 2:1–12; Psalm 50:1–6; 2 Corinthians 4:3–6; Mark 9:2–9

Opening Prayer

Holy One, Light of light, God of all creation,
  as once you showed yourself to the disciples in Jesus,
  glowing in a blaze of light,
  you shine in our hearts with the knowledge of grace,
  with the promise of abundant, overflowing life.

We see you in the great river that flows beside the city,
  running wild and full,
  promising more than enough water
  for all whose lives depend on it.

We see you in a single tulip,
  standing taller than its neighbors,
  unwilling to wait for warmer weather
  to unfurl its impossibly bright, red flower.

We see you in the story of Elisha,
  who begged for a double share of the spirit of prophecy
  as his teacher Elijah let go of earthly life.

And we see you in the faces of your people,
  members of your holy Body,
  on the street outside and here among us,
  transfigured in the light of your love.

As we stand marveling at the beauty of your presence,
  fill us with your Holy Spirit,
  so that we may become one with Christ,
  who lived and died and rose to eternal life,
  an eternal blessing for the world. Amen.

═══ **Thanksgiving and Praise** ═══

Light of light, True God of Truth,
  in every age you send us prophets,
  to help us hear your voice,
  to show us the way to come closer to you.

We give you thanks for the prophets of long ago,
  and for the prophets hidden among us,
  longing to share the glory they have seen.

We give thanks for the voices of children
  who have not yet learned to silence
  the questions that live in ancient stories.

We give thanks for the voices of elders,
  whose years are filled with stories
  of life and love and faith.

We give thanks for the voices of neighbors,
  whose stories of far-away places
  we hear in the light of your love.

For all these prophets, and for all your many gifts,
  we give our thanks and praise,
  aloud and in the silence of our hearts.

═══ **Petition and Intercession** ═══

Christ, our light, and Light of the world,
  though you shine brighter than brightest day,
  too many people still live in shadows
  cast by the brokenness of the world.

We pray for children whose voices cry out in hunger,
  in pain from abuse,
  in fear and loneliness from the absence of a parent.

We pray for elders who cannot speak,
  whose words are lost to stroke or disease,
  whose voices are stilled in solitude and loss.

We pray for neighbors,
  on the street outside and here among us,
  who live with heartache and with grief,
  for all who have forgotten how to hope.

We pray for a world that is filled with sorrow,
  that every hurt and anger
  might be transfigured into joy.
And for what else shall we pray?

LENT

FIRST SUNDAY IN LENT

Genesis 9:8–17; Psalm 25:1–10; 1 Peter 3:18–22; Mark 1:9–15

Opening Prayer

God of sea and sky, God of earth and wind,
  in the time of Noah,
    you set your bow of colors in the heavens as a promise,
    as the sign of the everlasting covenant
    between you and all creation.

In the time of Jesus,
  you tore apart the heavens,
    and your Spirit landed on him like a dove
    as the sign of good news
    of the coming of your holy reign.

In this season of Lent,
  you call us to repentance and renewal,
    to remember that we belong to you.

Fill us with your Holy Spirit,
  so that our fragile, earthen vessels may join as one,
    becoming ever more the loving, grace-filled Body
    of the one who lived and died and rose again
    as we gather in his name. Amen.

Thanksgiving and Praise

God of sea and sky, God of earth and wind,
  we give thanks for the rainbow,

and for the everlasting covenant
between you and all creation.

We give thanks for the beauty of the world:
  for a field of purple crocus;
  for bright flags snapping in the breeze;
  for smiling strangers on a city street.

We give thanks for our first breath each morning,
  and for the peace of sleep each night;
  we give thanks for pipes and pumps
  that bring safe water into our homes and offices;
  we give thanks for computers and telephones
  that keep us in touch with loved ones far away;
  we give thanks for those who work in dangerous jobs
  so that others might be comfortable and safe.

And we give thanks for this holy season,
  this time to learn from your teachings what is right,
  this time to follow more closely in your way.
  And for what else shall we give thanks?

Petition and Intercession

God of sea and sky, God of earth and wind,
  your bow of colors in the heavens
  is the sign of the everlasting covenant
  between you and all creation.

You have promised to care for all your creatures,
  that never again will you destroy the earth
  for the sins of humankind.

And yet we hear daily of flood and earthquake,
  storm and disaster,
  famine and disease.

Your creatures cry out to you in distress:
  we cry out with all who are in pain
  and beg you for mercy.

We pray for release for all who are captive
   to misery and sorrow;
   for all who fear and all who grieve;
   for all who hunger and thirst;
   for all who live with rage and violence.

As we bring our prayers for ourselves and for others
   whether aloud or in the silence of our hearts,
   remember your promise, Holy One,
   and save this broken world.

SECOND SUNDAY IN LENT

Genesis 17:1–7, 15–16; Psalm 22:23–31; Romans 4:13–25;
Mark 8:31–38

Opening Prayer

God of covenant and promise,
   you fill the world with sunlight and with rain,
   with bright yellow daffodils,
   with tender buds on branches,
   trembling on the edge of spring.

Long ago, you promised Abraham and Sarah
   that they would be the ancestors of multitudes,
   even though they despaired,
   thinking they were too old
   for the miracle of new birth.

Today, we are the heirs to that promise,
   yearning to see the tender signs of your bright future,
   trembling beyond the storms and darkness
   that sometimes threaten to overwhelm us.

Holy Maker of sunlight and of storms,
   help us to remember your promises,
   so that we may be a beacon of hope,
   the light of Christ to one another
   and to the world around us.

▨▨▨▨▨ Thanksgiving and Praise ▨▨▨▨▨

God of darkness and of light,
  we give you thanks for the rain that softens the ground,
  for the soft, early-morning sunshine
  that opens our eyes to the promise of spring.

We give you thanks for the birds who chatter loudly
  when we walk too close to their hidden nests.

We give you thanks for the children who fill the sidewalks,
  walking in exuberant groups on their way to school.

We give you thanks for highways and quiet paths,
  for the gifts of fasting and prayer, and
  for the inner darkness of Lent
  that illuminates our hearts and allows us to see your face.
  And for what else shall we give thanks this day?

▨▨▨▨▨ Petition and Intercession ▨▨▨▨▨

God of every time and every place,
  you have promised that the poor shall eat and be satisfied.

Yet all around us,
  we see people who have no food,
  no shelter,
  no safety.

Hear the cries of those in need, Holy One!
Comfort all who are in pain,
  all who mourn,
  all who wake in the night,
  crying out to you.

Send your wisdom to those who would lead our nation,
  and to the leaders of the other nations of the world.

Help us to know what to do,
  and what not to do,
  that the world may know your love.

We pray for all these things, and for so much else besides.

Aloud and in the silence of our hearts,
we pray for those we have never met.

We pray for our own needs and for the needs of those we love.
and for those who cannot pray for themselves.

THIRD SUNDAY IN LENT

Exodus 20:1–17; Psalm 19; 1 Corinthians 1:18–25; John 2:13–22

Opening Prayer

God of past and future,
long ago you gave us rules to live by:
do not steal, do not lie, do not kill—
and promised that the rain would fall,
and the sun would shine,
and you would be our God.

In another time, you sent Jesus,
to show us your power and your grace;
to teach us how to love each other
as extravagantly as you love
the gnarled branches of cherry trees
daring to put forth early blossoms,
the sturdy tulip leaves
just poking up above the ground,
the small creature that digs up the garden
while we are locked in the darkness of night.

Today, you call us to remember
the improbable abundance of creation;
the foolish wisdom of the cross,
the mystery of Christ, who rose from the dead
and lives among us and in us and around us.

Help us to know ourselves
as your holy temple,
the living Body of Christ,
the vessel of your holy wisdom and power.

Let the words of our mouths
  and the meditations of our hearts,
  be acceptable to you, Holy One,
  our Rock and our Redeemer. Amen.

═══ **Thanksgiving and Praise** ═══

God of past and future,
  God of today and every day,
  we give thanks for the overflowing abundance
  with which you fill the world.

Birds and flowers, wind and sunshine,
  all remind us of your generous grace,
  the unmerited gift that is our life in you.

Our grateful praise, our joy and gladness
  in the beauty of the world,
  in the embrace of friends and family,
  in the life and death and new life in Christ,
  spill out of our mouths as laughter and song,
  and fill our hearts with pleasure and delight.

You, who are our true Wisdom and power,
  our guide through the foolishness of the world,
  hear our praise and our thanks
  offered now in spoken words
  and in the silent temples of our hearts.

═══ **Petition and Intercession** ═══

God of past and future,
  of memory and promise,
  even as our hearts break open with thanks,
  the tears of your people echo through our gratitude.

We pray for those who mourn,
  that you will bring them comfort and consolation.

We pray for those who live in pain
  or in sickness of body or mind,
  that you will bring them healing and relief.

We pray for those who are oppressed,
  that you will bring them justice and mercy.

We pray for those whose lives
  are bound by war and violence,
  that you will bring them peace.

We pray for friends and loved ones,
  we pray for those here present,
  we pray for distant strangers,
  we pray for those who lead the nations,
  we pray for those who cannot pray for themselves,
  we pray for our own needs and grieving.

And for what else shall we pray?

FOURTH SUNDAY IN LENT

Numbers 21:4–9; Psalm 107:1–3, 17–22; Ephesians 2:1–10;
John 3:14–21

Opening Prayer

O wonderful Fountain of blooming life,
  we gather here to celebrate the good news
  that we are not alone.

We gather as a community, sprouting leaves of hope,
  a wiry muscle of justice,
  a cell of pollen in the body of Christ.

We come to remember what it means to be faithful.
  We come to remember how it is to labor against great odds.
  We come to remember that the future depends not on us,
  but on you.

Be with us, God of all creation,
  so we can worship you in spirit and in truth,
  for we have come to claim our place among your people,
  the people of the risen Christ. Amen.

▬▬ **Thanksgiving and Praise** ▬▬

Mysterious Maker of this reality we know as life,
  we come this bright, spring morning
  to celebrate our presence with you.
We came this morning through a blossom blizzard,
  a flying testimony to the power of life,
  a pink and white reminder
  that you will bring renewal to the earth each year,
  no matter what we do.

We come today
  to bring our praise, for all the goodness of your rich creation,
  to bring our thanks for your redeeming love.

We thank you for the joy of life and creativity
  that stand against the gravity of entropy and death,
  like water lifted from the salty seas today
  to make tomorrow's rain.

We thank you for your miracles of life, and love, and hope,
  and for the consciousness that lets us swim
  the swelling river of your ongoing creation.

Hear now our prayers of praise and thanks,
  for all the wonder of this place and time
  where you have planted us.
We offer them aloud here in this sanctuary,
  and in the silence of our hearts.

▬▬ **Petition and Intercession** ▬▬

Loving Beacon of family and community,
  We know how pain and loss are looming large
  for nations, families, and people all around the world.

We hear the news of war and violence;
  we watch as people struggle for the upper hand
  in marketplace and politics;
  we know the pain of illness, age, and loss.

We gather here to pause from all our busy caring
and take this time to offer up the burdens that we carry.

As Moses listened to your guidance,
and lifted up a serpent made of bronze to save his people
from the snakes that plagued them in the wilderness,
we sit beneath this empty cross.

They prayed for life, and you were there to save them.
We pray for healing from so many complicated maladies
and wait to know your healing presence in this time.

Joyful Giver of unending hope,
pour your Holy Spirit into us until it overflows,
remind us of the call to service
that you bring us through the risen Christ,
and turn us out to face the pain and suffering of this time,
so we can let your living water flow
into those painful places
where hope and joy have lost their foothold.

O Holy One, we raise our prayers for those in pain and need,
and for ourselves,
for we know how it is to wander in the wilderness.

Fifth Sunday in Lent

Jeremiah 31:31–34; Psalm 51:1–12; Hebrews 5:5–10; John 12:20–33

Opening Prayer

Ever-surprising, ever-faithful, ever-merciful Lover of creation,
you lavish us with cherry blossoms,
bright pink and glowing white,
floating above deep blue, wind-whipped waves.

You fill your world with tulips and woodpeckers,
with forsythia and robins,
with redbud and bluebirds,
with storm clouds and open sky.

You show yourself to us in all these things,
 calling us to prayer,
 to worship,
 to knowing ourselves
 as members of your holy Body.

Renew once more the covenant
 you made with our ancestors,
 put your law of love within us all
 and write it deeply upon our hearts,
 for we would be your people,
 and you shall be our God. Amen.

Thanksgiving and Praise

Ever-surprising, ever-faithful, ever-merciful Lover of creation,
 we give thanks for the overflowing abundance
 with which you fill the world.

Birds and flowers, wind and sunshine,
 all remind us of your generous grace,
 the unmerited gift that is our life in you.

Our grateful praise, our joy and gladness
 in the beauty of the world,
 in the embrace of friends and family,
 in life and death and new life in Christ,
 spill out of our mouths as laughter and song,
 and fill our hearts with pleasure and delight.

You, who are the bread of life,
 the cup of healing for all the nations,
 hear our praise and our thanks
 offered now in spoken words
 and on the silent altars of our hearts.

Petition and Intercession

Ever-surprising, ever-faithful, ever-merciful Lover of creation,
 even as our hearts overflow with thanks,
 the tears of your people wash over and through us.

We pray for those whose pain is so great
   that they cannot see the beauty around them,
   or feel the love that flows from heart to heart.
We pray for all who are hungry,
   that they will have both food and love.

We pray for all who thirst,
   that they will have both water and peace.

We pray for all who mourn,
   that they will find both comfort and joy.

You, who are the bread of life,
   the cup of healing for all the world,
   hear our prayers for all who are in need.

PALM/PASSION SUNDAY (SIXTH SUNDAY IN LENT)

Liturgy of the Palms: Mark 11:1–11; Psalm 118:1–2, 19–29
Liturgy of the Passion: Isaiah 50:4–9a; Psalm 31:9–16;
Philippians 2:5–11; Mark 14:1–15:47

Opening Prayer

Holy Word, holy Breath, holy Mystery,
   on this day of Palms and Passion,
   you call us to remember your life and death among us.

You call us to witness your triumphal procession,
   your challenge to worldly power,
   your humble service to those who love you,
   your self-giving in bread and wine.

You call us to be present
   at your final meal as incarnate being,
   at your prayer in the garden of Gethsemane,
   at your agony and death upon a cross.

As we wave our palms of anticipation,
   waken us into awareness of your presence
   within us, among us, and around us,

that we may become joined with you
as members of the incarnate, risen Body of Christ, our Savior.
Amen.

▬▬ Thanksgiving and Praise ▬▬

The psalmist says,
  Give thanks to God, for God is good.
  God's steadfast love endures forever.

And like the psalmist,
  we give thanks to you,
  holy Mystery,
  for all the wonders of creation:
  for thunderstorms and daffodils,
  for tender green leaves and bright red tulips,
  for bald eagle chicks and hammering woodpeckers,
  for seagulls and sunshine and high-running rivers.

As the Body of Christ,
  we give thanks for this day of remembrance,
  for processions with palm leaves,
  and for the Passion of Jesus,
  and the Way of the cross.

In the boundless grace of your Holy Spirit,
  we give thanks for breath and for life,
  for the gift of your holy Word, your holy wisdom,
  within us, among us, and around us.

And for what else shall we give thanks?

▬▬ Petition and Intercession ▬▬

Holy Word, holy Breath, holy Mystery,
  be gracious to us, for your world is in distress;
  your people waste away from grief, soul, and body.

Too many lives are spent with sorrow,
  too many years with sighing;
  the strength of many fails because of misery,
  and their bones waste away.

We pray for those who are the scorn of all their adversaries,
  a horror to their neighbors,
    an object of dread to their acquaintances.

We pray for those who have passed out of mind
  as if they were already dead;
    for those who live like broken vessels,
      with terror all around.

We trust in you, Holy One;
  you are our God.

This time is in your hand; deliver your people
  from the hand of their enemies and persecutors.

In the boundless grace of your Holy Spirit,
  we pray that your face will shine upon all your creation,
    and that you will bring wholeness and peace
      within us, among us, and around us.

And for what else shall we pray?

THE RESURRECTION OF CHRIST

Easter Sunday

Acts 10:34–43; Psalm 118:1–2, 14–24; 1 Corinthians 15:1–11;
John 20:1–18

Opening Prayer

Alleluia! Christ is risen!
Holy Mystery, you call us to this joyous moment,
  to celebrate the good news of the resurrection,
  to see the new promise of life everlasting.
  Through your grace,
  we have traveled with Jesus through the forty days of Lent.
We have joined the disciples,
  waving palms on his triumphal entry into Jerusalem;
  our feet have been washed,
  and we have eaten and drunk in the presence of Christ.
Like the disciples, we have fallen asleep in the garden,
  waking to realize that Jesus must die on the cross.
Now we stand,
  blinking our eyes in amazement at the empty tomb,
  wondering at the miracle that you have accomplished,
  astonished at this good news, the mystery of faith in you:
  Christ has died! Christ is risen! Christ will come again!
By your spirit, make us one with Christ and in Christ,
  that we might be a holy people,

spreading the good news of resurrection
through all the world. Amen.

Thanksgiving and Praise

Alleluia! Christ is risen!
Loving Bringer of more gifts than we can ever name,
  this good news is greater than we can understand,
  astonishing us with the extravagance of your grace.

In halting words, in faltering wonder,
  we can only begin to thank you
  for this day of Christ's resurrection,
  for this feast of love and awe.

And so we thank you for lesser things,
  for the everyday miracles of sunrise and moonlight;
  of bright orange day lilies and deep red roses;
  of freshly-baked bread and the laughter of children.

We give thanks for friends who call from distant lands,
  and for quick conversations over the back fence;
  we give thanks for bicycles and computers,
  for electric lights and indoor plumbing,
  for the neighbor's cat sleeping on the back porch,
  and the dog next door with wildly wagging tail.

For all these things, and so much more,
  in spoken words and silent gratitude,
  we give our thanks and praise
  to the One who gives us all our days.

Petition and Intercession

Alleluia! Christ is risen!
  And yet our cup of joy is never full
  as long as the least of our brothers and sisters
  lives in brokenness and pain.

Bountiful Healer of all the world,
  on this day of resurrection,
  we pray that you will bring comfort to all who grieve.

We ask that you stop the cycles of oppression and violence
  that fill our world with hatred and fear,
  end the wars that kill your children,
  and place your holy peace into the hearts of all humankind.

As we stand wondering at the empty tomb,
  for what else shall we pray?

THE GREAT FIFTY DAYS

The Easter Season

SECOND SUNDAY OF EASTER

Acts 4:32–35; Psalm 133; 1 John 1:1–2:2; John 20:19–31

Opening Prayer

God of soft spring rain and white-petaled dogwood,
  God of extravagant love,
  God of all that is and all that shall ever be,
  you call us to celebrate
  your life and death and new life among us.

Like the disciples who sold their possessions
  and laid them at the feet of the apostles
  so that no one would be in need,
  we bring our whole lives to the foot of the cross,
  trusting the promise of eternal life
  in your resurrection.

As we look for your new promise,
  make your presence known to us
  in our song and in our silence
  and in the moving of your Holy Spirit among us. Amen.

Thanksgiving and Praise

God of thunderstorms and rainbows,
  God of exuberant laughter,
  God of birth and death and eternal life,

you have given us the gift of yourself,
  poured out for the healing of the world.

Our thanks are not enough for all your many gifts to us,
  but gratitude is all we can offer,
  the only thing that we can give
  to the One who is the source of all.

And so we give thanks for the changing seasons,
  the newness of spring,
  the lengthening days,
  the lilac and hyacinth and redbuds,
  the twitters and songs of nesting birds,
  all the freshness and delight
  of a reawakening world.

We give thanks for friends who remember our birthdays,
  for cakes and candles and small tokens of their love;
  we give thanks for deep conversation,
  for moments when our souls seem to touch
  and dance together in your holy light;
  we give thanks for the many languages of love
  in which your people give thanks throughout the world.

And we give thanks for your holy apostles,
  who carried the good news wherever they went,
  and whose words today
  continue to bring new hope and promise.
  And for what else shall we give thanks?

Petition and Intercession

God of daylight and starlight,
  God of endless comfort and consolation,
  God of birth and death and eternal life,
  our cup of thanksgiving overflows
  into prayers for the healing of this broken world.

You have promised that you will heal the sick,
  bind up the brokenhearted,

free the captives,
and that your peace will fill all the earth.

And yet the news is filled with war and suffering,
with violence and despair,
with stories of greed and need,
of broken families and broken lives.

We pray for all who need your comfort,
your healing, your consolation,
that in your presence they will find
all that they need.

We pray for guidance and help,
for strength and for courage,
that we may be your holy Body,
interceding for others
and pleading for ourselves.

Hear us, Holy One, in the prayers of our lips
and the silence of our hearts.

THIRD SUNDAY OF EASTER

Acts 3:12–19; Psalm 4; 1 John 3:1–7; Luke 24:36b–48

Opening Prayer

God of abundance and new life,
today a sea of bright, pink primroses appeared
where yesterday there were only tightly-curled green buds.

The bare, dead stick, planted in the ground last fall,
today has brave, new leaves, drinking in the warmth of spring.

Everywhere we look,
we see signs of your extravagant energy,
breaking open the tombs that imprison us,
like a sprig of fragrant mint
pushing upwards towards the sunlight,
cracking open the hardest cement sidewalk.

Holy, mysterious, Fountain of joy,
  help us to say "yes" to your invitation
  to enter into the morning of new life,
  to celebrate the astonishing mystery
  that Christ is risen today, and every day. Amen.

Thanksgiving and Praise

God of forgiveness and new beginnings,
  we give you thanks for this new day,
  for opening our eyes to each new morning,
  for reminding us that Christ is always risen.

We give you thanks for sunshine and for rain,
  for morning and evening,
  for starlight and moonlight,
  and, yes, for electric lights, too.

We give you thanks for simple meals
  and extravagant feasts;
  for music and dancing,
  for silence and solitude,
  for hugs from friends and smiles from strangers,
  for walks in the park and the bustle of city streets.

We give you thanks for all the moments that fill our lives,
  aloud or in the silence of our hearts.

Petition and Intercession

God of healing and new hope,
  our gratitude for all these gifts reminds us
  of the broken, empty places that still remain,
  near and far away.

The endless, aching need of the world
  is beyond what human hands can fill,
  and so we pray that you will provide what we cannot.

We pray that you will guide those who make decisions,
  and that you will protect those who live under their rule.

We pray for those who live in fear of violence,
  and for those who make them feel afraid.

We pray for those who live in mansions,
  and for those who live on the street.

We pray for those who have too much,
  and for those who have too little.

We pray for those who live in sickness and in pain,
  and those who find ways to bring them relief.

We pray for those who have asked us to pray,
  and for those who cannot pray for themselves.

We pray for all who need our prayer,
  and we pray for our own needs and weakness.

And for what else shall we pray this day?

Fourth Sunday of Easter

Acts 4:5–12; Psalm 23; 1 John 3:16–24; John 10:11–18

Opening Prayer

Beloved Shepherd,
  you gave your life in love,
  and in love you rose,
  calling your disciples
  to be your holy, risen Body.

You call us to acknowledge that you are our Savior,
  to heal in your name
  and to love one another so much
  that we lay down our lives for one another.

You give yourself to us in soft, spring days,
  in starlit nights,
  in the whistles and hoots of courting birds,
  and the playful dance of two butterflies
  in the middle of a parking lot full of cars.

As your holy, living Spirit flows among and through us,
  make our fragile, earthen vessels
  overflow with praise and wonder. Amen.

Thanksgiving and Praise

Loving Shepherd,
  your goodness and mercy are all around us,
  restoring our souls.

You lead us along shorelines and mountain paths,
  on busy city streets and quiet, country lanes,
  offering us a feast of love and blessing.

You give yourself to us in sacred stories,
  in familiar poems,
  in parables and proverbs
  and the words of those who testify
  to your presence among them.

Hear, now, our prayers of praise and thanks,
  our words and our silence,
  our astonishment at this gift of life in you.

Petition and Intercession

Gentle Shepherd
  lover and spirit,
  you call us to your table
  even when we are beset with trouble.

Pour out your goodness and grace
  on all who grieve,
  on all who fear,
  on all who live with pain.

Lead our nation, and all the world,
  into your paths of peace,
  and let our cups overflow with mercy.

Hear us as we pray for those we love,
  for those we fear,

for those we have never met,
and for ourselves,
in spoken words and in the silence of our hearts.

FIFTH SUNDAY OF EASTER

Acts 8:26–40; Psalm 22:25–31; 1 John 4:7–21; John 15:1–8

Opening Prayer

Blessed, holy God of all eternity,
 you look with favor on those who believe in you,
 and redeem them.

Source of all creation,
 you have come among us as the fertile Vine of love,
 showing us that every branch that learns to love
 will bear much fruit,
 and still be pruned to love more deeply.

As Philip helped the Ethiopian understand,
 by your love, the poor shall eat and be satisfied,
 and all the ends of the earth shall remember and turn to you.

By your love, we gather this morning in joyful worship,
 to celebrate the power of Christ
 returned to life from death,
 calling us into a faith-filled future.

Be with us as we worship in the name of the risen Christ.
Amen.

Thanksgiving and Praise

God of all creation, we celebrate the good news,
 that you are love.

We celebrate the power of new life filled with promise,
 the hopeful vision of a new heaven and new earth.

We watch the fields, springing green,
 drinking in the rain, reaching for the sun.

We hear the promise of summer in the song of every nesting bird.
Holy Maker of this day,
  you have shown the mercy promised to our ancestors;
  you have remembered your holy covenant
  with all creation,
  you have given us the promise of new life in Christ.

The dayspring from on high has broken in upon us
  bringing us peace in the midst of toil,
  and we are grateful for the call to serve you in so many ways.

Hear now our prayers of praise and thanks,
  for all the blessings you have given to the world this day.

Petition and Intercession

Loving Christ, you came to bring good news to everyone.
Through your atoning sacrifice you freed us
  to reach out to those who are weary and heavy-laden,
  so that they might find rest,
  healing for their wounds and illnesses,
  comfort for their despair and grief,
  and new hope in the face of tribulation.

God of healing love,
  like Christ we would take your burden upon ourselves.
Show us how we can learn to love one another,
  for we know we are called to be your Body
  in this time and place.

Healing Holy Spirit, we raise our prayers
  for those who have no dayspring in their lives,
  the homeless and the lonely,
  the sick and dying,
  those whose bodies and spirits cry out in pain.

Hear now, O God, our prayers for those in need,
  as we raise them up for healing in the name of Christ,
  who walks with us, guiding our feet into the way of peace.

Sixth Sunday of Easter

Acts 10:44–48; Psalm 98; 1 John 5:1–6; John 15:9–17

Opening Prayer

O holy Maker of the universe,
  we come today to sing to you a new song,
  a song of bud and blossom,
  a song of thanks for love within community,
  a song of hope for future blessings
  we cannot yet understand.

Fill us, Holy Mystery, with vision and compassion
  so we may know that resurrection comes from you,
  for we gather in the presence of the risen Christ. Amen.

Thanksgiving and Praise

God of field and valley,
  the gift of Easter is poured out everywhere around us.

The buttercup, the dandelion, and the dogwood
  shout with tongues we understand without translation.

Promise of a vibrant future
  flies like maple birds on single wings,
  trusting there will be a place to root and grow
  no matter where they land.

Hurting hands stretch out for help,
  chorusing like pond frogs,
  giving thanks for strength enough
  to ask for what they need.

O God of Easter gladness,
  we bring our prayers of thanks like clusters of asparagus,
  thrusting up from cold, wet earth
  to lift the taste of new life, bright and clean,
  into the warming, fragrant air.

That dandelion thrusting through the broken pavement,
  shouting golden good news to the litter

and the rusted hulks of old communities,
that vibrant weed must be a sign of hope,
a sign of seeds to come.

We give you thanks that you are present,
even when we wonder if it's true.

May we hear tongues of buttercup and dandelion,
dogwood and asparagus
extolling God with joy and hope!

Hear now, O God of Easter gladness,
our own prayers of praise and thanks.

▬▬ **Petition and Intercession** ▬▬

O God of Easter hope,
it's hard to see your promise of new life
in littered parking lots where whole communities
sit like rusting cars, their hoods thrown open in disgust,
their seats, once safe abiding places for the human odyssey,
now torn apart by selfish rats.

We know so many places where hope is hard to find,
where war and famine turn the sprouting fields to mud,
where anger and despair
are bold enough to mock the good news of the risen Christ.

Holy Wellspring of love,
we watch the life and death of Jesus
and the resurrection of Christ,
and pray for strength and discernment
to lay down our lives for our friends,
one bright, faithful day at a time.

God of Easter hope,
we claim the promise of this resurrection season,
and dare to pray for those whose lives seem empty,
whose hopeful hands are empty.

Hear now our prayers for those in pain and need,
and for ourselves,

for we would be part of future blessings
you already have in mind.

Seventh Sunday of Easter

Acts 1:15–17, 21–26; Psalm 1; 1 John 5:9–13; John 17:6–19

Opening Prayer

God of words and wisdom,
  God of beginnings and endings,
  God of truth and hope,
  you lead us into each bright, new morning,
  inviting us to listen as the sparrows and wrens and robins
  announce the coming of the dawn;
  inviting us to watch as the first golden trumpet of the daylily
  opens its mouth to the sun.

You call us to delight in your presence,
  to be like trees planted by streams of water,
  giving shade to all who pass by,
  and yielding fruit in due season.

As we sing and pray and share the stories of our life in you,
  help us to remember
  that you are always with us and around us and among us,
  and that Christ is always risen. Amen.

Thanksgiving and Praise

God of hope and wonder,
  God of earth and sea,
  God of love and glory, we give you thanks
  for all the ordinary wonders of each new day:
  for bees and butterflies, for primrose and pansy,
  for the sweetness of strawberries
  and the tartness of lemonade.

We give you thanks for the countless forms of beauty
  that tell us of your abundant love:

for all the colors of skin and hair and eyes
that adorn the members of your Body,
for all the languages and sounds in which we sing and pray,
for all the hopes and dreams,
that help us to live the vision of your holy realm.
Because Christ is always risen,
we give our thanks and praise to you
aloud and in the silence of our hearts.

Petition and Intercession

God of vision and power,
God of love and hope,
God of compassion and comfort,
even as we give thanks for so much
we hear the cries of the lost and broken,
yearning for an end to fear and pain.

Each morning's news brings word
of war and famine,
of violence and oppression,
of injustice and cruelty.

Our bodies are subject to illness and disease,
our friends and loved ones die,
our neighbors fall prey to those who would harm them,
and earthquake, fire, and flood destroy the homes
of rich and poor alike.

We pray for all who live with heartache and sorrow,
we pray for all who work to ease the pain of others,
we pray for all who give their lives so that others might live.

Because Christ is always risen,
we pray aloud and in silence
for all who need our prayers,
in the name of the Risen One.

PENTECOST

Acts 2:1–21; Psalm 104:24–34, 35b; Romans 8:22–27; John 15:26–27, 16:4b–15

Opening Prayer

God of fire and wind,
   God of speech and silence,
   God of future and past and this present moment,
   your Spirit is among us
   as it was with the disciples
   on that first day of Pentecost.

Like them, we stand in awe,
   feeling your holy fire
   flowing through our hearts,
   loosening our tongues
   to speak the good news of your eternal love.

Like them, we feel the rushing wind,
   and hear the sound of thunder
   that calls us to live the vision that you have shown us.
Pour our your Spirit among us,
   that this fragile, earthen vessel that is the church
   may live as the Body of Christ. Amen.

Thanksgiving and Praise

God of future and past and this present moment,
   God of fire and wind,
   God of speech and silence,

we give you thanks for all the languages that humans use
to praise you and give you thanks.

We give you thanks for poetry and essays
and stories and sermons,
for waltzes and marches and hymns and wordless tunes,
for paintings and statues and the drawings of children,
for leaping and running and twirling with outstretched arms.

Most of all, we give you thanks for giving yourself to us,
for helping us in our weakness,
for teaching us how to pray.

The psalmist cries, "I will sing to the Holy One as long as I live,
I will sing praise to my God while I have being."
Aloud and in silence,
let us, also, give our thanks and praise to God.

▬ Petition and Intercession ▬

God of speech and silence,
God of fire and wind,
God of future and past and this present moment,
even as we give thanks for so much
we hear the whole of creation groaning,
waiting for good news that never seems to come.

Murder and violence,
war and destruction,
sickness and pain,
poverty and need are everywhere we look.

When will it end, O God?
When will your promised reign of peace be real
for all your hurting people,
for all your aching world?

Pour out your Spirit upon us gathered here today,
praying aloud and in silence
for the healing of the world.
And when we do not know how to pray,
let your Spirit pray for us with sighs too deep for words.

ORDINARY TIME

The Sundays after Pentecost

Trinity Sunday (First Sunday after Pentecost)

Isaiah 6:1–8; Psalm 29; Romans 8:12–17; John 3:1–17

Opening Prayer

Eternal One, Incarnate Word, Abiding Spirit,
  your voice calls to us
    in the loud crack of thunder in the midst of a storm,
    in the chirping birdsong of early morning,
    in the roar of traffic and the quiet footfall on a forest path.

You call to us in dreams and visions,
  in the voices of our neighbors,
  in the silent whispers of our hearts.

You call us here to remember your holy Word,
  and to celebrate the love of Jesus,
  who gave his life and calls us to follow him
  for the healing of the world. Amen.

Thanksgiving and Praise

Eternal One,
  we give you thanks for all creation,
  for daylilies and woodpeckers,
  for dark, roiling clouds and pouring rain,
  for cool nights and sunlit mornings,
  and for the bodies that you gave us
  so that we can know your world.

Incarnate Word,
  we give you thanks for the love you taught us,
  for forgiveness and healing,
  for serving and leading,
  for dying and rising,
  for teaching us how to live in you.

Abiding Spirit,
  we give you thanks for moving among us,
  for joy and pleasure,
  for laughter and loving,
  for hope and commitment,
  for living within us and around us and through us.
  And for what else shall we give thanks?

Petition and Intercession

Eternal One,
  in gratitude for all these things,
  we praise your triune name.
  And still, we cry out to you,
  aching with all that is broken
  in this troubled world.

We pray for the leaders of nations,
  for generals and admirals,
  for bishops and ministers,
  for executives and professionals,
  that all who lead and all who follow
  will hear and do your loving will.

Incarnate Word,
  we pray for those who are poor and hungry,
  for those whose bodies are bleeding and broken,
  for those who live in daily fear,
  for all who are desperate and oppressed,
  that your loving touch will heal their wounds
  and free them into life in you.

Abiding Spirit,
in the silent groaning of our hearts,
and in the words of our mouths,
we pray for your comforting presence,
bringing hope and salvation
to us and to this troubled world.

SUNDAY BETWEEN MAY 22 AND MAY 28 INCLUSIVE (IF AFTER TRINITY SUNDAY)

PROPER 3, ORDINARY 8

Hosea 2:14–20; Psalm 103:1–13, 22; 2 Corinthians 3:1–6;
Mark 2:13–22

Opening Prayer

O steadfast, forgiving Redeemer of the fallen,
you call us to become new wineskins,
vessels for the new wine of your good news.

You call us to live each day
filled with awareness that you are always present,
seeing your generous Spirit
in the brilliant abundance of bright azalea hedges,
in creamy white dogwood blossoms tinged with red,
in peonies whose petals bloom in such profusion
that our hearts burst with joy at the very sight.

Open our hearts to follow you
as Levi followed Jesus when he called,
for we gather in the name of that same Savior,
Jesus, who is the Christ. Amen.

Thanksgiving and Praise

God of compassion and mercy,
your love endures forever.

Patient, empowering Healer of the brokenhearted,
we give you thanks that you are

the power that forgives our iniquity,
the physician that heals our disease,
the overwhelming power that crowns us
with steadfast love and mercy.

Holy One, we are so deeply thankful
that you are merciful and gracious,
slow to anger and abiding in steadfast love.

Our thanks overflows
for the surprising ways you lead us to places
where pain and sorrow seem to have the upper hand,
then show us how to be the channels of your holy love
by simply being present.

Holy God of healing love,
receive our prayers of praise and thanks,
our gratitude for the empowering comfort
of your presence in our lives.

We offer you our thankful exclamations
and our silent praise-filled meditations.

Petition and Intercession

Patient, empowering Healer of the brokenhearted,
we know, deep down within,
that we are living in the midst of pain
we are not able to understand, or heal.

We know so many painful places in the world these days
where the best efforts of caring people
are not enough.
We know how hard so many have labored
to solve the challenges of poverty, disease,
and lack of opportunity.

Holy, steadfast, forgiving Redeemer of the fallen,
we bring to you the heavy needs for hope and healing,
the burdens we have been carrying
for those we know and love,

and for so many others,

whose pain and suffering we only hear about.

Holy God of compassion and mercy,

we lift aloud our prayers for those in pain and need,

and honor them in the silence of our hearts,

bringing them into the healing harmony

of your holy presence,

O Maker of all that has ever been.

Sunday between May 29 and June 4 inclusive (if after Trinity Sunday)

Proper 4, Ordinary 9

1 Samuel 3:1–10, (11–20); Psalm 139:1–6, 13–18; 2 Corinthians 4:5–12;
Mark 2:23–3:6

Opening Prayer

Holy Painter of lingering rhododendron blossoms,

Weaver of the vinca carpet springing up

to hide the oak leaves donated to the earth last fall,

Mother of the daffodil who's told her children,

"Now's your naptime,"

when so many other garden residents are fresh and green,

we gather on the edge of summer,

ready to celebrate the Good News

that all of us are called to be your people.

Come, loving Maker of the universe,

fill us with your Holy Spirit,

clear our ears to hear the many ways you speak to us,

for we gather in the name of your holy,

chosen one, our Messiah, who is Jesus the Christ. Amen.

Thanksgiving and Praise

Exciting, vibrant Gardener of creativity,

we've come to celebrate the good news

that you are with us.

We've come together to share our stories,
  celebrate the joys and sorrows of our lives,
  and tell each other of the signs and wonders we have seen
  that let us know that you are in our midst.
Like Samuel, we know that you have called us into being,
  and that you call us each to live a life of faithful service,
  if we can only listen to your quiet voice.
We thank you that you've known us intimately
  since long before we came into this world.
We thank you for the gift of life,
  for healing love that knits together broken bones
  in body, spirit, and community.
Hear now our prayers of praise and thanks,
  our psalms of wonder,
  our celebrations of the life you animate
  throughout the universe.
  We offer them aloud and in the silence of our hearts.

Petition and Intercession

O holy Fount of every blessing,
  your passion for diversity is clear.
  You make each leaf, each cat, each bird,
  each one of us, unique.
  We marvel at the breadth of your imagination,
  and we strive in vain to love creation
  with the grace you pour out without ceasing.
Although we find life easier
  if we can guess where you are taking us,
  we know the future is beyond our divination.
We know the love
  you poured into the world through Christ
  can overcome the pain and suffering we see around us.
We pray for trust to bring our pain and grief to you,
  believing that your love is present
  even in the uttermost places of despair.

Hear now, O holy Healer,
 our prayers for those in need,
 and for ourselves, for we are broken, too,
 in ways we may not understand.

Sunday between June 5 and June 11 inclusive (if after Trinity Sunday)
Proper 5, Ordinary 10

1 Samuel 8:4–11, (12–15), 16–20, (11:14–15); Psalm 138;
2 Corinthians 4:13–5:1; Mark 3:20–35

Opening Prayer

Creative, generous Sovereign of life,
 gentle, renewing Wellspring of grace,
 persistent, forgiving Mystery of faith,
 you have created all that is, seen and unseen,
 knowing our inmost thoughts and desires,
 and loving each of your creatures beyond measure.

The world you have made is full of delights—
 cool, sun-drenched mornings with deep blue skies,
 red-leafed Japanese maples,
 and fast-running mountain streams
 that burble and sing with joy.

You offer these pleasures to all,
 without regard for wealth or station,
 warning us of the dangers of putting our faith in rulers,
 and calling us to be your brothers and sisters
 in doing your will.

Open our minds and hearts to know your will,
 so that we may more perfectly be your Body,
 filling the world with grace and peace. Amen.

Thanksgiving and Praise

Persistent, forgiving Mystery of faith,
 you pour out your blessings on all your creatures,

sustaining our every breath,
  renewing our lives in every moment.

In all things, we give you thanks with our whole hearts,
  singing our praises for your steadfast love,
  for nourishing our souls
  and giving life to every cell of our bodies.

We give you thanks for the everyday miracles
  of rich, hearty bread and cool, clean water,
  for surprising moments of deep connection with colleagues,
  for photographs that remind us of other times and places.

Even when our hearts are heavy,
  we give you thanks for your eternal love.

And for what else shall we give thanks this day?

Petition and Intercession

Gentle, renewing Wellspring of grace,
  in your eternal love, you teach us
  to care for all of your creation.

When mountain streams and mighty rivers
  become too dirty to drink,
  when garbage fills the deep trenches of the ocean floor,
  when the air itself becomes a poisonous brew,
  we cry out to you.

We cry out for all who sleep in doorways,
  for all whose waking moments are filled with danger,
  for all who have no money, no job, no prospects.

We cry out for all whose bodies are filled with pain,
  for all whose minds are clouded with grief or despair,
  for all whose days are a blur of fatigue.

We cry out to you in our own pain, too,
  begging for healing, for protection, for peace.
Aloud and in silence, we bring our prayers,
  our trust, our desire for the healing of the world.

SUNDAY BETWEEN JUNE 12 AND JUNE 18 INCLUSIVE (IF AFTER TRINITY SUNDAY)

PROPER 6, ORDINARY 11

1 Samuel 15:34–16:13; Psalm 20; 2 Corinthians 5:6–10, (11–13) 14–17; Mark 4:26–34

▬▬▬ Opening Prayer ▬▬▬

God of wheat and mustard seeds,
  God of parable and story,
  God of breath and hope,
  you hold us in your hand,
  and anoint us as heirs with Christ.

As we sing your praises,
  as we declare your steadfast love,
  let us know your holy presence
  in the songs we sing, in the words we speak,
  in the movements of our bodies,
  and the tokens of your love,
  laid upon the altar before us. Amen.

▬▬▬ Thanksgiving and Praise ▬▬▬

God of breath and hope,
  God of parable and story,
  God of wheat and mustard seeds,
  we thank you for the gift of forgiveness,
  for the gift of love,
  for the gift of your presence among us.

We give thanks for the old and the young among us,
  for new visions and ancient tales,
  for the songs of the psalmist,
  for the vision of prophets,
  for the courage of those who have walked in your ways.

We give you thanks for swift-flowing mountain streams,
  for placid ponds and stone-lined brooks,

for running water from the kitchen tap,
for clear, cold water on a hot, dry day.

We give you thanks for fathers and grandfathers,
for brothers and uncles,
for cousins and husbands,
for friends and companions,
for the men who share their lives with others
with strength and compassion and love.

We give you thanks for all these gifts,
and for the many more that fill our hearts with gratitude
and our mouths with words of praise.

Petition and Intercession

God of parable and story,
God of wheat and mustard seeds,
God of breath and hope,
you have promised to be father to the fatherless,
to protect and care for all who are in need.

We pray for those who suffer,
for those who have no food or homes,
for those who do not know human love,
for those who live in fear and pain and silence,
for those who cry out for comfort and for help.

We pray for presidents and politicians,
for bureaucrats and business owners,
for lawyers and doctors and poets and painters,
for farmers and bricklayers and those who dig ditches,
for soldiers and peacemakers,
and for all whose work is more burden than calling.

We pray for the earth and for all of its creatures,
we pray for our loved ones
and for those we do not know.

We pray for ourselves, for our pains and our heartaches.
And for what else shall we pray?

SUNDAY BETWEEN JUNE 19 AND JUNE 25 INCLUSIVE (IF AFTER TRINITY SUNDAY)

PROPER 7, ORDINARY 12

1 Samuel 17:(1a, 4–11, 19–23), 32–49; Psalm 9:9–20;
2 Corinthians 6:1–13; Mark 4:35–41

Opening Prayer

Ruler of sea and wind, we hear your voice
  in the crack of thunder, deep in a stormy night.
  We see you in the towering clouds,
  the flash of lightning and the pouring rain,
  and in the freshness of the early-morning garden
  where each green leaf and branching stalk
  reaches out to your embrace.

Like the leaves and branches
  stretching toward the sun,
  we reach out for your love,
  knowing that you are always in us
  and around us and among us.

You pour out your grace on all your creatures,
  making yourself known in all the world.
  We sing your praises,
  as we rejoice in all that you have done. Amen.

Thanksgiving and Praise

Ruler of sea and wind,
  source of compassionate love,
  we are overwhelmed with joy and gratitude
  for the gift of your grace and love.

And, as though this were not enough,
  you continue to pour out your gifts upon us,
  raining goodness and peace around us
  and through us and within us.

In receiving these great gifts,
  and many more than we can name,

our hearts overflow with gratitude,
as we give thanks,
aloud and in the silence of our hearts.

Petition and Intercession

Breath of God, compassionate Healer,
like the disciples on a stormy sea,
we are afraid for ourselves and for others
in a world that is full of hurt and pain.

We pray for the broken and battered,
for the lonely and broken-hearted,
for the scattered and lost,
for the crowded and captive,
for warriors and peacemakers
and those who sail on troubled waters.

We pray for those who mourn,
and those who live in fear;
for those who have too much
and for those who have nothing at all.

Source of compassion,
Savior of all who suffer,
healing breath of God,
we beg you to still the storms that trouble our souls,
as you hold the world in your eternal embrace.

SUNDAY BETWEEN JUNE 26 AND JULY 2 INCLUSIVE
PROPER 8, ORDINARY 13

2 Samuel 1:1, 17–27; Psalm 130; 2 Corinthians 8:7–15; Mark 5:21–43

Opening Prayer

Holy Beloved, holy Lover, holy Spirit of love,
  you are bigger than our wildest dreams,
  closer than our very breath,
  creator of stars and planets,
  healer of every broken heart.
We come like the woman who bled for twelve years,
  like the centurion whose daughter had died,
  like ones who have power
  and ones who have nothing,
  wanting only a word or a touch from you.
As we gather in your holy presence,
  speak to our hearts,
  touch our minds,
  and feed our souls,
  that we may become more fully your holy church,
  the living, loving, breathing Body of Christ on earth. Amen.

Thanksgiving and Praise

Holy Beloved, holy Lover, holy Spirit of love,
  You hear the prayers of all your people,
  in all the languages of all the peoples of earth.

You hear the silent whispers of the heart,
  the stumbling words of the little child,
  the mumbles of those who have forgotten how to speak.

In words and in silence, we give thanks
  for those who work tirelessly to put out wildfires,
  for those who rescue people from flood,
  for those who lend a hand wherever there is need.

We give thanks for life and for breath,
  for love and for friendship,
    and for your ever-flowing grace.

And for what else shall we give thanks?

Petition and Intercession

Holy Beloved, holy Lover, holy Spirit of love,
  our hands are open,
    holding on to nothing but the hem of your garment;
  our hearts are open,
    breaking with the pain of the world.

Out of the depths of our own yearning for wholeness,
  we cry out to you to heal every broken heart
  and every broken body.

We pray for soldiers and sailors and pilots and peacemakers,
  for all who live threatened by the weapons of war.
  Like David weeping over Saul and Jonathan,
  we weep for the blood of the fallen
  in every place where violence rages,
    and for their mothers and fathers and sisters and brothers,
    their children and spouses,
    their friends and also their enemies,
    for every life is precious and every heart knows grief.

We pray with those who suffer in silence,
  and we pray with those who wail their lament.
  For them and for us, we beg for your healing touch,
  your comforting word, your eternal compassion.

Sunday between July 3 and July 9 inclusive
Proper 9, Ordinary 14
2 Samuel 5:1–5, 9–10; Psalm 48; 2 Corinthians 12:2–10; Mark 6:1–13

Opening Prayer

Eternal One, Incarnate Word, Abiding Spirit,
  we ponder your steadfast love
  here, in the midst of the city,
  and as we travel to mountains,
  the seashore,
  or distant lands.

Your abundant grace
  pours out over all the earth.
  Your hands are filled with justice,
  and your ways are the ways of peace.
Like the disciples who went from town to town
  healing the sick and casting out demons,
  we know that you are always with us
  and around us and among us,
  filling us with love for all of your creation,
  anointing us with the power of your spirit,
  calling us to become your holy Body. Amen.

Thanksgiving and Praise

Abiding Spirit, Eternal One, Incarnate Word,
  the astonishing grace of forgiveness
  takes us into Paradise,
  as our hearts overflow with gratitude.

We give thanks for waking up each morning,
  and for the solace of sleep each night.

We give thanks for the tart, sweet blueberries of summer,
  for the breezes that soften the heat,
  for the promise of vacation travel,
  and for the safe return of those we love
  from distant places.

We give thanks for hugs and for handshakes,
  and for the smile of a stranger
  who waves us ahead as we wait to turn left in heavy traffic.

We give thanks for the tools that make our lives easier,
  for hammers and screwdrivers,
  for computers and telephones,
  for dishwashers and power drills,
  and for knowing how to use them.

We are thankful that we can live into the vision of love
  that you have set before us.
And for what other wonders and miracles
  shall we give thanks today?

▬▬▬ Petition and Intercession ▬▬▬

Incarnate Word, Abiding Spirit, Eternal One,
  like Paul, to whom was given a thorn in the flesh
  that he might not be too elated with visions of Paradise,
  we, too, suffer with the brokenness of creation.

We hear of terrorists planning to bomb public places,
  of ancient enemies continually at war,
  of our own people in uniform
  dying and killing in some distant land,
  and we groan in anguish, pleading for peace.

We know of children who have no homes,
  parents who have no work,
  people who have nothing but the tattered clothes they wear,
  and we call out in distress, pleading for justice.

We learn that a loved one has cancer,
  a friend is in pain,
  our own bodies betray us,
  and we weep with grief, pleading for healing.

Hear us, Holy One, as we pour out our hearts to you,
  aloud or in words that only you can hear.

SUNDAY BETWEEN JULY 10 AND JULY 16 INCLUSIVE
PROPER 10, ORDINARY 15

2 Samuel 6:1–5, 12b–19; Psalm 24; Ephesians 1:3–14; Mark 6:14–29

Opening Prayer

God of abundance and mystery,
  the earth and all that is in it belongs to you.
  Your voice is in the whirring sound of cicadas,
  singing of your glory in choirs too numerous to count.
  Your face is in the tall, sturdy sunflowers,
  turning their yellow petals
  towards the light of your splendor.
  Your touch is in the rain that splashes on hot sidewalks,
  the steamy mist rising again towards the clouds,
  the water running downwards towards rivers and seas.

Like David, who danced before the ark of the covenant,
  our hearts and bodies, too, leap with joy when you call us,
  and the sounds of music and laughter fill the air,
  as we thrill to the movement of your Holy Spirit.

Blessed are you, Holy One, who has blessed us in Christ
  and chosen us to be your children,
  so that we might live for the healing of the world. Amen.

Thanksgiving and Praise

God of grace and abundance,
  we give you thanks for adopting us into your family,
  for the grace that you pour out on us so abundantly,
  even when our hearts are not pure
  and our hands are not clean.

We give you thanks for the pileated woodpecker,
  its crimson head a brightly moving flare
  against the brown hulk of a fallen tree.

We give you thanks for farms and gardens,
  for so many zucchini and peppers and berries
  that we have to share them with our neighbors.

We give you thanks for the everyday miracles
  that we forget to notice:
  for telephones that connect us to family and friends,
  for trains and buses that take us where we need to go,
  for microwave ovens that heat up our food
  when it is too hot to turn on the oven.

We give you thanks when gateways that seem barred and locked
  open at your holy Word;
  when paths that are filled with stumbling blocks
  suddenly beckon towards an open future.

We give you thanks for days filled with wonder,
  and nights of restful sleep.

Aloud and in silence, we give you thanks
  for all the gifts and graces of our lives.

▬▬ Petition and Intercession ▬▬

God of mystery and grace,
  even in the midst of your abundant gifts
  there is heartache and sorrow and evil and pain.

Even as Jesus proclaimed the coming of your realm,
  Herod sent soldiers to cut off the head of John the Baptist.

Even as we believe that your realm is among us
  and around us and within us,
  our hearts sink when we hear of oppression and violence,
  of leaders who live in extravagant wealth
  while the people do not have enough to eat.

Even as we do what we can to heal the sick,
  to clothe the naked,
  to love our neighbors as ourselves,
  we cry out to you for the justice and peace
  that only you can bring.

Hear our prayers for the swift coming of your realm, Holy One,
  as we speak them in words
  or hold them silently in our hearts.

SUNDAY BETWEEN JULY 17 AND JULY 23 INCLUSIVE
PROPER 11, ORDINARY 16

2 Samuel 7:1–14a; Psalm 89:20–37; Ephesians 2:11–22;
Mark 6:30–34, 53–56

Opening Prayer

Eternal One, all of creation delights in your blessings;
  every creature lives only by your grace.
In your abundant, astonishing love,
  strengthen us in our inner being
  with power through your abiding Spirit,
  that Christ may dwell in our hearts through faith,
  as we are rooted and grounded in love.
As you form us into your holy Body,
  make us know the love of Christ
  that surpasses all understanding and knowledge,
  so that we may be filled with all the fullness of you. Amen.

Thanksgiving and Praise

Abiding Spirit, our joy in your blessings is beyond measure,
  our delight in your gifts is more than we can name.

We give thanks for birds and bicycles,
  for strawberries and sailboats,
  for beaches and mountain cabins and walks in the woods.

We are grateful for the long, hot days of summer,
  for ice cream and swimming pools,
  for deep conversations in the darkest hours,
  and the relief of air conditioning
  when it is too hot to sleep.
We give thanks for the love of friends and family,
  for children and parents and cousins
  and all the tumbling confusion
  of celebrations and memories.

To you, who are able to accomplish abundantly far more
  than all we can ask or imagine,

we bring our thanks and praise
aloud and in the silence of our hearts.

Petition and Intercession

Incarnate Word,
  long ago the crowds followed you from place to place
  because they saw the signs you performed
  for the healing of the world.

Today, we still follow you,
  longing for your healing touch,
  longing for your mysterious power to make us whole.

We pray for the hungry crowds who fill our cities,
  for children and women and men who have no homes,
  for those whose bodies are filled with pain,
  and for those whose days are filled with weeping.

As we hear of war and destruction,
  of violent death,
  of yet more refugees,
  of yet more fear and hatred,
  our hearts break again and again.

We beg you to speak a healing word
  to the leaders of nations,
  to those who think that bombs and guns
  will somehow salve their wounds,
  to those who fight because they don't know what else to do.
  Lead us and them to the ways of peace.
And for what else shall we pray?

Sunday between July 24 and July 30 inclusive
Proper 12, Ordinary 17

2 Samuel 11:1–15; Psalm 14; Ephesians 3:14–21; John 6:1–21

Opening Prayer

Eternal One, you call us to listen for your voice,
   to look all around us,
   to learn from you how each of our lives
   may be lived as prayer.

You call us to eat and drink at your table,
   to receive the bread of life and the cup of salvation,
   to become your holy Body
   as we grow in the warmth of your love.

In this celebration
   of the life, death, and resurrection of the Word made flesh,
   fill us with joy and gladness,
   so that we might become worthy vessels
   for your Holy Spirit. Amen.

Thanksgiving and Praise

Abiding Spirit, we rejoice in your presence among us,
   and give thanks for the gifts of life and love
   that you spread out as a feast
   for a world that hungers and thirsts for you.

We give thanks for the heat of summer
   that makes us move a little more slowly
   and reminds us to savor the sweetness
   of peaches and berries,
   the cool, ripe roundness of melons and grapes.

We give thanks for the sound of thunder
   that signals a coming storm,
   for raindrops that slake the thirsty land,
   that fill up the rivers
   with the water of life.

We give thanks for friends and for family,
   for phone calls and emails,
   and safe returns from faraway places.
   And for what else shall we give thanks?

Petition and Intercession

Incarnate Word, in gratitude for all these gifts
   our hearts are breaking as we hear
   a world which is groaning in pain.

Every day,
   the newspaper brings another tale of rockets and gunfire,
   the television brings pictures of death and destruction,
   and we pray that the violence will stop.

And even if there were no war,
   every day there is still the ordinary brokenness of life.
   We pray for those who need clean, safe homes;
   we pray for those who need jobs;
   we pray for those who mourn;
   we pray for those who live in danger and fear;
   for those who are in pain,
   for those who grieve,
   for those who cannot pray for themselves.

Aloud and in silence,
   we pray for all who hunger and thirst for you.
Have mercy on us, and on all your creation,
   according to your steadfast love.

SUNDAY BETWEEN JULY 31 AND AUGUST 6 INCLUSIVE
PROPER 13, ORDINARY 18

2 Samuel 11:26–12:13a; Psalm 51:1–12; Ephesians 4:1–16;
John 6:24–35

Opening Prayer

Holy God, hidden Source of life,
  we come hungry for the comfort of your forgiveness.

These summer days,
  when many of our familiar routines are different,
  bring us to unexpected places.

Unfathomable Mystery,
  Holy Spirit of care,
  we come today to celebrate our place in your creation.

We come to be healed in your presence,
  to find the peace that passes understanding,
  and open the door to those around us.

We pray that your healing spirit will fill us
  until we overflow in love,
  for we gather in the name of our Savior,
  who is Jesus the Christ. Amen.

Thanksgiving and Praise

God of love, we know the beauty of your creation.
Our senses overflow with tastes, and smells,
  and touch too delicate for words,
  and every one a precious gift from you.
God of mystery,
  like a cup in a waterfall
  our hearts run over with the richness of this life
  you pour out on the earth.

We celebrate the rich variety of gifts you offer us
  to build community and work for peace and justice
  here and in the many ordinary structures of our lives.

Hear now our prayers of praise and thanks,
  praise for the richness of your never-ending gifts,
  and thanks for eyes to see, and ears to hear,
  and fingertips to touch.

And for what else shall we offer thanks and praise?

Petition and Intercession

Unfathomable Mystery,
  source and substance of all being,
  we gather here like pilgrims
  searching the shoreline for you,
  hungry for the good news you have come to share.

We hear you challenge us to work for food that endures,
  that heals the rough and broken places in our lives,
  the pain we carry in our bodies and our hearts,
  the hunger in ourselves and others for reconciliation.

O God, we claim your promises
  that when we care enough to share our selves,
  there will be enough for all:
  enough forgiveness,
  enough healing,
  enough compassion.

We claim your promises
  for those we know who are in pain,
  and those more distant,
  whose lives are only sad and painful stories in our ears.
Hear now our prayers for those who suffer
  as we share them in community
  and lift them in the silence of our hearts.

Sunday between August 7 and August 13 inclusive
Proper 14, Ordinary 19

2 Samuel 18:5–9, 15, 31–33; Psalm 130; Ephesians 4:25–5:2;
John 6:35, 41–51

Opening Prayer

Out of the depths we cry to you, O Holy One.
  God of all creation, hear our voices.

Let your ears be attentive to the voice of our supplications
  as we gather to worship you,
  to sing a new song to you,
  to raise our prayers of praise and thanks,
  our cares and our concerns.

Fill us with your Holy Spirit, we pray,
  for we gather in the name of our Savior,
  who is your firstborn, Jesus the Christ. Amen.

Thanksgiving and Praise

God of justice and mercy,
  God of love and forgiveness,
  God of change and new beginnings,
  we come to you this day,
  filled with wonder for the power of your mighty presence
  in all of this creation.
We think we know so much,
  but when we turn out the lights
  we are confronted by stars without number,
  stars that you created long before you imagined us into being.
All-nourishing Bread of Life,
  we thank you for showing us
  how to speak loving truth to our neighbors.
Open our hearts to the wonder of your wisdom;
  give us the eyes of a child,
  to see the miracle in each ripening seed.

Hear our prayers, O God of all creation,
  hear us as we bring our thanks
  for the richness of this world you are creating.
Receive the prayers we share aloud in this community,
  and those we ponder in the silence of our hearts.

Petition and Intercession

God of love, more than those who watch for the morning,
  our souls wait for you.

You call us to lives of righteousness,
  to speak the truth to our neighbors,
  to refrain from sin even when we are angry,
  to let no evil talk come from our mouths,
  to put away all bitterness and anger,
  to forsake our rights to wrangling and slander.

God of unending compassion,
  you call us to forgive one another, as you have forgiven us.

Give us the insight and commitment
  to respond in faithful love.

Holy Redeemer,
  we pray for those whose lives are scarred by wrath and anger,
  by malice and slander and pain.

Our souls wait for the presence of your healing power.
Holy Source of all salvation,
  lead us to the bread of life, we pray,
  then transform us
  so that we may be part of the Bread of Life to others,
  a loving, healing presence in these troubled times.

We lift our prayers for those in pain and need,
  and for ourselves, that we might be part of your good news.

SUNDAY BETWEEN AUGUST 14 AND AUGUST 20 INCLUSIVE

PROPER 15, ORDINARY 20

1 Kings 2:10–12, 3:3–14; Psalm 111; Ephesians 5:15–20; John 6:51–58

▰▰▰ Opening Prayer ▰▰▰

Eternal One, Inspiring Spirit, Bread of Life,
  you call us to praise you,
    to sing psalms and hymns and spiritual songs,
    making melody to you in our hearts.

You call us to listen for your voice,
  to look at the world around us,
  to attend to the whispers of our hearts.

You call us to become prayer,
  and so we offer our lives to you.

Fill us with your Holy Spirit,
  and teach us to live
  as members of the living Body
  of your holy child, Jesus, who is the Christ. Amen.

▰▰▰ Thanksgiving and Praise ▰▰▰

Eternal One, Inspiring Spirit, Bread of Life,
  with our whole hearts,
  we praise your holy name.

We give thanks that you have loved us,
  even before we know how to love,
  and that from you, we have learned to love others.

We give thanks for every movement towards peace,
  for every moment
  in which your wisdom overtakes our folly,
  for teaching us how to walk in your ways.

We give thanks for friends and family,
  for work and for leisure,
  for strawberries and watermelon,

and all the cool, juicy fruits of summer.
And for what else shall we give our thanks and praise?

Petition and Intercession

Eternal One, Inspiring Spirit, Bread of Life,
  like Solomon, who prayed for an understanding mind,
  help us to discern good from evil.

When pain and suffering fill our world,
  when all around us is grief and sorrow,
  help us to know what to do,
  when to act,
  and when to wait for you.

We pray for newborn babies,
  just opening their eyes to the world,
  and for those who are approaching the end of their days.

We pray for children who have trouble in school,
  and for those who have no schools to go to.

We pray for young men and women just starting to work,
  and for those who have lost the work
  that gave their lives meaning.

We pray for all whose days are passed in pain,
  and for all whose lives are poured out in caring.
Aloud and in silence, let our lives become prayer,
  interceding for the healing of the world.

SUNDAY BETWEEN AUGUST 21 AND AUGUST 27 INCLUSIVE

PROPER 16, ORDINARY 21

1 Kings 8:(1, 6, 10–11), 22–30, 41–43; Psalm 84; Ephesians 6:10–20; John 6:56–69

Opening Prayer

How lovely is your dwelling place,
  Holy Mystery, holy Breath, holy Lover!

Our souls long, indeed faint for your presence;
  our hearts and bodies sing our joy to the living God.

In the sultry heat of summer's end,
  we feel your refreshing breath in soft, evening breezes;
  we hear your voice in the whirring hum of cicada song;
  we see your light shining through the glitter of falling stars.

In our prayers and in our singing,
  in our words and in our silence,
  bring us ever closer to your heart and will.

Holy Mystery, holy Breath, holy Lover,
  our strength is in you alone.
  Clothe us in your loving power,
  so that we may live in you
  and become your people. Amen.

Thanksgiving and Praise

How lovely is your dwelling place,
  Holy Mystery, holy Breath, holy Lover!

To live with you is joy,
  and we praise you without ceasing.

You are our sun, our shield,
  the giver of honor and grace.

You never fail to bless those who walk with integrity.
  Blessed are all who trust in you.

We give thanks for life and breath,
  for body and blood,
  for the spirit that gives life,
  for the bread of heaven
  that is your eternal Word.

And for what else shall we give thanks?

Petition and Intercession

How lovely is your dwelling place,
Holy Mystery, holy Breath, holy Lover!

But in this broken world,
life does not always seem lovely.

We grieve with those who mourn,
we ache with those who live in pain,
we cry out with those who hunger and thirst,
we plead for those who live in fear.

Hear the prayers that we pray to you today,
that we may see this hurting world
with your eyes of love and compassion.

Hear the plea of your servants and of your people,
gathered in your lovely dwelling place,
the cries and silent whispers
of all who need your healing grace.

Sunday between August 28 and September 3 inclusive

Proper 17, Ordinary 22

Song of Solomon 2:8–13; Psalm 45:1–2, 6–9; James 1:17–27;
Mark 7:1–8, 14–15, 21–23

Opening Prayer

Creator of lights, Light of the world,
you bring into being all that is good,
all that is true,
all that sustains our lives.

Your voice is in the storm and in the silence,
in the song of the turtledove,
in the pounding of the woodpecker,
in the soft sounds of water dripping from the eaves,
and in the hearts of those who yearn for justice.

We hunger for your perfect love,
and thirst for your perfect peace.
And so you call us to gather at your table,
to feast on your holy Word,

to drink the cup of salvation,
poured out for the healing of the world.

Bless our stumbling words of prayer and praise,
and fill us with your spirit of love,
as we offer ourselves to you
in the name of the living Christ. Amen.

Thanksgiving and Praise

Creator of lights, Light of the world,
we thank you for all that is good,
all that is true,
all that sustains our lives.

You give us senses of smell and sight,
of hearing and taste and touch,
so that we might know and enjoy the world around us.

You give us the fresh scent of lavender,
the muskiness of wet leaves,
the roughness of pine cones,
the caress of a lover,
the yeastiness of fresh bread,
that we might always be aware of your loving presence.

When we rejoice at the birth of a child,
when we celebrate the long life of a friend,
when we dance to the changing beat
of life's complicated rhythms,
we give you our thanks and praise
in the words of our lips and in the silence of our hearts.

Petition and Intercession

Creator of lights, Light of the world,
we pray that your goodness
will heal all the hurts that fill us with despair.

War and violence, rage, and oppression,
divorce and abandonment,

accidents and disease—
the news is filled with sadness and pain.

Each person we pass on the street has a story of loss;
each person we know has stories of sorrow.

When we grieve at the death of a loved one,
when we mourn for the loss of our livelihood,
when we ache for the end of a relationship,
we plead with you for solace and comfort for ourselves
and for a world that aches for your healing Word.

And for what else shall we pray?

SUNDAY BETWEEN SEPTEMBER 4 AND SEPTEMBER 10 INCLUSIVE

PROPER 18, ORDINARY 23

Proverbs 22:1–2, 8–9, 22–23; Psalm 125; James 2:1–10 (11–13), 14–17; Mark 7:24–37

Opening Prayer

Holy Mystery, holy Lover, holy Breath,
you shower your creation with abundant life,
and fill the world with grace beyond measure.

Each day, some new facet of your creation
takes us by surprise:
we hear a sudden crack,
and turn to watch a slender tree
fall in the woods on a sun-filled afternoon;
the full moon emerges from its veil of clouds,
giving enough light to see colors in the garden;
a stranger smiles at us,
and the day becomes filled with possibility.

Today you invite us to look for more surprises
in the faces of those around us,
in the words of hymns both new and old,
in the hopes and dreams of a world that longs for peace.

You invite us to say "yes" to you,
  to one another,
  and to all creation.

Fill our minds with wisdom
  and our hearts with love,
  as we learn, once more, what it is to be your people,
  one small expression of the universal,
  grace-filled, living Body of Christ. Amen.

Thanksgiving and Praise

Holy Lover, holy Breath, holy Mystery,
  all of creation breathes a vibrant "yes,"
  and we, too, say "yes"
  in gratitude for your astonishing, abundant grace.

We say "yes" to blue skies and thunderclouds;
  to puppies and kittens
  and a family of deer grazing in the park.

We say "yes" to lifelong friends and new acquaintances,
  to babies and elders
  and long-lost relations who want to share old stories.

We say "yes" to the lonely and forgotten,
  to the hungry and homeless,
  to those who ask only for one kind word.

We say "yes" to all these
  as our hearts break open with gratitude
  and our voices speak our thanks and praise,
  to you, who first said "yes" to us.

Petition and Intercession

Holy Breath, holy Mystery, holy Lover,
  even in the abundant "yes" of creation,
  a broken, hurting world still hears too much of "no."

Rage and violence break tender hearts,
  war and terrorism maim and kill,
  oppression overturns the common good.

Our hearts still ache with the shock of ancient wounds,
  our minds go numb with the magnitude of need.

And so we plead with you and beg for your holy "yes."
  Give sight to the blind,
  speech to the silent,
  hearing to those who have closed their ears
  to the sound of your holy, healing Word.

Comfort those who mourn,
  bring peace to those who fear,
  give relief to those who live with pain and loss.

Holy One, hear the prayers of those who can speak,
  and those whose pleas are hidden in their hearts.

SUNDAY BETWEEN SEPTEMBER 11 AND SEPTEMBER 17 INCLUSIVE

PROPER 19, ORDINARY 24

Proverbs 1:20–33; Psalm 19; James 3:1–12; Mark 8:27–38

Opening Prayer

Holy Wisdom, you cry out in the streets,
  calling us to hear your voice,
  to heed your counsel,
  to live in your holy ways.

The heavens tell your glory,
  and the very sky tells the genius of your work.

Day carries the news to the day,
  and night carries the message to the night,
  without a word,
  without a sound,
  without a voice being heard,
  and yet their message fills all the world.

We, who have heard this astonishing message,
  gather now to share the good news of your presence
  within us and among us and around us,

conforming us ever more truly
to the living body of the crucified and risen Christ. Amen.

══ Thanksgiving and Praise ══

Jesus asked, "Who do you think that I am?"
And, with the disciples, we confess and give thanks:
Jesus is the Christ,
through whom we are loved and forgiven.

In the reality of this love,
everything else is gift:
the sun and sky, the night and stars,
the earth on which we walk,
the air that fills our lungs and lifts our spirits,
the food that fills our bellies and delights our senses,
even life itself.

So, with the psalmist, we cry,
God's just demands delight the heart.
God's clear commands sharpen vision.
God's faultless decrees stand forever.
God's right judgments keep their truth.
Keeping them makes us rich.
And for what else shall we give our thanks and praise?

══ Petition and Intercession ══

Holy Maker of all that is,
in your wisdom you give and take away,
you make and destroy,
you number our days and each hair on our heads.
In your loving-kindness,
and remembering your promises,
we pray that you will comfort those who mourn,
bring healing to those who suffer in body or in mind,
and freedom to those who are oppressed.
We pray for an end to violence and war around the world,
and in our cities and our homes.

For peace and for wisdom, we pray aloud and silently,
in the name of Jesus, who is the Christ.

Sunday between September 18 and September 24 inclusive

Proper 20, Ordinary 25

Proverbs 31:10–31; Psalm 1; James 3:13–4:3, 7–8a; Mark 9:30–37

Opening Prayer

Holy Wisdom, holy Breath, holy Maker of all,
you show us what is good,
and invite us to celebrate with all of your creation.

You give us blue skies and towering clouds,
crowds and solitude, conversation and silent reflection,
anticipation and memory, certainty and hope,

As we gather now to share the good news of your presence
within us and among us and around us,
help us to know that you are always with us,
forming us into the living body
of the crucified and risen Christ. Amen.

Thanksgiving and Praise

Holy Wisdom, holy Breath, holy Maker of all,
you show us what is good,
and shower us with blessings.

Jesus said that the last shall be first,
and the one who would be first
should be servant of all.

We give thanks for all who work for justice,
for those who pour out their lives making peace,
for those who serve in hospitals and homeless shelters,
for those who try to stop the violence they see
and replace it with love.

We give thanks for those who bring music to our ears
and hope to our hearts,
for those who brighten the world with visions of abundant life,
for those who tell new stories of wonder and delight.

We give thanks for valiant women and for righteous men,
for all who have heard God's word and follow the call
to be Christ to everyone they meet.
And for what else shall we give our thanks and praise?

Petition and Intercession

Holy Wisdom, holy Breath, holy Maker of all,
you show us what is good,
and promise to draw near to us
when we draw near to you,
to watch over all your people in their distress.

And so we pray that you will comfort those who mourn,
bring healing to those who suffer in body or in mind,
and freedom to those who are oppressed.

In a time when violence seems to be all around us,
we pray for peace and for wisdom
to calm the voices that incite others,
and to heal the divisions that lead to hatred and fear.

We pray for those who seek elected office,
that they may speak thoughtfully and respectfully,
and seek the good of all.
Aloud and in silence,
we pray in the name of Jesus, who is the Christ.

SUNDAY BETWEEN SEPTEMBER 25 AND OCTOBER 1 INCLUSIVE

PROPER 21, ORDINARY 26

Esther 7:1–6, 9–10, 9:20–22; Psalm 124; James 5:13–20; Mark 9:38–50

Opening Prayer

O Holy God, who made us in your image,
 we gather as your people.

We come,
 hungry for the stories that will connect us with our past,
 with each other and with you.

We come to offer praise and thanks for being on our side,
 for calling us to stand with you when we were threatened.

Reveal yourself to us, we pray, for we gather in your name,
 Creator, Redeemer and holy, healing Presence
 here among us. Amen.

Thanksgiving and Praise

O Holy One who is beyond our wildest imagination,
 we know that you are blessing everyone
 who trembles in the presence of your power,
 all those who walk in your ways,
 as part of your faithful people!

We eat the fruit of the labor of our hands, the bread of toil,
 and we are happy,
 for we know that you have been with us in the toil,
 as you will be with us in the celebration.

O God, you made us with a longing for each other,
 and placed that longing at the very heart
 of our relationships with one another
 and with the universe around us.

We bring you praise and thanks
 for all the wonder of your closely knit creation,
 and for the power of love and compassion.

Hear now our prayers of praise and thanks,
  for all the richness of this wild, always-emerging reality.

Petition and Intercession

God of all creation, we know our help comes from you.
But sometimes we find it hard to understand
  how you can be among us,
  and around us, and within us,
  and still there seems to be
  so much pain and sorrow in the world.

We see the spoiled fruit of broken promises,
  the wounds of pent-up anger,
  the pain of relationships betrayed.

We long for healing,
  for those around us whose lives are burdened
  by poverty and disease,
  for those in places where the anger flares
  as violence and war,
  and for ourselves, for we know all too well
  how we contribute to the pain around us.

O Holy God of love,
  help us speak truth to power,
  as Esther did in advocating for her people.

Hear now our prayers for those in need,
  and for ourselves,
  for we would be your servants in this time and place,
  salt of the earth, a faithful flavor of your holy realm.

We offer you our prayers for those in pain and need
  by sharing them aloud with our community,
  and raising them within the silence of our hearts.

SUNDAY BETWEEN OCTOBER 2 AND OCTOBER 8 INCLUSIVE

PROPER 22, ORDINARY 27

Job 1:1, 2:1–10; Psalm 26; Hebrews 1:1–4; 2:5–12; Mark 10:2–16

Opening Prayer

O God of love and mystery,
  we come because you have chosen us,
  gathering as your people.

O God, be with us in this hour;
  bind us together in your covenant of love and service;
  fill us with the power of your Holy Spirit.

Holy Fountain of forgiveness,
  we gather in the name of our Savior, Jesus the Christ. Amen.

Thanksgiving and Praise

How wonderful and how mysterious are your ways, O God,
  how beautiful is your creation!

We gather here this morning
  in the cool warmth of a summer remembered.

We gather because we need to know
  that we are in your midst,
  that you are in our hearts.

We come to pray together,
  to remind ourselves that this is your creation,
  that all your paths are steadfast love and faithfulness.

We give thanks that even as you stood with Job
  through all his painful trials,
  so you will stand with us.

God of acorns falling to the ground
  and fat onions already buried there,
  we put our trust in you.

Give us glimpses of your glory,
  images of your love for all creation,
  words of praise and thanks that we can share with you.

Hear now our prayers of praise and thanks
  for all the wonders of this time.
We offer them aloud in this sacred space,
  and lift them in the silence of our hearts.

Petition and Intercession

God whose love is everlasting,
  loving Christ who always heals those who are ready,
  Holy Spirit of love and healing and tender compassion,
  we come because you have called us,
  we come to you because you love us.

And even as we give thanks that you are with us,
  O God of love and mystery,
  we come tired from tugging at the burdens of this world.

We see so much pain and suffering.
We feel the burdens of injustice,
  and we want the world to be free.

We know that you have promised your loving presence
  to heal the sick and bind up the brokenhearted,
  yet there are so very many broken hearts.

We pray for healing of tensions within our community,
  for healing from political strife around the world,
  for healing from the devastation of storm and fire and flood.

We pray for all those
  who have abandoned hope for justice in our land,
  who have lost faith in the ideal of democracy.

O God of love and mystery,
  plant our roots in fertile soil,
  water us with love and wisdom
  and lead us on the path you are making before us,
  for you are the God of this unfolding universe,
  leading us on the path of peace and justice.

Hear our prayers for healing, in others and in ourselves.

WIN A $100 GIFT CERTIFICATE!

Fill in this card and mail it to us—
or fill it in online at

**skylightpaths.com/
feedback.html**

—to be eligible for a
$100 gift certificate for
SkyLight Paths books.

SKYLIGHT PATHS PUBLISHING
SUNSET FARM OFFICES RTE 4
PO BOX 237
WOODSTOCK VT   05091-0237

Fill in this card and return it to us to be eligible for our quarterly drawing for a $100 gift certificate for SkyLight Paths books.

We hope that you will enjoy this book and find it useful in enriching your life.

Book title: _____

Your comments: _____

How you learned of this book: _____

If purchased: Bookseller _____ City _____ State _____

Please send me a free SKYLIGHT PATHS Publishing catalog. I am interested in: (check all that apply)

1. ❑ Spirituality
2. ❑ Mysticism/Kabbalah
3. ❑ Philosophy/Theology

4. ❑ Spiritual Texts
5. ❑ Religious Traditions (Which ones?) _____
6. ❑ Children's Books

7. ❑ Prayer/Worship
8. ❑ Meditation
9. ❑ Interfaith Resources

Name (PRINT) _____

Street _____

City _____ State _____ Zip _____

E-MAIL (FOR SPECIAL OFFERS ONLY)

Please send a SKYLIGHT PATHS Publishing catalog to my friend:

Name (PRINT) _____

Street _____

City _____ State _____ Zip _____

SKYLIGHT PATHS® Publishing   Tel: (802) 457-4000 • Fax: (802) 457-4004

Available at better booksellers. Visit us online at www.skylightpaths.com

SUNDAY BETWEEN OCTOBER 9 AND OCTOBER 15 INCLUSIVE

PROPER 23, ORDINARY 28

Job 23:1–9, 16–17; Psalm 22:1–15; Hebrews 4:12–16; Mark 10:17–31

Opening Prayer

Constant, delivering Creator of all,
  you show us what is good,
  and teach us how to be your people.

You are present in the brisk autumn air
  in the first edges of red and gold among the leaves,
  in the bright stars that linger alongside the crescent moon
  in the hour just before dawn.

Before you no creature is hidden,
  no decision is too secret for you to hold.

You search us out and know us,
  breathing life into ancient stories,
  filling our hearts with hope,
  even when the news fills our eyes and ears
  with destruction and despair.

As we discern the shape of our commitments,
  we ask you, who once became human and died on a cross,
  to live among us again today,
  leading us into new life in you. Amen.

Thanksgiving and Praise

Deep, mysterious Breath of life,
  you give us laughter and sunlight,
  life-giving rain and the bright autumn leaves.

You hold all of creation in your hands,
  filling it with blessings beyond our wildest dreams.

All that we have, all that we know comes from you,
  and so we thank you for love and for beauty;
  for bright, new homes and comfortable, old rooms;

for exciting stories from distant lands and old, familiar tales;
for friendship that lasts for a lifetime;
for the smile of a stranger when we feel all alone.

Rejoicing in the good news of your love,
we give thanks for the chance to trust you,
joined together as members
of the holy, living Body of Christ.

Hear, now, our prayers of thanksgiving and praise,
aloud and in the silence of our hearts.

━━━ Petition and Intercession ━━━

Caring, compassionate Healer of broken lives,
how hard it is to enter the realm of God,
when all around us we hear of death and illness,
of violence and destruction.

Because we trust in your promises to wipe away all our tears,
we pray for consolation for those who mourn,
for comfort for the sick and dying,
and for strength for those who care for them.

We pray for honesty and humility in those who seek to govern,
for wisdom to discern the path to wholeness,
and for courage to make good decisions for the benefit of all.

We pray that you will bring justice and compassion
to places where now there is only oppression and retribution,
understanding and hope
where now there is only anger and fear.

We pray for those who have asked us to pray,
and for those who cannot pray for themselves.

We pray for those who are close to us,
and for those whose needs are only a story from far away.

We pray for the needs of others,
and for the healing of our own fears.

And for what else shall we pray this day?

SUNDAY BETWEEN OCTOBER 16 AND OCTOBER 22 INCLUSIVE

PROPER 24, ORDINARY 29

Job 38:1–7, (34–41); Psalm 104:1–9, 24, 35c; Hebrews 5:1–10; Mark 10:35–45

═══ Opening Prayer ═══

Mysterious, wonderful Architect of the future,
  we come together this soft, fall morning
  to celebrate the knowledge that we are in your midst.

We marvel in the way you set the earth on its foundation
  so that it shall never be shaken.

We celebrate the way you call us into the future
  you reveal to us only as fast as we move toward it.

We treasure the call to love and justice
  you draw gently from our hearts.

We celebrate the knowledge that we are in your midst.
Reveal your presence to us, O God of all creation,
  for we gather in the name of our Savior,
  who is Jesus the Christ. Amen.

═══ Thanksgiving and Praise ═══

O God of all creation, how manifold are your works!
The glowing maple preening in the gentle afternoon sun,
  the brave crickets in the warm, enfolding dark,
  and families of geese moving at your inner bidding,
  each testify to the coming of a new tomorrow,
  a time of change,
  a time of endings that make way for new creation.

And, holy Maker of the seasons and cycles of life,
  you've brought us to a turning point ourselves,
  calling us to be with you on the way by serving others.

We celebrate the way you call us into an unfolding future
  as a fragile earthen vessel of love and justice

for those we serve, and those they touch,
and those who hear the story
of your compassion and forgiveness.

We thank you for the stirring of new call
that whispers in the wind of change.

Fill us to overflowing with the power
of your holy, creative compassion,
for we would heed your call to live our life together
as one small part of the body of the risen Christ.
Hear now our prayers of praise and thanks,
for all the wonder of your rich reality.

Petition and Intercession

Holy loving Creator of all,
we watch in helpless anguish
as smoldering conflict in distant lands flares into bloodshed.

There seems to be so little we can do
except to pray for understanding, tolerance, and forgiveness
among the angry, weary people
whose lives have been so battered
by forces that seem to be beyond control.

We watch as hopes for new beginnings in many different places
seem tossed about like butterflies before a thunderstorm.

And there are those much closer to us
whose fear and pain seems overwhelming.

Holy God of harvest plenty,
hear now our prayers for those who do not have enough—
enough protection from violence, and hunger, and disease,
enough hope to start again.

We raise them up aloud, and in the silence of our hearts.

SUNDAY BETWEEN OCTOBER 23 AND OCTOBER 29 INCLUSIVE

PROPER 25, ORDINARY 30

Job 42:1–6, 10–17; Psalm 34:1–8, (19–22); Hebrews 7:23–28;
Mark 10:46–52

Opening Prayer

Holy Shaper of new dreams,
  you open our eyes to astonishing visions,
  inviting us to see a world of overflowing abundance
  where everyone has all that is needed,
  and all are embraced in a circle of love.
You call us to rejoice in an upside-down world,
  where blind people see,
  where the last are the first and the first are the last,
  where rich people give all that they have to the poor.
When the news fills our eyes and ears
  with death and destruction,
  we ask you, who once became human and died on a cross,
  to live among us again
  helping us to fulfill your dream of justice and peace. Amen.

Thanksgiving and Praise

Faithful Giver of hope and promise,
  you give us laughter and sunlight,
  storm clouds and shadows.
You hold all of creation in your hands,
  surprising us with blessings
  just when we think that all has been lost.
We give thanks for the flame-red leaves that linger in trees,
  and flutter around our ankles as we walk down the street.
Rejoicing in the good news of your unending love,
  we give thanks that you have called us
  to be members of your holy, living Body,

the eyes and ears and hands and feet of Christ
carrying your light into a darkening world.

Hear, now, our prayers of thanksgiving and praise,
aloud and in the silence of our hearts.

Petition and Intercession

Faithful Restorer of all that is lost and broken,
when the dark hours of night seem to stretch out forever,
we struggle to remember that dawn will surely come.

We beg you to save us from the monsters of despair,
to free us from our fears,
to take away our burdens,
to comfort all whose hearts are broken,
to heal all who bear wounds in body or spirit.

As you open our eyes to the world around us,
we pray for all who live without love,
for those who live without hope,
for those who have lost their vision of a better world.

Aloud and in silence,
we pray for glimmers of hope and glimpses of glory,
blessings of faith in dark and troubling times.

And for what else shall we pray?

Sunday between October 30 and November 5 inclusive
Proper 26, Ordinary 31

Ruth 1:1–18; Psalm 146; Hebrews 9:11–14; Mark 12:28–34

Opening Prayer

Holy Wisdom, holy Lover, holy Breath,
you call us to love you
with all our heart and all our soul and all our mind,
to love our neighbors as we love our very selves.

Just as Ruth followed Naomi into a strange land,
  we follow your call to be your people,
  not knowing where we will go
  or how we will live along the way.

As we walk in the footsteps of those who have gone before,
  we learn to trust only you,
  the God of heaven and earth and all that is in them,
  the God to whom we pray
  in the name of Jesus, who is the Christ. Amen.

▬▬▬ Thanksgiving and Praise ▬▬▬

Holy Wisdom, holy Lover, holy Breath,
  the earth is yours and all that is in it,
  the world, and those who live in it;
  oceans and rivers,
  mountains and valleys,
  city and forest
  all belong to you.

We give you thanks for the glorious colors of autumn,
  for the sight of our breath in the bright, cold dawn;
  for the rustling carpet of leaves along the path;
  for the deep, purple light left in the sky just as the sun sets.

We give you thanks for stories of loyalty and love,
  of trust and hope and caring,
  of strangers who became members
  of the family of faith.

We give thanks for candle-lit pumpkins flickering on doorsteps,
  beckoning costumed children towards handfuls of treats.

We give thanks for scary stories and happy endings,
  for customs and traditions that connect us through the years.

We give thanks for all the love that surrounds us,
  for all that we know and all that we hope for,
  aloud and in the silence of our hearts.

Petition and Intercession

Holy Wisdom, holy Lover, holy Breath,
  we love you with all our heart and soul and mind,
  we give you thanks for all the moments of our days,
  for the earth and the sea and all that is in them.

And still we long for more.

We long for you to bring justice to those who are oppressed,
  to give food to those who hunger,
  to set the prisoners free,
  and open the eyes of those who refuse to see.

We pray that you will lift up
  those who are bowed down with pain,
  watch over travelers who feel lost and alone,
  take care of widows and orphans
  and all who have no help but you.

We pray for loved ones and for strangers,
  for our own needs,
  and for all who need our prayers.
  And for what else shall we pray this day?

SUNDAY BETWEEN NOVEMBER 6 AND NOVEMBER 12 INCLUSIVE

PROPER 27, ORDINARY 32

Ruth 3:1–5, 4:13–17; Psalm 127; Hebrews 9:24–28; Mark 12:38–44

Opening Prayer

God of Ruth and Naomi,
  of Boaz and Obed and Jesse and David,
  and all of our ancestors in faith,
  we come to you like widows
  bringing all that we have,
  all that we are.
In return, you fill us with dreams,
  with visions of justice and peace,
  with fantasies of a world that has put an end to war.

You fill our eyes with glorious color,
  the brilliant red leaves of a Japanese maple
  piling in drifts against the rich, black earth;
  the golden leaves of oak trees,
  flying in the wind against a deep, blue sky.

Accept our meager gifts of song and prayer,
  and fill our hearts with your abundant love,
  that we may become your hands and feet and heart,
  filling the world with good news
  in the name of Jesus, who is the Christ. Amen.

Thanksgiving and Praise

Holy Maker of color and sound,
  we give you thanks for the beauty that surrounds us,
  and for the senses you have given us
  so that we can perceive it.

We give you thanks for changing seasons,
  for warm days and chilly nights,
  for the rustle of leaves in a brisk breeze,
  for pots of bright pansies
  hoping for a spot in someone's garden.

We give you thanks for good conversation,
  for food and wine and laughter and fun,
  for hard questions and thoughtful answers,
  for silliness and seriousness,
  and all the little moments that make up a life.

In silence and in spoken words,
  we give you thanks for all these gifts.
  And for what else shall we give thanks?

Petition and Intercession

Holy Fulfiller of our wildest dreams,
  when Ruth and Naomi had nothing,
  you gave them more
  than they could ever imagine or desire.

Like them, we come to you with nothing but our lives,
    asking for your blessing,
    asking for you to fill our hearts with hope.

We pray for those who have won elections,
    that they may govern wisely and fairly;
    for those who have lost,
    that they may accept the decisions with grace;
    and for our country and for the world,
    that new leaders and new dreams
    will bring an end to war and injustice in every land.

We pray for all who care for the sick and dying;
    for all who do the hard, dirty work
    of keeping our cities clean,
    growing our food,
    and moving goods from one place to another;
    for all who work long hours at low pay,
    and for all who have no work at all.

Holy One,
    you, who provide for the poor,
    bring comfort to widows and orphans,
    heal the sick,
    and advocate for the oppressed,
    hear now our pleas and our prayers,
    aloud and in the silence of our hearts.

Sunday between November 13 and November 19 inclusive

Proper 28, Ordinary 33

1 Samuel 1:4–20, 2:1–10; Hebrews 10:11–14, (15–18), 19–25;
Mark 13:1–8

Opening Prayer

There is no one like you, Ruler of the Universe,
    God of all of creation.

There is no one but you, in whom we trust,
in whom we live and move and have our being.

In this time of changing seasons,
you remind us that pouring rain and bright blue skies,
howling wind and sunbaked afternoons,
blazing red maple leaves and sodden, brown mud
all come from you.

Like Hannah, who trusted in your promise,
and gave her only son into your service,
we come to serve you with all our being:
with bodies that shiver in the wind
and welcome the autumn sun's bright rays;
with minds that thrill to the thought of your power;
with souls that thirst for your love.

Though we hear of wars and disasters,
we remember your promise
to put your laws into our hearts,
filling us with the intoxicating wine of your Holy Spirit
so that we may more completely be
the earthly Body of the risen Christ,
in whose name we pray. Amen.

Thanksgiving and Praise

Blessed are you, our God,
Creator of all that is,
who has given us life, and sustained us
and brought us to this time.

Blessed are you,
who has poured out blessing upon blessing,
filling our eyes with the sight of golden trees,
lit as if from within by a nearby streetlight;
our ears with the sound of leaves,
crunching underfoot with every step;
our mouths with the taste of crisp apples
and our hearts with the abundance of your love.

Blessed are you,
   who poured out your life in love,
   dying on a cross so that we could understand
   the meaning of forgiveness,
   and rising again so that we could understand
   the meaning of eternal life in you.

Our hearts exult in your many gifts,
   too numerous to count,
   so astonishingly generous
   that we blink our eyes in wonder.

We cannot thank you enough,
   but our thanks and praise is all we have,
   spoken aloud or in the silent gratitude of our hearts.

▬▬ Petition and Intercession ▬▬

Blessed are you, our God.
   You, who are known as Healer of the sick,
   Comforter of the weary,
   Mother and Father of the orphan,
   you know our pains and sufferings,
   our fears and our anguish,
   our hopes and our longings,
   even before we can name them ourselves.

Still, we need to pour out our hearts to you,
   to pray for an end to war,
   for an end to the violence that seems to surround us,
   for an end to the endless cycle of hurt and revenge.

We pray that you will give wisdom
   to those who lead our nation
   and to leaders around the world
   who seek answers to the problems of their people.

We pray for those who suffer from famine and earthquake
   and fire and flood;
   for those who mourn and for those who long for death;

for those who need to work and for those who cannot;
for those who cannot pray for themselves,
and for our own needs.

And for what else shall we pray?

THE REIGN OF CHRIST

SUNDAY BETWEEN NOVEMBER 20 AND NOVEMBER 26 INCLUSIVE

PROPER 29, ORDINARY 34

2 Samuel 23:1–7; Psalm 132:1–12 (13–18); Revelation 1:4b–8; John 18:33–37

Opening Prayer

O holy Mystery, Ruler of all this complex creation,
  we gather to give ourselves to you
  in thanks and celebration.

We come from many places,
  filled with hopes and fears,
  hungry for a quiet spot
  where we can share our load.

We know this is a place where we connect with you,
  a place of Sabbath rest,
  a place where love and understanding,
  healing and forgiveness
  flow like quiet streams beneath a piercing, icy sun.

Help us follow where you lead us,
  for we would be your people,
  one small part of the body of the risen Christ,
  gathered here to sing and pray and celebrate
  in the name of our Savior, who is Jesus the Christ. Amen.

▬▬▬ Thanksgiving and Praise ▬▬▬

Holy shepherd of your faithful flock,
  we see how you have led us to this place.
This is a time when the bright reality of your holy city
  is dimmed by violence and fear,
    and still we know your presence in so many ways.

We watch the season turn so sharply
  that we're caught off guard,
    surprised by early nights
    with icy moonlight guiding our way home.

We watch with hopeful expectation
  as new ideas for ministry spring forth
    here and in other places where hope shines brightly
    in the darkness of despair.

We give you thanks for the comfort of tradition
  and the delight of discovery.
And now, O Holy One, what other thanks
  do you invite?

▬▬▬ Petition and Intercession ▬▬▬

Holy Alpha and Omega,
  you teach us that your holy realm is mystery:
    not of this world yet very close at hand,
    for you are love.

We pray for wisdom and compassion
  to let your love flow through us,
    bringing life and hope to those in pain and need.

We worry,
  and we reach out to help,
    and we regret that there is not enough time to do more.

We ache for the pain we see
  in places where there seems to be no healing:
    the schoolyard squabbles in our government,
    the homeless facing lonely days and freezing nights,

the tragedy of violence in distant lands
and right around the corner.

What can we do to help?
O God of love and hope,
  hear now our prayers for those in need,
  and for ourselves, for we are needy too.

We lift them in the safety of this holy place,
  and in the silence of our heavy hearts.

Year C

ADVENT

FIRST SUNDAY OF ADVENT

Jeremiah 33:14–16; Psalm 25:1–10; 1 Thessalonians 3:9–13;
Luke 21:25–36

Opening Prayer

Holy Maker of deep and mysterious promises,
  lead us in your truth and teach us,
    for you are the God of our salvation;
      we wait for you every day of our lives.

You have promised to be a God of mercy and steadfast love,
  a trustworthy guide
    when the future seems dark and dangerous.

You have promised that your realm is near,
  a realm of peace and plenty and joy.

You have promised to be with us,
  even to the end of the world.

In these days of waiting,
  help us to prepare our hearts and minds
    for living each moment in your eternal realm.

Teach us how to say "yes" to your promise,
  to live as the Body of Christ,
    bearing your gifts into a world
      filled with signs of your coming. Amen.

━━━ Thanksgiving and Praise ━━━

God of faithfulness and steadfast love,
  how can we thank you enough for the joy that we feel
  for all that we have already been given?

We give thanks for the love
  that endlessly pours out from you,
  filling our hearts with gladness
  and spilling over into love for one another.

We give thanks for the first frost of winter,
  the bright, full moon in a starry sky,
  the icy sparkles that dance on early-morning gardens.

We give thanks for music and silence,
  for friendly bus drivers and walks in the woods,
  for conversations that take us into the hard places
  that open our hearts to each other's pain.

Most of all, we give thanks for the promise of your coming,
  for the mystery of your holy child, Jesus, who is the Christ.
  And for what else shall we give thanks this day?

━━━ Petition and Intercession ━━━

God of mercy and justice,
  in this time of waiting,
  of not knowing what will happen next,
  people are filled with grief and sorrow
  over disasters that have already come,
  with fear of what is coming upon the world.

We hear of great storms and terrible droughts,
  of climate change that will destroy the life that we know.

We hear of governments challenged,
  of new nations recognized,
  of threats of war and conflict.

We hear of economic troubles,
  less money available to help those in need,

while more and more people live
without food or shelter or hope.

Trusting in your promises, we pray for peace,
in our homes, on our streets, and around the world.

We pray for leaders, both here and in every country,
that they will make just decisions,
a blessing for all the people
whose lives are affected by their decrees.

We pray for all who live in sickness or in pain,
for those who grieve and those who are dying,
for those who have asked us to pray
and those who cannot pray for themselves.

For all this and so much more,
we pray aloud or in the silence of our hearts.

SECOND SUNDAY OF ADVENT

Baruch 5:1–9 or Malachi 3:1–4; Luke 1:68–79; Philippians 1:3–11;
Luke 3:1–6

Opening Prayer

Blessed are you, eternal Light of the world,
for you have spoken
through the mouths of your holy prophets,
promising to remember your covenant with your people,
so that we might serve you in holiness and righteousness
even to the end of the world.

You give us night skies filled with stars and scudding clouds,
and mornings hiding behind thick veils of fog.
Pull back the foggy curtains that veil our eyes
so that we may see your radiance
glowing in the faces of each person we see.

Fill us with your luminous love,
so that every word we speak is a blessing to all,

a sparkling reflection of your holy presence
in us, and around us, and through us.
Make us live as your holy Body,
a beacon of hope in a world that is filled with darkness.
Amen.

Thanksgiving and Praise

Blessed are you, boundless Source of grace,
for you cover us with the beauty of your glory,
and show us your splendor in all that you have made.

We give you thanks
for the bright glitter of the morning star,
bravely shining in the first, pink flush of dawn.

We give you thanks
for the intricate web of dark, wet branches,
outlined against the deep blue sky of evening.

We give you thanks for the warmth of friendship,
for songs and for laughter,
for gift wrap and glitter,
for cookies and cocoa,
and for the exuberant abundance of your unfailing love.

Aloud and in silence, we give our thanks
for all that we can name,
and all that we do not even notice.

Petition and Intercession

Blessed are you, compassionate Savior,
for you have looked favorably on all your people
promising that the dawn from on high
will break upon the world,
giving light to those who sit in darkness
and in the shadow of death.

In this season of short days and long nights,
we pray that you will shelter those who sleep outdoors,
protecting each one who lives in fear of violence,

and strengthening those who pour out their lives
that others may live.

In these days of waiting for the light,
  we pray that you will bring freedom
  to all who are oppressed,
    healing to all who are broken in body or spirit,
    and comfort to all who mourn.

In these days of preparing the way for your coming,
  we pray that you will grant wisdom to all who make the rules,
  give courage to all who must follow them,
    and guide those who wage war into the ways of peace.

For the needs that are known to us,
  and for the needs that are known only to you,
  we pray aloud or in the silence of our hearts.

THIRD SUNDAY OF ADVENT

Zephaniah 3:14–20; Isaiah 12:2–6; Philippians 4:4–7; Luke 3:7–18

Opening Prayer

Faithful, life-giving Mystery,
  long ago, you sent John to baptize the people,
  to proclaim the good news of the coming of Christ.

Today, you send messengers of your coming reign
  in stories of unexpected generosity
  on city streets and country highways;
  in grace-filled conversations with strangers
  on street corners and subway stations;
  in the thoughtful gesture of a neighbor
  who sweeps up the last leaves of autumn
  from every front stoop on the block.

Even when we are afraid of a future
  that looks like the end of the world,
  you remind us that you are always with us.

As we gather in the name of the One who came
  and is to come again,
  fill us with your peace;
  teach us to sing your praises;
  and guard our hearts and minds
  until we shout aloud and sing for joy. Amen.

━━━ Thanksgiving and Praise ━━━

The psalmist says, "Surely God is our salvation;
  We will trust, and will not be afraid,
  for the Holy One is our strength and our might;
  give thanks to God, call on God's holy name;
  make known God's deeds among the nations;
  Sing praises to the Holy One, for God has done gloriously;
  let this be known in all the earth!"

And we do give thanks:
  for sparkling mornings and moonlit nights,
  for asters and mums and late-blooming daisies;
  for bare, black branches outlined against a deep blue sky.

We give thanks for promises made and promises kept,
  for parties and food pantries,
  for the excitement of crowds and moments of solitude,
  for the good news of your presence among us.

For all this, and for more than we can ever know,
  we give our thanks and praise.

━━━ Petition and Intercession ━━━

Life-giving, comforting Redeemer,
  you have given your word
  that we should not worry about anything,
  but in everything, by prayer
  and supplication with thanksgiving,
  let our requests be made known to you.

In the wake of hurricanes and tornadoes,
  and newspapers filled with violence and war,

we want to believe your promise to bring an end to disasters
to deal justly with oppressors,
to gather in the outcasts
to heal all who live with daily pain.

We pray for students and teachers,
for parents and children,
for salesclerks and customers,
and all who are preparing as if for the end of the world.

We pray that you work in us and among us and through us
that we may be agents of healing and hope to those around us;
and that you will bring relief to all
whose hurt is beyond our power to help.

We pray for the coming of your Anointed One,
for the promised day of peace and plenty,
for wisdom to recognize that your reign has already begun.

For all that we can name,
and all that we have forgotten,
we pray aloud and in the silence of our hearts.

FOURTH SUNDAY OF ADVENT

Micah 5:2–5a; Luke 1:46b–55; Hebrews 10:5–10;
Luke 1:39–45, (46–55)

Opening Prayer

Holy God of this unfolding creation,
the long dark nights of waiting are nearly behind us.

This people who have walked in darkness
begin to see the light.

We have been living in a land of darkness,
but the light is on the way.

That light is the Light of the world, O God,
your presence here as one of us,

as part of us,
as new beginning born within us.

O come, O come, Emmanuel! Amen.

Thanksgiving and Praise

O God of all creation,
we pace the waiting room, filled with hope and fear.

We hope that your coming
will truly bring a peace that fills our hungry hearts.

We fear our hopes are more than you will share.
The dawning brightness all around us
reaches for a sense of hope hidden deeper than the pain,
and we give thanks.

Our chosen family of faith is gathering,
and scattering,
to celebrate this time of new beginnings,
and we give thanks.

Your promised light is coming once again to shine around us,
and we give thanks.

Fill us with a child's love we pray,
so we can fill this room with prayers of praise and thanks
for all your gifts of life and hope!

Petition and Intercession

O Holy One, the bright lights and the glitter all around us
make it hard to see
that there are people living in the shadows,
people who cannot meet their own needs,
let alone reach out to help meet the needs of others.

We see them lined up, every night,
waiting for the doors of shelters to open.

We see them standing in the median,
risking life and limb to ask for nickels and dimes
to help them make it through the night.

We see them underneath the bridge just down the street,
sheltered from the rain,
but shivering in the bright light that shows us clearly
how they're trying to protect their meager possessions
with black plastic bags.

And sometimes, in that bright but barren spot,
I catch a glimpse of how it was
for Mary and Joseph to find the only spot for them
that night so long ago
when Jesus came to live among us,
and the only shelter they could find was in the barn.

A barn!
Restore us, O God of Hosts.
Let your face shine that we might be saved,
saved to reach out to those who live this night
with grief and hunger well beyond our knowing.

Hear now, O God of new beginnings,
our prayers for those in pain and need,
and for ourselves,
for we would be part of your healing presence
on this night of new beginnings.

CHRISTMASTIDE

FIRST SUNDAY AFTER CHRISTMAS DAY

1 Samuel 2:18–20, 26; Psalm 148; Colossians 3:12–17;
Luke 2:41–52

Opening Prayer

God of life and love,
  holy Mystery of wildness and order,
  prolific Giver of everything,
  today we come to celebrate the mystery of your gift of life,
  the wonder of your gift of consciousness,
  the great joy of your gift of Christ among us.

O Holy One,
  we know that you are here,
  among us and around us and within us.

We pray now that you will draw our hearts together
  in one act of worship,
  as we have drawn ourselves together in this place;
  that you will blend our voices
  into a vibrant note of thankfulness and hope.

Let us know deep down in our bones
  that we are not alone,
  that you are here with us on the Way,
  for we've gathered to sing and pray and celebrate
  in the name of Jesus,
  newborn again among us as the Messiah. Amen.

Thanksgiving and Praise

God of life and love, holy Mystery of wildness and order,
  like Mary and Joseph,
    who fled to Egypt when you warned them through a dream,
    we listen for your call in these uncertain times.

We wait with praise and thanksgiving rising from within.
This cold morning at the end of a turbulent year,
  we raise our voices with the angels and the seas,
    the mountains and the flocks.

We marvel at all the signs of change, and hope, and new life:
  the celebration of your coming among us as a child,
    the coming of a new year.

Holy Lover of all of life,
  help us remind each other
    that each one of us is part of your good news,
    part of your message of hope and mystery and wonder,
    part of the body of the living Christ.

God of all creation, hear now our prayers of praise and thanks
  as we share them aloud with each other
    and offer them to you from the silence of our hearts.

Petition and Intercession

God of life and love, holy Mystery of wildness and order,
  although we celebrate, the pain is never far away.
We know so many places of brokenness and separation;
  so much anger and distrust.

Like children, we want to know the reason why.
Why is there violent death in our schools and on our streets?
Why do so many people have no work,
  no way to support themselves?

Why have we cut ourselves off from each other?
Why can't the leaders of all nations
  find paths to peace *and* justice?

Holy Mystery,
Creator who has made us without full understanding,
hear our prayers for those in pain and need.

Second Sunday after Christmas Day

Jeremiah 31:7–14; Psalm 147:12–20; Ephesians 1:3–14;
John 1:(1–9), 10–18

Opening Prayer

God of life and new birth,
prolific Creator of everything,
you make the wind blow
and the waters flow throughout the land.

In the beginning was the Word,
and the Word is love, for God is Love.
Wise, searching Maker of life,
you have found us here, huddled in this little band,
wondering whether this is the palace of Herod
or the stable of Christ.

We came because we saw something that looks,
in some ways, like a star.

We came because we wanted to be near you
and there were others here
who sounded like they'd also seen a star.

We stumbled, and fell in through the door,
and found ourselves gathered
at a familiar table of forgiveness.

The wonder is, you met us where we were,
and welcomed us as we are,
hungry for your love and nowhere near perfect.

We come to worship you
in the name of our Savior, Jesus the Christ. Amen.

Thanksgiving and Praise

Holy Source of light and life,
 you've sent the true light,
 which enlightens everyone,
 into the world, and we give thanks.

You come among us as an infant,
 a light unto the world,
 a light to all the nations,
 and we give thanks.

As we are born in this new way,
 you welcome us as your daughters and sons,
 and we give thanks.

We are so thankful for the blessing of your presence.
O Holy One, we lift our praise and thanks
 that you have chosen to make your home
 with mortal creatures like us,
 that you have promised to wipe away our tears
 and lift the pain of death.

Hear us as we lift our hearts to you in prayer,
 full of praise and thanks.

Petition and Intercession

Unpredictable, redeeming Mystery of faith,
 we come together as a burdened people.

Our hearts are often heavy
 with the pain of living in these mean-spirited times.

We know so many people
 whose lives are filled
 with illness, grief, warfare, or isolation.

We reach out, as best we can,
 to help find clothing and shelter, food and compassion
 for those in need.

Help us, O holy Fount of every blessing,
  help us find the strength to realize your gift,
  that all should eat and drink and take pleasure in their toil.

Show us the star.

Help us to see the signs of this time,
  and keep us ready for the journey,
  for we offer now the prayers of our hearts,
  our prayers for those whose spirits teeter on the edge,
  and for ourselves,
  for we would be your faithful people,
  praying in the name of the Messiah, who is Jesus the Christ.

THE EPIPHANY OF CHRIST

Isaiah 60:1–6; Psalm 72:1–7, 10–14; Ephesians 3:1–12;
Matthew 2:1–12

Opening Prayer

God of astonishing grace,
  the good news of your coming rings out in every direction,
  lighting up the world with your radiant glory,
  showing forth in every raindrop and snow crystal,
  in every sunrise and sunset,
  in every bird
  that finds a morsel of food on the frozen ground,
  in every smile of blessing
  that celebrates the first days of a new year.

Like the Magi who greeted the Christ Child in Bethlehem,
  help us to see the miracles that you set before us,
  to lift up our eyes to the riches
  that you spread before us each day,
  and to rejoice in the mystery of your presence
  flowing among us and around us and through us.

Captivate us with your love,
  and overwhelm us with joy,
  so that we may see ourselves
  as the holy, living Body of Christ,
  born in human flesh for the healing of the world. Amen.

▰▰▰ Thanksgiving and Praise ▰▰▰

God of endless mercy,
  in forgiving our sins, our mistakes, our foolishness,
  you give us, instead, the boundless riches of life in Christ,
  and we can do nothing but give our thanks.
We give thanks for cold, bright mornings
  that fill our eyes with sunshine that reminds us of your glory.
We give thanks for stark, bare branches,
  scratching out invisible words of praise on grey, cloudy skies.
We give thanks for friends and family
  who enfold us in warm hugs that remind us of your love.
We give thanks for the daily food that nourishes our bodies
  and reminds us of the heavenly feast you spread before us.
Aloud and in silence, we offer our thanks and praise
  for all these simple gifts and for all that we have not noticed,
  for the endless abundance of all that you have made.

▰▰▰ Petition and Intercession ▰▰▰

God of eternal compassion,
  as we remember the gifts that fill our lives,
  the injustice and pain of a broken world
  fill our hearts with sorrow.
We pray that you will give those who govern in every land
  your justice and your righteousness.
  May they defend the cause of the weakest of the people,
  give deliverance to those in need,
  and make an end to all oppression.
We pray that you will bring healing to those who are in pain,
  comfort those who mourn,
  and give vision to those who cannot see
  the glory that you spread around us.
We pray for those who are near to us,
  and for those who are far away;

we pray for friends and family,
and for those whom we have never met;
we pray for our own needs,
and for those who cannot pray for themselves.

And for what else shall we pray this day?

ORDINARY TIME
The Sundays after Epiphany

BAPTISM OF CHRIST
(FIRST SUNDAY AFTER EPIPHANY)
ORDINARY I

Isaiah 43:1–7; Psalm 29; Acts 8:14–17; Luke 3:15–17, 21–22

Opening Prayer

Holy, loving Mystery of life,
  we gather here to celebrate the gifts you bring,
    the gifts you give to others,
      the gift you are through your holy call upon our lives.

We come to celebrate the blessing of your presence in this time.
Living Spring of comfort and renewal,
  we pray that we might know your presence
  with us in this hour
  as we celebrate Jesus' baptism,
    a sign of your incarnate reality. Amen.

Thanksgiving and Praise

Wonderful, comforting Lover of creation, Messenger of new life,
  we glimpse you stirring in the wet soil of winter,
    brooding over every bulb and seed,
      whispering quietly to us as we face our future.

For generations you have called forth faithful people,
  called them each by name
  to love, and serve, and care for this reality.

We've come because we've heard your still, small voice,
  or seen that star,
  or felt an emptiness that only you can fill.
We're here because we want to be near you
  and share this sense of call with one another.

We marvel at the power of your presence,
  and bring our thanks for all the places
  where we know the power of your creative love.

Hear us as we lift our hearts to you,
  full of praise and thanks,
  offering our prayers aloud and in the silence of our hearts.

▬▬ Petition and Intercession ▬▬

Unfailing Source of healing and forgiveness,
  it is so comforting to be here
  where we know we can be fed.

Whenever we come here,
  we carry with us hurts and hungers,
  some of them well up from deep within,
  and some of them come crashing in upon our consciousness
  like garbage trucks with brakes locked,
  spinning slowly toward us on the clear ice of our lives.

God of healing wisdom and compassion,
  we are so thankful that not only do you call us
  to move out beyond the streetlights of our experience,
  but that you go there with us,
  promising to keep flood and fire from overwhelming us.

Holy Mystery of Life,
  hear us as we offer you the prayers of our hearts,
  our prayers for those in pain and grief,
  our prayers for those who teeter on the edge.
In the name of our Savior,
  who is Jesus the Christ, we pray.

SECOND SUNDAY AFTER EPIPHANY
ORDINARY 2

Isaiah 62:1–5; Psalm 36:5–10; 1 Corinthians 12:1–11; John 2:1–11

Opening Prayer

Holy, empowering Artist of creation,
how precious is your steadfast love!

We come to celebrate the feast you offer
from the abundance of your house,
the delights we share with others
as we share the gifts you give so freely.

We celebrate the story of the first miracle by Jesus,
as he brought overflowing hospitality
to the wedding feast at Cana,
demonstrating your loving presence
in that time of celebration.

Come, now, O Holy One,
come close to heal and teach us in our hearts,
come help us celebrate as well,
for we gather in the name of our Savior,
who is Jesus the Christ. Amen.

Thanksgiving and Praise

Holy, creating Artist of life,
we catch glimpses of your power in the universe,
the unexpected fountains of forsythia and quince
announcing the return of life and light.
We thank you for modern martyrs
who give their lives in calling us to dream
of justice and reconciliation
and to give our lives to make those dreams become reality.

How precious is your steadfast love, O God.
All people can take refuge in the shadow of your wings.
You call us to celebrate the variety of your gifts,

making sure that we are each equipped
to serve the common good in different ways—
some bringing wisdom and knowledge,
others faith and healing,
and still others prophecy and the discernment of gifts.

Hear now our prayers of praise and thanks
for all that you have done to bring this world to life.

▬ **Petition and Intercession** ▬

Great, healing Artist of love,
it seems that joy is always mixed with pain,
and each of us is burdened by a most important problem.

When we forget you,
these burdens threaten to immobilize us, isolate us,
cut us off from one another and from you.

And yet we know, because your presence has been real for us,
we know that all of your creation is connected,
every stone and grain of sand,
every drop of rain and muddy floodcrest,
every frightened child,
all the sick and lame,
and those who have forgotten where they came from.

All of your creation is firmly cradled
in the healing warmth of your embrace.

O faithful, liberating Artist of new beginnings,
we pray for those in need of healing and reconciliation.

We pray for those cut off from community
by violence, hatred, racism, and oppression.
We pray for children,
and for their hopes and dreams.

Hear now our prayers as we share them aloud
and lift them up in the silence of our hearts.

Third Sunday after Epiphany
Ordinary 3

Nehemiah 8:1–3, 5–6, 8–10; Psalm 19; 1 Corinthians 12:12–31a;
Luke 4:14–21

Opening Prayer

Holy God, our Rock and our Redeemer,
  we've gathered here this cold winter morning
  to help each other know
  that all of this creation is in your loving arms.

O Giver of that perfect law that promises to revive the soul,
  maker of those true and righteous ordinances,
  we pray that you will fill us with that Holy Spirit,
  for we gather as one tiny part of the body of the risen Christ,
  a beacon of the hope and light and love we claim
  for this day and the days to come. Amen.

Thanksgiving and Praise

Wonderful Architect of culture and community,
  holy Lover of life,
  we've come from near and far
  to share with those we love this special hour with you.

We marvel at your wisdom:
  the way your commandments
  enlighten the eyes of the faithful;
  the way you help us make the holy day a day of celebration;
  the way you call us to the joyful task
  of being one particular part of your vast creation.

We marvel at how you mold each one of us
  into a unique part of your body,
  and how each part has its own important role to play
  in our life together.

Holy Creator of all that we cannot imagine,
  we offer now our prayers of praise and thanks,

our prayers of wonder and hope,
for all that you are doing in these days
to nourish a hopeful future for our world.

We lift them in our hearts,
and share them aloud in this sacred space.

▬▬▬ Petition and Intercession ▬▬▬

God of hidden hope,
the clustered white narcissus on the window sill
are nearly finished with their premature celebration.

Planted just a month ago, these plump, dark bulbs,
resting on damp marbles,
gave not a hint of all the hidden glory that was yet to come.

And now that small community of just four bulbs
is reaching for the snowy window,
tall and lovely, clearly ready for the bees that will not come.

Are they a waste, because they bloomed too soon?

Did we do wrong, by forcing them to bloom before their time?

Or is their call to keep us faithful to the waiting time we are in,
to help us know, in ways no words can shape,
that there will be a time for us to bloom as well, if we can wait.

For everything there is a season,
and every part of the body of the risen Christ is important,
even when it feels like we are nothing but an elbow.

Holy God of new beginnings, we offer now our prayers
for those who are leading the nations of this world
as we search for ways to build community,
to share the bounty and the joy of your creation,
and to share the pain and trouble,
trash and selfish preoccupation, that mark so much of life.

Holy Lover of the universe,
we bring our heavy burdens:
bundles of concern and care too much for us to carry,

threats to peace and safety,
the pain of illness, the grief of death and loss.

We offer now our prayers for those in pain and need,
and for ourselves, for we can feel the dagger of despair
dimpling the softness underneath our chins.

Hear now our prayers of petition and intercession,
spoken aloud and raised up in the bright silence of our hearts.

Fourth Sunday after Epiphany
Ordinary 4

Jeremiah 1:4–10; Psalm 71:1–6; 1 Corinthians 13:1–13; Luke 4:21–30

Opening Prayer

Holy God, great liberating Rock of salvation,
we have gathered in this place to celebrate the good news,
that you are a fortress for your people,
a sheltering oak for every creature.

O quiet, healing Lover of all creation,
we come to you because you have come to us,
and loved us into community.

Liberating God, we pray that you will fill us
with the knowledge of your presence with us,
for we gather in the name of our Savior,
who is Jesus the Christ. Amen.

Thanksgiving and Praise

Great liberating Lover of creation,
the life that quietly withdrew last fall
from every dying leaf and stalk
is coming back.

You've loosed the ropes of winter
from a clutch of tiny snowdrops,
feet bundled in a leafy blanket to protect against the frost.

You've given heart to cardinals,
  who spend the early morning hours hoping out loud for spring.
O holy nurturing Dawn of life,
  the quiet epiphanies of late winter are all around us,
  and we respond with gratitude and thanks.
Hear now the prayers we bring,
  the words we share and the images that blossom in our hearts.

▬▬ Petition and Intercession ▬▬

Great, giving Heart of happiness,
  when all the world seems cold and wet
  it's somehow easier to find the places
  where there doesn't seem to be love enough to go around.

The holidays are long behind us now,
  and we seem to miss their tinsel distractions
  as we step out in the cold.

We watch as little signs of hope are tossed aside,
  like Jesus in his own hometown,
  a voice for change and healing,
  rejected just because it came from someone too familiar.

We want to hear that voice of Christ today,
  those promises that prophecy will be fulfilled,
  but somehow it is often easier for us
  to see the problem, rather than the Gospel.

The frozen ground is everywhere,
  and snowdrops in the yard are hard to see,
  and harder to believe.

Hopeful, invigorating Messenger of spring,
  we bring our prayers for those in pain,
  for those whose burdens keep them in the cold,
  for those whose sorrow flows like winter rain.

Hear now our prayers for faith,
  and hope,
  and love.

We lift our prayers as part of your body
   incarnate in this time and place,
   the body of Christ, Immanuel,
   God among us.

Fifth Sunday after Epiphany
Ordinary 5

Isaiah 6:1–8, (9–13); Psalm 138; 1 Corinthians 15:1–11; Luke 5:1–11

Opening Prayer

Holy God, giver of bright, frigid nights and crisp, winter days,
   we gather here to pray and sing,
   and celebrate your mysterious presence in our time.

You send angelic messengers to assure us of your healing love,
   then ask, "Whom shall I send?"
And touched by that love, we dare to reply,
   "Here we are."

Lift us up, we pray, as we gather in your presence
   to celebrate your saving love that risks the cold
   to grow in secret, making ready
   for the coming of a new season of fruit and flower.

Show us the path in this bright new dawn,
   for we gather in the name of the resurrected Savior,
   who is Jesus the Christ. Amen.

Thanksgiving and Praise

God of winter waiting,
   thanks for sending those reminders,
   those little signs that hope is still alive,
   that fresh new life is just around the corner.

Yesterday, bright moss and sprouting grass
   was pushing through the snow beside the creek,
   sparkling in the presence of fresh water
   from your Dayspring on high.

And wasn't that a cardinal calling clear on the frigid air,
  looking for community in barren oaks
  that offer neither food nor shade?

Even when the growth of your unfolding story
  does not match the calendars we keep so carefully,
  even when the fish elude us on the other side of the boat,
  we know you are at work,
  and we give thanks.

The psalmist reminds us that
  although you are mighty beyond imagination,
  you regard the lowly
  and keep your distance from the haughty.

We are reminded that although these days
  we walk in the midst of trouble,
  you will preserve us against the wrath of our enemies.

We give you thanks, O wonderful, healing God,
  for all the richness of your creation,
  and for the time and place you've called us to,
  this time, this place.

Hear now our prayers of praise and thanks,
  for all the richness of your new creation.

Petition and Intercession

Holy God, great sparkling Dawn of creativity,
  we gather together here this morning,
  drawn by the persistent power of your knowing love.

The cold drives home a fresh awareness
  of those who struggle by themselves.

For some the struggle is to make a difference;
  others want to find a friend, or overcome the pain,
  and others fight to stay alive on days like this.

Your words of hope cut through the chill,
  that those who follow where you lead
  will find their nets full to overflowing.

You lead us into a fresh concern for those in need.

Hear now our prayers for those we know,

  and those we only know about.

O Holy One, we lift our prayers

  in the Spirit of the resurrected Christ,

  spoken aloud, and lifted up in the silence of our hearts.

SIXTH SUNDAY AFTER EPIPHANY
ORDINARY 6

Jeremiah 17:5–10; Psalm 1; 1 Corinthians 15:12–20; Luke 6:17–26

Opening Prayer

O God of love and reconciliation,

  we gather here this morning,

  praying to know your presence among us.

Lover of the outcast,

  you establish equity and bring justice

  even where we see no cause for hope.

It is good to gather in this familiar place,

  to share our silence and our celebration,

  to wait patiently for your exciting mystery to come upon us.

O Holy One, we pray that you will join us in song and prayer,

  give us eyes to see the truth that has been invisible till now,

  fill us with the Holy Spirit

  that transfigured our Savior, Jesus, who is the Christ. Amen.

Thanksgiving and Praise

God of creation and re-creation,

  holy Painter of the coming spring,

  God of all those fat robins

  hunting for just the right place to nest and raise a family,

  the wind and rain you sent

  scattered tiny emerald shoots of wild tulip all across the yard,

  to let us know that we are not alone:

  good news rising from the mud.

You are the refuge of the faithful,
  planting them in community
  like trees planted by flowing streams,
  they will be nurtured by your love when times are tough.
O God, we've come together,
  filled with praise and thanks for being part of your creation.
  Hear us as we name the joy and wonder
  we have known this week.

Petition and Intercession

Holy Spirit of healing and compassion,
  we know that there are many people
  for whom this life is not good news.

We pray that those who are poor will be led into your holy realm,
  that those who hunger will be filled,
  and those who weep and mourn
  will know the joy of your blessed love deep within their hearts.

We know that healing is a mystery,
  a weaving of hope and opportunity and courage
  that overcomes the fraying, tearing force
  of wearing down and running out,
  a victory for order over chaos.

We know those who need help:
  healing for their bodies or their spirits,
  their relationships or their finances,
  their homes and communities.

We lift up those we love, and pray for healing,
  and also those whose pain and fear and loss
  we have not felt ourselves, but know about.
Hear now our prayers for those in pain and need,
  and for ourselves, for we would be healed
  and sent as bearers of your good news
  of love and reconciliation.

SEVENTH SUNDAY AFTER EPIPHANY
ORDINARY 7

Genesis 45:3–11, 15; Psalm 37:1–11, 39–40;
1 Corinthians 15:35–38, 42–50; Luke 6: 27–38

Opening Prayer

O God of unexpected welcome,
  we've come not knowing just quite what to expect.

The story of Joseph and his brothers fills us with wonder.
There the brothers were,
  in Egypt where they had fled to escape famine,
  only to be welcomed by their brother, Joseph,
  whom they had sold into slavery.

Welcomed, forgiven, and provisioned
  with opportunities for survival and prosperity.
We come to rejoice in your holy generosity,
  to share with one another
  those brief and often unexpected glimpses
  of your Good News that help us through dark times.

We come to pray and sing and celebrate
  the hope that keeps us on the path with you.

Come, Holy One,
  come let us know that you reach out to welcome us,
  for we gather to worship and praise you
  in the name of Jesus, who is the Messiah. Amen.

Thanksgiving and Praise

Holy Guide and Guardian of our faith,
  we marvel at the unexpected way
  you bring us to those moments of reconciliation.

We stand with Joseph's brothers,
  struck dumb by sudden awareness
  that not only had he survived being sold into slavery,
  but that he had gone ahead

to prepare a place of safety and sustenance
where they could live through the famine.

Compassionate, caring Guardian of exiles,
we praise you for your care,
your promise that the meek
will have full measure of the inheritance
you have set aside for those you love.

We pray for the imagination to understand quickly
when your good news connects with us
in ways we could not anticipate.

Holy God, receive our prayers of praise and thanksgiving,
for your power over all,
and for the joy we find along the way with you.
And for what else shall we give thanks and praise,
    O Holy One?

Petition and Intercession

God of loving compassion, we hear your guidance
on how to live into the mystery of your realm.

We are called to love our enemies,
do good to those who hate us,
bless those who curse us,
and pray for those who abuse us.

Holy Healer of the ungrateful and the wicked,
we know so many places
where pain and suffering feel overwhelming.

And when we contemplate your call to care
for those who seem to be the sources of that pain,
the task seems more than we can bear.

God of compassionate self-giving,
help us grow into useful parts of your healing, loving body
here on Earth, the body of the risen Christ.

Hear now our prayers for those who suffer pain
and grief and need,

and for ourselves as we seek to add our lives
to the power of your Body here and now.

Eighth Sunday after Epiphany
Proper 3, Ordinary 8

Sirach 27:4–7 or Isaiah 55:10–13; Psalm 92:1–4, 12–15;
1 Corinthians 15:51–58; Luke 6:39–49

Opening Prayer

O God, it is good to give thanks to you,
to sing praises to your name, O Holy One;
to declare your steadfast love in the morning
and your faithfulness by night.

Holy One you call us to come together
to celebrate being in your presence.

At the works of your hands we sing for joy, O God;
hear our songs and our prayers.

Fill us with the Holy Spirit
that filled our Savior, Jesus, who is the Christ. Amen.

Thanksgiving and Praise

We thank you, holy Source of creation and re-creation,
for new life springing into being all around us.

We thank you for those purple crocus blossoms
you dropped beside the road last night while we slept.

We thank you for returning cardinals,
whose sharp song severs the tired bonds of winter.

We thank you, too, for signs of new birth,
fresh opportunities in our community,
for understanding, healing, and forgiveness.

O holy, warm Blanket of reconciling love,
we bring our prayers of praise and thanks
for being part of your creation,

sharing them aloud in this community
and offering them in the silence of our hearts.

Petition and Intercession

Holy Spirit of healing and compassion,
  we know that there are many people
  for whom life does not feel like good news:
  those who have no home,
  those who grieve the death of their loved ones,
  those who suffer illness and trauma,
  those whose spirits are burdened or broken,
  those who are alone against their will,
  those who fear they have been abandoned
  by society and community.

We pray to be part of your healing Word,
  called forth like snow and rain
  to water the earth and bring forth
  sprout and seed of peace and justice.

Sometimes it takes a shift in our perspective
  to open up our hearts to let your healing love
  flow through to others.

Sometimes we need to see and claim our limits
  before we can be much help.

May we be parts of the Body of Christ,
  going forth in joy to live out your call,
  and being led home by your loving Holy Spirit
  to declare your steadfast love and faithfulness.

Holy One, help us see the logs in our own eyes,
  so we can help each other
  clear our vision and get ready to help others.

We know those people who need help,
  healing for their bodies or their spirits,
  their relationships or their finances.

We lift up those we love and pray for healing,
   in the name of your healing presence among us,
   our Savior, who is Jesus the Christ.

NINTH SUNDAY AFTER EPIPHANY
PROPER 4, ORDINARY 9

1 Kings 8:22–23, 41–43; Psalm 96:1–9; Galatians 1:1–12; Luke 7:1–10

Opening Prayer

Holy One, there is no God like you!
You keep covenant and steadfast love
   for all who walk before you with all their heart.

You guide and protect even those who do not know you,
   calling us to enfold them into our hearts
   and know them as your beloved people.

You give yourself to the world with selfless abandon,
   covering flowering trees with countless fragile petals,
   filling the seas with millions of fish,
   and the sky with stars as numerous as sand on the beach.

Long ago, you gave yourself to us in Jesus,
   who lived and taught in Galilee
   and healed all who came to him in faith.

Grant us the faith to accept these gifts,
   so that we may learn how to be the Body of Christ,
   living our lives as a gift for the world. Amen.

Thanksgiving and Praise

Holy One, Holy Three, there is no God like you!
You healed slaves and the children of rulers in Galilee,
   brought good news to those who lived in fear,
   and set the prisoners free.

We give you thanks for astonishing miracles,
   and for all the ordinary gifts that fill our lives:
   for the touch of a gentle breeze,

for the sight of falling petals,
for the sound of footsteps on a gravel path.

We give you thanks for giving yourself to us,
that we might live for the sake of the world.
And for what else shall we give thanks this day?

Petition and Intercession

Creator of all, Spirit of truth, Healer of all who come in faith,
there is no God like you!

We hear the good news and believe,
rejoicing when those who live in darkness
suddenly see the light,
when those who are imprisoned suddenly walk into freedom.

But when miracles like those do not happen every day,
we begin to think that there is no end to pain,
and we cry out to you.

We pray for an end to endless violence
in faraway places and on the streets at home.
We pray for an end to the endless pain
of illness and diminishment and grief.

We pray for an end to all the ways
that the light you give to each of us is dimmed
by loneliness, depression, and despair.

We pray for all who suffer,
we pray for all who are in need,
we pray for ourselves,
that we may be the good news that someone longs to hear.
Aloud and in silence, we pray for the healing of the world.

TRANSFIGURATION (LAST SUNDAY AFTER EPIPHANY)

Exodus 34:29–35; Psalm 99; 2 Corinthians 3:12–4:2;
Luke 9:28–36, (37–43)

Opening Prayer

God of Moses and Elijah,
  God of Miriam and Mary,
  God of history and of the future,
  when Moses came down from the mountain,
  his face reflected the radiance of your presence,
  filling the people with awe because he had heard your voice.

When Peter and John and James went up to the mountain,
  they saw your face in the face of Jesus,
  shining like sun on a windswept morning.

Today, you show us your glory in the glitter of melting snow,
  in the bright flash of a hunting hawk's wing,
  in the hands of strangers pushing a car stuck on an icy street,
  in the smiles of neighbors wading through slush and ice.

Today, you call us to be your light in the world.
  Help us become what you call us to be:
  a beacon of peace and justice and love and hope,
  the radiant, living Body of the risen Christ. Amen.

Thanksgiving and Praise

God of prophets and poets,
  God of land and sea and air,
  God of all that is seen and all that is unseen,
  you have given us this day,
  this hour, this moment.

With grateful hearts, we see your face
  shining in the faces of those we love,
  in the laughing eyes of children sledding down a long hill,
  in the hopeful glance
  of the person who asks us for our change,

in the selfless work
of those who shovel and plow and salt the roads.

We give thanks for the moments of beauty that surprise us—
the unexpected gift of silence in a busy city,
the graceful bow of a branch laden with snow,
the brilliant glitter of ice shards on the path before us.

We give thanks for the simple pleasures of body and mind—
for strong muscles that lift and bend,
for warm soup and crusty bread,
for scarves and gloves and hats and boots,
and a place to come in out of the cold.

Aloud and in our hearts,
we give thanks for all that we can name,
and all the gifts that we forget to notice.
And for what else shall we give thanks this day?

Petition and Intercession

God of healing and salvation,
you have given the gift of life to all your creatures,
but the goodness of your creation lies broken,
shattered with the weight of anger and loss,
heartbreak and sorrow.

Like the father who begged the transfigured Jesus
to heal his son,
we pray for the healing of all who are in pain,
all who need your comfort and your presence.

We pray that you will bring peace where there is violence,
plenty where there is want,
hope where there is despair.

Aloud and in silence, we pray for all the needs we know of,
and for those that are known only to you.

And for ourselves, we ask only to know and do your will
as members of the radiant, living Body of the risen Christ,
as we offer our prayers of petition and intercession.

LENT

FIRST SUNDAY IN LENT

Deuteronomy 26:1–11; Psalm 91:1–2, 9–16; Romans 10:8b–13;
Luke 4:1–13

Opening Prayer

O God, we come from many different places,
  bearing many different joys and pains.
We gather here, a band of pilgrims on the Way with Jesus.
We gather, praying that your angels might bear us up,
  might comfort us as we live into the temptations
  that confront us on every side.

O Holy Host of sacrificial reconciliation,
  let your Holy Spirit bind us into one community,
  so we remember how it is to be your people
  as we worship you this crisp, late winter morning,
  wrapped in the warm comforter of your love,
  in the name of Jesus the Messiah. Amen.

Thanksgiving and Praise

God of cold sun and gentle rain
  bathing every corner of the yard
  until the unremembered fur of some great green beast
  washes to the surface,
  we marvel at the signs of life
  that rise so boldly from the mud.

What have you revealed,
  O God of new surprises?

Are those green spikes
  the artifacts of some forgotten battle,
  some struggle between death and life
  where life has claimed the upper hand?

Holy One, we know that you lead us into this land,
  the place where we do what we can
  to raise up fresh living sprouts of peace and justice.
Help us have the courage
  to bring to you the first fruits of our labors:
  injustices confronted, laws changed, needs met.

O God, you are always giving us
  something new to wonder about!

Our lives are filled with things we must be doing.
We work so hard to fill our barns and bank accounts,
  yet we can see your hand at work in all the busyness.

We thank you for the gift of life,
  for the gift of your love hidden in the fruits of our labor;
  for the cold damp of winter
  and the fresh green life that pushes in to take its place,
  we give thanks to you, O God.

Hear now those prayers of praise and thanks,
  spoken aloud and lifted up silently in our hearts.

Petition and Intercession

O God, there is always so much more to do
  than we think we have time and energy to engage,
  so much pain and suffering around us to confront or ignore.

We pray, remembering all those
  throughout this city and across the world
  who hunger but find no relief.

We pray, remembering all those
  throughout this city and across the world
  who suffer harsh conditions, bondage, and affliction,
  the pain of isolation or the anguish of war.

We lift up all these whose needs we know,
  remembering the lessons of Jesus' ministry
  and your promise of deliverance.
O Holy One, hear our prayers for those in pain and need.

SECOND SUNDAY IN LENT

Genesis 15:1–12, 17–18; Psalm 27; Philippians 3:17–4:1; Luke 13:31–35
or Luke 9:28–36, (37–43a)

Opening Prayer

O Holy Mystery of love,
  unknowably powerful Giver of life,
  we gather here this morning
  to help us see the love that binds us to each other,
  the life that binds us all to you.

Be present to us, here among us,
  all around us,
  deep within us.

Gather us under your wing for this brief time of celebration,
  for we come in the name of that one
  who moved through death to find new life,
  your chosen child, our Savior, who is Jesus the Christ. Amen.

Thanksgiving and Praise

O God of unfathomable promises,
  you came to Abram and Sarai in the late afternoon of life,
  and promised them their children, yet unborn,
  would be more numerous than the stars.

You promised them an answer for their people,
  an answer so unexpected it left them speechless.

O God, your love is like those almost unseen threads
that link us to each other
and to the world beyond our doors,
tough threads of care and compassion,
cords of action and reflection.

O God, we praise you for your power of creation.
We raise up times and places
where even though it seemed too late,
your loving presence made a way
through all the cold confusion to a place of life.

We thank you for the unexpected bounty of your love,
the way you bring us in, like peeping chicks,
to find the safety of your widespread, brooding wings.

O God, hear now our prayers of praise and thanks,
our words, our sighs, the silent groaning of our hearts.

Petition and Intercession

Great, brooding Mother Hen,
we know you care for everything you are creating.

We know your wings are wide enough
to gather everyone.

We give you thanks for healing those who suffer and are ill.
And yet, we know so many people
who seem to be beyond your love.

Help us to know that they are also in your loving care.
Show us how to be your wings of love,
so we may offer healing compassion and hope
to those whose pain we touch.

Loving, healing God, hear now our prayers
for those who suffer, those who mourn,
and for ourselves, for we are hungry to be healed.

And for what else shall we pray, O Holy Lover of life?

THIRD SUNDAY IN LENT

Isaiah 55:1–9; Psalm 63:1–8; 1 Corinthians 10:1–13; Luke 13:1–9

Opening Prayer

Ineffable Mystery of life, cosmic Jeweler,
   who crafts those brazen daffodil and royal crocus gems
   and sets them in a spiked emerald crown;
   Holy Source of life and fresh new growth,
   we gather here like ants
   drawn to some damp sweetness on the earth.

Our hearts leap up as we experience
   the stirring of this season.

Holy Maker of this lively reality,
   we come to drink the cold, clear water of life
   from the ever-flowing spring of your love.

Help us tend the stream and keep the water clear for others,
   even as we celebrate the goodness of your nourishing love,
   for we would let the world know that we are your people,
   gathered in the name of Jesus, who is the Christ. Amen.

Thanksgiving and Praise

Gracious, invigorating Wellspring of reality,
   we marvel at the rich intricacy of all that you have made:
   sun and moon and stars without number;
   ancient trees and butterflies
   and more grains of sand than we can count;
   rain and dew and snow and streams
   that water the desert into life.

All these are part of your unfathomable richness.
How many and wonderful are your works,
   holy Architect of this reality.

We praise you for the fullness of the life we know.
Hear now those prayers of praise and thanks
   for all of your most wonderful creation.

━━━ Petition and Intercession ━━━

O holy, loving Healer of creation
  your steadfast love is better than life.
We come to you,
  knowing that we have despoiled things in so many ways.

It only takes us minutes to consume
  what has taken eons to create,
  the trees that carry news and advertisements to our door,
  the fuel that moves our cars,
  the ozone that protects us from the sun.

How easily we forget
  that you have called us to be stewards of your creation.

How easy it can be
  to think that we are so small and insignificant
  that there is nothing we can do to change the way
  our culture treats the health of our world and all that is in it.

Holy God,
  you give us every reason to learn how to live as stewards,
  caring for the richness of reality.

Help us listen;
  help us hear;
  help us learn to care for what you've made.

Help us answer the call you sound
  to care for this fragile earthen vessel we call home.

Hear now, O holy Fountain of life,
  the prayers we offer for those in need,
  and for ourselves, for we long to be made whole.

FOURTH SUNDAY IN LENT

Joshua 5:9–12; Psalm 32; 2 Corinthians 5:16–21; Luke 15:1–3, 11b–32

Opening Prayer

O holy Wind of life and growth,
  and bright canary blossoms thrusting from the cold, wet earth,
  we gather here to join our hearts and voices
  in praise and celebration of the wild fullness of your creation.
We come because you call us.
We come because we've learned
  that there are others here who'll help us find the path to you.

We come because we know
  that fundamental loneliness is, at its core,
  a hunger for your love.

Fill us with your Holy Spirit, O God of reconciliation,
  for we gather in the name of our risen Savior,
  who is Jesus the Christ. Amen.

Thanksgiving and Praise

God of life and love,
  Holy God of every living thing,
  wonderful Mother of the daffodil,
  imaginative Creator of the whale and the ant;
  we know your being is beyond our wildest imagination,
  and still we try to find the words to say how great you are.

We celebrate the ways you satisfy our hunger for community,
  by bringing us together in one body,
  to celebrate the meaning of the risen Christ,
  for us and for each part of your creation.

We give you thanks that we can share our lives,
  that we can celebrate with one another.

We praise the power of forgiveness
  that makes it possible for each of us to start again.

Holy God of mystery,
  whose love has kept our world in being since the dawn of time,
  we praise you for the richness of the feast of life
  you make for us each day.
Hear now our prayers of praise and thanks,
  for all the riches you provide.

▬▬ Petition and Intercession ▬▬

Holy, loving God,
  your tender care for all that you have made is so much more
  than any parent could bestow
  on even the most forgiven prodigal child,
  and we know so many who seem to be laboring in the pigsty
  of some far forsaken land.
We pray that you would call them
  home from pain and suffering,
  home from misery and fear.
We pray for those whose suffering seems generated,
  like the prodigal, by their own decisions.
We also pray for those who seem to be the victims
  of a life they did not choose.
O mighty Wind of healing,
  whose workings we will never really understand,
  hear now our prayers for those in need,
  and for ourselves,
  for we have needs for healing and forgiveness
  that may be understood by you alone.
In quiet speech and groaning silence,
  we hold our prayers aloft,
  and toss them out into your mighty wind of love.
Receive us now, O Holy One, as you receive our prayers,
  for we offer them from this body of the living Christ,
  the crucified and Risen One from Nazareth,
  our Savior, Jesus the Redeemer.

FIFTH SUNDAY IN LENT

Isaiah 43:16–21; Psalm 126; Philippians 3:4b-14; John 12:1–8

Opening Prayer

Living Word, everlasting Fountain, renewing Breath,
  you speak the world into being each moment,
  changing midnight darkness into pale, blue morning,
  making new buds appear
  on branches that were bare only yesterday,
  filling the cold, wintry air with the heady promise of spring.

You call us to feast on your living Word,
  to drink at the fountain of wisdom,
  to rejoice in the mystery that you are preparing.

You call us to share in the sufferings of Jesus,
  that we may be one with him, and one with you.

Help us to know the power of resurrection,
  so that we may more fully be the Body of Christ
  sent for the healing of your beautiful, broken world.

Amen.

Thanksgiving and Praise

Renewing Breath, living Word, everlasting Fountain,
  you wash away our sins in the waters of forgiveness,
  and wipe away our tears with your eternal love.

We give you thanks for mornings and evenings,
  for daffodils and crocus,
  for the last cold wind of winter,
  and the first warm afternoons of spring.

We give you thanks for the work and play that fill our days,
  for nights of restful sleep and wakeful waiting,
  for long hours of easy conversation with friends,
  for brief moments of grace-filled new connections.

We give you thanks for ancient treasures and new wonders,
  for books and computers, for art and for science,

for the moments in which you suddenly appear,
  making order in the chaos of our lives.

We give you thanks for all that we notice,
  and all that we forget.

  And for what else shall we give thanks this day?

Petition and Intercession

Everlasting Fountain, renewing Breath, living Word,
  you have promised to make a way in the wilderness,
  to fill the desert places of our lives
  with cool, running rivers of delight;
  to save the lost, heal the sick,
  and restore the fortunes of those who have nothing.

And still, everywhere we look there are people in need,
  people whose lives are broken
  by poverty, disease, and violence.

And so, in our weakness, we cry out to you,
  may those who go out weeping,
  come home with shouts of joy.

Aloud and in silence,
  we pray for all whose lives are filled with tears.

Palm/Passion Sunday (Sixth Sunday in Lent)

Liturgy of the Palms: Luke 19:28–40; Psalm 118:1–2, 19–29
Liturgy of the Passion: Isaiah 50:4–9a; Psalm 31:9–16;
Philippians 2:5–11; Luke 22:14–23:56

Opening Prayer

O wonderful Maker of bud and blade and blossom,
  we are astounded by the greening of your world.

Your care for all creation calls us to wake up;
  your creativity spills over,
  like the blizzard of blossoms swirling through the city;
  your steadfast love endures forever.

Holy Fount of eternal hope, this is the day which you have made.
Help us rejoice together,
  as one tiny blossom on the tree of faith,
  gathered in the name of Jesus of Nazareth,
  who is the Christ, redeemer of the world. Amen.

Thanksgiving and Praise

Holy Fount of eternal hope,
  we catch glimpses of new life on every side:
  beneath the cherry and the pear, the oak and maple,
  the ground has shadow once again.

The time is right, and we praise you.
These trees are drinking in the sun
  as buds fly open overhead, making life of earth and water,
  storing sunlight so they'll have enough this fall
  to make the seeds of future life, when the time is right.

And we give thanks.
The geese who've guarded nearby parks all winter
  are heading north to find their nesting place,
  just as their cousins who wintered somewhere else
  arrive to make their home beside the pond.

For faithful sentinels who help us remember the gift of life,
  we give thanks.
This is a time to celebrate our hopes, this passion day,
  the day we hold up Jesus' entry into Jerusalem,
  a day of hope and expectation
  for those who followed him then,
  a day of heavy hope and caution
  for those of us who know the story now.

Hear now our prayers of praise and thanks,
  O God of blooming passion.

Petition and Intercession

God of passionate commitment and renewal,
  this week we come carrying more than palms and petals

to mark your triumphal entry into Jerusalem.

We celebrate in hope, even as we carry fear and anger,
  pain and anguished resignation.

We watch as leaders bicker over power, politics, and taxes,
  with little mention of how many acres of field and forest
  were lost to parking lots this week alone.

We wait expectantly to learn which team will win,
  and scarcely think about the pesticides
  that slowly gather in the flesh of all that lives.

We borrow heavily against a future
  that you have created and called us to protect.

We need your loving wisdom
  to know which burdens we should carry,
  and which belong to you right now, and should be left alone.

Holy Maker of every bud and blade and blossom,
  give us the strength to stand with you this week;
  help us to hear your call to join you in the garden;
  hold us close as we walk with you
  through the valley of death.

For we would be a resurrection people,
  but first we need to wait with you.

Hear now the prayers of pain and passion;
  receive our burdens, O active, creating God of all.

THE RESURRECTION OF CHRIST
Easter Sunday

Acts 10:34–43; Psalm 118:1–2, 14–24; 1 Corinthians 15:19–26; John 20:1–18

Opening Prayer

Holy God of modern miracles,
  maker of new heavens and this new earth,
  we come rejoicing in all that you create.

We know ourselves as yours:
  children of God, reunited in Christ,
  enlivened by the Holy Spirit.

Fill us to overflowing with joy and thanksgiving,
  for we come this Easter morning to celebrate a mystery:
  Christ is risen! Alleluia! Amen.

Thanksgiving and Praise

God of miracles, we have been tested,
  our sisters and brothers have been chastened sorely,
  but we celebrate that we have not been given over unto death,
  that we are not left alone and hopeless.

For you have opened the gates of righteousness,
  that we may enter through them and give thanks to you.

You lead us to this place
  where we may know your presence.
You show us comfort and compassion.
You call us into ministry,

and turn us from the glare of selfish hunger
to find the sparkling water of obedience.

O holy God of miracles,
  we bring our praise and thanks for Jesus
  resurrected and returned to be among us;
  for miracles of love and reconciliation;
  for growth and change that promise new life for all the earth.

Hear now our prayers of praise and thanks,
  O holy Gardener of delight.

We raise our praise
  because the risen Christ has shared our earthly life
  and conquered death to end our strife.
  Alleluia, alleluia, and Amen!

Petition and Intercession

O holy God of miracles,
  we bring our burdens with us, too,
  even on this day of celebration.

We know so many whose oppression, isolation, pain and anger
  crowd the joy of resurrection from their sight.

Our hearts are heavy, even on this day of celebration,
  heavy with the burdens of those who suffer pain and illness,
  the burdens for those whose lives
  are bound up in the violence and destruction of war,
  the weight of grief and sorrow.

O holy God of resurrection miracles,
  we pray for those in pain and need,
  and for ourselves,
  that we may be an Easter people in this place.

Hear our prayers for those in need,
  the words we speak,
  the thoughts that fill our minds,
  the sighs and groans too deep for words.

THE GREAT FIFTY DAYS
The Easter Season

SECOND SUNDAY OF EASTER

Acts 5:27–32; Psalm 118:14–29; Revelation 1:4–8; John 20:19–31

Opening Prayer

Holy Maker of all this reality,
  God of pouring rain and redbuds,
  wonderful giver of justice and reconciliation,
  we come from many busy places
  ready to celebrate your dominance,
  your primal power to create reality.
Help us, O God of every thought and thing,
  help us to know your presence so completely
  that we are lifted into timeless time.
Give us hints, today, of what it is to be your people,
  nerve and sinew in the body of the risen Christ,
  in whose name we gather here
  to pray, and praise, and celebrate. Amen.

Thanksgiving and Praise

Holy God of fresh spring life rising from this wet earth,
  God of opening azalea and slowly uncurling fern,
  holy Giver of boiling buds and blossoms,
  we come today with overflowing thanks.
We thank you for the riot of color on every hill.

We thank you for the wily dandelion
  that comes to bloom before we even notice it has sprouted.

We thank you for relationships,
  and opportunities bursting open
  as we celebrate those unexpected changes
  in the path of life you open out before us.

Holy God of vernal resurrection
  we know how small we are,
  and still you fill us with your love.

Holy Maker of the cycle of life that brings us spring,
  we lift our prayers of praise and thanks to you,
  spoken aloud and lifted up
  in the grateful silence of our hearts.

Petition and Intercession

Holy Wellspring of hope and healing,
  we've brought our burdens with us
  into this time of celebration,
  our burdens and our fears and doubts.

We know how Thomas felt:
  "Unless I can feel the wound myself, I can't be sure …"
We want to give our doubts and cares to you,
  to know that we are doing what you want,
  to rise above the wavering uncertainty that fogs our faith,
  to celebrate the promise of your healing presence
  flowing through us.

Bring forth our hungers and our needs
  in speech and sound and sigh,
  and inner vision of your healing presence.

Come, Holy Spirit, lift us up, we pray,
  until our feet find somewhere solid as a base,
  a firm foundation rooted in your healing love.

Fill us with that love, Lord Christ,
  until we burst the moment we are touched by need,

for we would be a dandelion of the resurrection,
an early-blooming flower of the risen Christ.

O God of hope and resurrection,
hear our prayers for those in pain and need,
and for ourselves, for we have pains and needs as well.

Third Sunday of Easter

Acts 9:1–6, (7–20); Psalm 30; Revelation 5:11–14; John 21:1–19

Opening Prayer

Holy River of life-giving water,
you invite us to come and drink,
to fill ourselves with your love and grace,
to live in the resurrection power of your eternal life.

Every morning, you invite us to rejoice with you
in the pink and white drifts of cherry blossoms
that surprise us around every corner,
in the golden trumpets of daffodils
shouting alleluia to the shimmering air,
in the multicolored cups of tulips
opening their mouths to the warmth of the sun.

With every breath,
you invite us to drink in your overflowing bounty,
to sing your praises
as we walk along city streets and country paths,
to handle your garden, the earth,
as tenderly as a precious jewel, caught up in nets of glory.

Help us to follow you into everlasting life,
to feed all of your sheep with lavish abundance,
even as you fill our hearts
and minds and bodies to overflowing
with your holy presence. Amen.

══ **Thanksgiving and Praise** ══

Holy Fountain of abundant life,
  with every creature in heaven and on earth and under the sea
  we bless you and honor you and give you thanks
  for all the wonders that fill our lives.

We give you thanks for the resurrection
  of your holy child, Jesus,
  who lives among us and through us and in us,
  the living Body of Christ,
  doing your work in the world.

We give you thanks for stars and starfish and starlings,
  for thunderclouds and clouds of petals,
  flying ahead of a storm.

We give you thanks for picnics and banquets,
  for leisurely meals shared with friends,
  and for days when we are too busy to eat.

We give you thanks for revelations and visions,
  for ordinary days and even for sleepless nights.

Like the birds that greet each morning with song,
  we sing your praises aloud and in silence,
  giving thanks to your holy name.

══ **Petition and Intercession** ══

Holy Spring of compassion and healing,
  with our hearts overflowing with gratitude
  for all that we can name and all that we have forgotten,
  we also remember that too many lives are flooded with pain.

As we feel our own scars, and know our own emptiness,
  we pray that you will comfort and protect
  all who live with pain and fear,
  all whose lives are marked by violence,
  all whose mourning has not yet been turned into dancing.

As leaders make decisions that affect all of our lives,
  we pray for wisdom.

As seas rise and deserts grow, we pray for mercy.

As nations threaten war, we pray for peace.

We pray for those who are close to us

and those we do not know,

for those who do not believe that any prayers are heard,

and for those who have asked for our prayers.

We pray now aloud and in the silence of our hearts

for the healing of the world.

Fourth Sunday of Easter

Acts 9:36–43; Psalm 23; Revelation 7:9–17; John 10:22–30

Opening Prayer

Exquisite, invigorating Mentor of new beginnings,

we come today with open hearts, ready to be healed.

We come today with open minds, ready to be taught.

We come today with open souls, ready to be transformed.

We pray that your Holy Spirit will fill us up

until your love spills over every levee we might build,

and washes us into shameless acts of justice and mercy.

For we would be a part of your resurrected presence

in this time and place,

the body of the risen Christ. Amen.

Thanksgiving and Praise

Glorious, enlivening Sculptor of new life,

we celebrate these first warm days

as though we've never felt the sun before.

We thank you for the litany of celebration written by the iris,

fulsome purple heads with golden tongues,

lapping up these first hot days

like sheep beside the deep, still waters.

We thank you for the mocking bird,

whose song is so much bigger than its body

that we always look too far away to see the bird itself,
swaying on a power line,
  declaring the greatness of God with such a rich vocabulary
  that we often hear, in some new way,
  "Thank you, God, for giving us this day!"
Holy Womb of summer,
  we bring our prayers of praise and thanks,
  like hillsides of azalea blossoms,
  rich and full, in every clashing color.
Hear now, our prayers of praise and thanks,
  spoken aloud and lifted silently in our hearts.

▬ **Petition and Intercession** ▬

Tenacious, loving Wellspring of incarnation,
  we thank you that you call us here
  and show us how to listen to the still, small voice you use
  to guide us on the path to fuller faith.
We thank you for your promise to be with us
  in times of pain and stress.
Merciful, healing Artist of new hope,
  we need your spirit welling up within us,
  for there are many places
  where we face the depths of pain or illness, anger or isolation.
We pray for our relationships
  in families and ministries,
  and for our future as a church.
Hear now our prayers for those in pain and need,
  O holy Healer of the universe.

Fifth Sunday of Easter

Acts 11:1–18; Psalm 148; Revelation 21:1–6; John 13:31–35

Opening Prayer

O triumphant Source of all being,
  you are faithful in every word,
  and gracious in every deed.

We come together in this moment
  to recognize that you are the holy source of all things new.

We come to praise your infinite creativity,
  to give thanks for life in such abundance.

We unite our hearts and our voices
  as we worship the creator of the universe
  in the name of our Savior, who is Jesus the Christ. Amen.

Thanksgiving and Praise

Holy God,
  source of birth and life and death and resurrection,
  great living God who makes the heavens
  and the earth and the sea and all that is in them,
  Holy Lover of all creation,
  we come today to celebrate your presence with us
  in our lives and in our world.

You give us rains and fruitful seasons.
You satisfy our hearts with food and gladness.
You bring your people together in your presence
  with song and prayer,
  with love and deep compassion for the world you are creating.
Maker of the universe,
  we raise our prayers of praise and thanks to you,
  aloud, and in the silence of our hearts.

Petition and Intercession

Healing God of love,
  we know that you have given your disciples
  power to heal and to forgive.

There are so many places in our world that cry out for healing:
   the violence in distant lands,
   where ancient enmity clings
   to burdened hearts like barnacles;
   the pain and loneliness of illness;
   the fear of age and loss of capability;
   the trauma of communities torn apart
   by fear and drugs and hatred.

We know you stand ready to feed your faithful people,
   that you will send your healing, Holy Spirit.

We claim that promise for our time,
   and bring to mind and speech
   all those whose lives are heavy with fear and pain.

Hear now our prayers for those in pain and need.

SIXTH SUNDAY OF EASTER

Acts 16:9–15; Psalm 67; Revelation 21:10, 22–22:5; John 14:23–29 or
John 5:1–9

Opening Prayer

God of our ancestors in faith,
   God of Lydia and Paul,
   God of all our days,
   favor and bless us,
   revealing your ways to us and to all people.

You order creation with justice and grace,
   forming brilliant pink drifts of azalea blossoms
   and the four perfect, white petals of each dogwood flower.

You fill the air with the high-pitched chirp of sparrows,
   the cheerio call of robins,
   the harsh scream of the red-tailed hawk
   riding the thermals of late afternoon.

Long ago, you came to us in human form,
   living and teaching and dying on the cross,

and then living again,
   calling us to be your people.
Let your Holy Spirit flow among us and around us
      and through us,
   calling us and guiding us into becoming the Body of Christ,
   pouring out our lives until the whole world shouts with joy.
Amen.

Thanksgiving and Praise

God of life-giving water and fruit-bearing trees,
   God of city streets and country paths,
   God of all who search for peace and justice,
   we give you thanks for moonlight and sunlight
   and candlelight and streetlights,
   for dreams of the future
   and tales of events that happened long ago.
We give you thanks for the joy of new birth,
   and for long years filled with memory and hope.
We give you thanks for voices that sing and talk and laugh,
   for toes that tap and hands that clap.
We give you thanks for hugs and hellos,
   for letters and emails and texts and yes, even tweets,
   for all the ways that you have given us to say
   that we love one another.
Aloud and in silence, we give you thanks
   for all that we can name,
   and all that we do not even notice.
   And for what shall we give our thanks this day?

Petition and Intercession

God of hope and healing,
   God of promise and blessing,
   God of all who yearn for wholeness,
   our hearts are troubled by a world that is broken and in pain.

When the morning news is filled
  with stories of war and violence,
  of terrorists and tyrants,
  of corruption and graft,
  of racism and harassment,
  of lives destroyed by hatred and oppression;
  we pray that you will remember your people,
  and wipe away every tear.

When our loved ones fall ill,
  when our bodies fail us,
  when wildfires rage in the mountains or in our hearts,
  when the pain of the world is too much for us to bear,
  we cry out to you for comfort and for peace.

Holy God of the lost and the least,
  God of all compassion,
  God of love and peace,
  in words that are spoken aloud
  and in the wordless silence of our hearts,
  we bring our prayers for others and for ourselves to you.

Seventh Sunday of Easter

Acts 16:16–34; Psalm 97; Revelation 22:12–14, 16–17, 20–21;
John 17:20–26

Opening Prayer

Merciful, loving Champion of justice,
  we hear the wisdom of the psalmist:
  The heavens proclaim your holy righteousness,
  and all the peoples behold your glory.
  You love those who hate evil,
  preserve the lives of the saints,
  and deliver them from the hand of the wicked.
  Light dawns for the righteous, and joy for the upright in heart.

We celebrate your promise:
the light that shone in Christ is in the world today,
calling us to a life of faithful witness and celebration.

Therefore, O Holy One, we come to worship,
rejoicing in you and giving thanks together
for we are gathered as part of the living Body of Christ. Amen.

Thanksgiving and Praise

Holy, creating Leader of the faithful,
great redeeming Healer of the sick,
we gather in your presence
in grateful recognition of your majesty.

We marvel at the strength of life
that flourishes through storm and tribulation.

We celebrate the presence of your spirit
in faithful people everywhere.

We praise the joy that flows when people of compassion
seize the opportunity, like Paul and Silas,
to care for those who have imprisoned them,
rather than run free.
Hear now our prayers of praise and thanks
for all the richness of our vast creation.

Petition and Intercession

Lively, healing Maker of Easter,
we come because you call us to a deeper caring.

We come to share the mix of joy and sorrow
that is our life together.

We come with heavy hearts,
burdened by a world that looks as though
too many have forgotten
that their lives must rest in you for meaning.

Our dreams of peace
are troubled by memories of war and hatred.

We know so many whose nights are haunted
  by the agony of violence within the home, or family, or clan.

And there are those who gave their lives
  believing that their sacrifice would save us
  from the terror that was stalking them.

Most clever Potter of the vessel of life,
  you made each one of us unique
  from elements that are so much alike.

You came among us in the human Jesus
  to let us see what life can mean
  when it is fully rooted in your love.

Help us lift the crosses lying in the streets.
Help us reach out in love across the tiny fissures
  that seem to separate us from each other.

Help us be Christ to those to whom you send us.
Hear now our prayers for those in need,
  for those we know,
  and those whose stories pile rough wood
  upon the fires of our compassion.

God of all creation, we lift our prayers to you,
  counting on the power of continuing creation
  you showed us in the life of Jesus, who is for us, the Christ,
  good news of reconciliation and forgiveness.

PENTECOST

Acts 2:1–21; Psalm 104:24–34, 35b; Romans 8:14–17;
John 14:8–17, (25–27)

Opening Prayer

O God, how great and wonderful is your holy creation,
the earth itself and all the beings who call it home,
the sun and all our sister planets,
and galaxies that stretch far beyond our vision.

We marvel at the power of your imagination!
Holy Maker of this complex thing that we call life,
we gather here to praise you
for the power of your Holy Spirit loosed among us,
singing of the Good News like a chorus of cicadas,
calling us to life.

We gather here this morning in the name of Jesus,
who is our hope and our salvation. Amen.

Thanksgiving and Praise

Holy Wind that blows whenever and wherever it wills,
teach us to honor the wild wind of heaven.

Mover of that colorful community blooming in the meadow
and the bright rivulets that cascade through,
delivering the water of life,
open us to the mysterious movement of your Holy Spirit,
the giver of life who is the servant of no other force.

We rejoice in the gifts you give so carefully to every
   creature,
   the strengths and vulnerabilities
   that give shape and energy to our environment
   and our community of relationships.

Lift us up above our selfish interests,
   spread our concerns to the limits of our awareness,
   and beyond to new understanding of what it means
   to be your loving, cocreating people.

Hear now, O holy Wind of creation,
   our prayers of praise and thanks.

Petition and Intercession

Holy, healing Fire,
   we know that we are called to carry your good news,
   your healing love,
   to those who are in pain and need.

And even as we try,
   we see so many places where pain and arrogance
   seem to have the upper hand,
   places where your healing love is needed,
   some of them too far away for us to touch,
   and some we've turned away from out of fear.

We see the shame that grips the hearts of prisoners,
   the pain of those
   whose bodies, minds or spirits carry some disease,
   the blindness of those
   whose only goal is satisfaction of their own desires.

Show us what it means to give ourselves,
   to bring the promise of your good news
   to the world we're called to serve.

We raise our prayers,
  knowing that you are moving deep within us,
  calling us to be your people, the people of the risen Christ.
Holy One, receive our prayers for those in need
  as we offer them aloud
  and lift them up in the silence of our hearts.

ORDINARY TIME

The Sundays after Pentecost

TRINITY SUNDAY (FIRST SUNDAY AFTER PENTECOST)

Proverbs 8:1–4, 22–31; Psalm 8; Romans 5:1–5; John 16:12–15

Opening Prayer

Maker of wisdom and hope,
　Spirit of truth and delight,
　Lover of all creation,
　you make the moon and the stars to give light to the night,
　thunderstorms to water the earth,
　and gentle breezes to cool a steamy afternoon.

You have called us to be your people,
　to share your word in song and story and silence,
　to rejoice in your presence,
　to know that you are the source of all life and love.

As we gather in your holy name,
　help us to see the glory that shines in each face,
　to share the love that you have poured into our hearts,
　and to delight in the hope and joy of life in Christ. Amen.

Thanksgiving and Praise

Spirit of truth and delight,
　Lover of all creation,
　Maker of wisdom and hope,
　you have made us mortals just a little lower than you,
　pouring your love and grace into our lives
　beyond all that we can begin to imagine.

We give you thanks for the small blessings of each moment,
  for the air that enters our bodies with each breath,
  and flows out again whether we are awake or asleep;
  for the raucous orange trumpets of daylilies
  whose leaves shrivel to nothing each winter,
  only to return in extravagant abundance
  with the heat of summer;
  for phone calls and emails and hugs and smiles
  that connect us to one another and to you.

We give you thanks for the beasts of the field,
  the fish of the sea, the birds of the air,
  for all that we see and hear and feel
  and touch and taste and smell,
  for all that we know and all that we have yet to know.

And for what else shall we give thanks this day?

Petition and Intercession

Lover of all creation,
  Maker of wisdom and hope,
  Spirit of truth and delight,
  you fill our hearts with grace and love until they overflow,
  breaking under the weight of the pain of the world.

We ask for your comfort to those who suffer
  in body or mind,
  that you will give strength to those who care for them,
  courage to those who love them,
  and peace to all who mourn.

We ask for your mercy for the birds and fish and people
  whose lives are darkened
  by oil fouling the waters and the land.

We ask for your blessing and help for the women and men
  who serve in places of violence and danger,
  on ships at sea and on bases around the world,
  for the families that wait for them to return

and for those who know
that their loved ones will never come home.

Holy God, Holy One, Holy Three,
we pray for all who are in need of prayer,
for those we love and those we do not know,
for our own needs
and for those who cannot pray for themselves.

Aloud and in silence we bring our prayers to you.

Sunday between May 22 and May 28 inclusive (if after Trinity Sunday)

Proper 3, Ordinary 8

Sirach 27:4–7 or Isaiah 55:10–13; Psalm 92:1–4, 12–15;
1 Corinthians 15:51–58; Luke 6:39–49

Opening Prayer

Holy God, you declare your steadfast love in the morning,
and your faithfulness by night.

We gather here today,
as one tiny part of your infinitely rich creation.

We bring our thanks for life, and light, and love.
Bright Fountain of diversity,
fill us with your loving presence, we pray,
as we gather here in the name of your redeeming presence,
Jesus, who is the Christ. Amen.

Thanksgiving and Praise

God of all Creation, it is good for us to give thanks to you,
to praise your holy name,
and so we come to sing and pray and celebrate,
to share in this community the fruits of faith.

We thank you for the way the meadow grows,
each colony of flower and grass is different,
yet they join together in a vibrant testimony to life.

We thank you for the way each one of us
   stands out as someone different,
   each one bringing some dimension of reality
   that no one else will offer.

We praise you for the way your Holy Spirit
   buoys up our differences,
   helping us to see the treasure
   you have planted uniquely in each heart,
   and how our differences can help us
   learn to love and honor even strangers whom we've never met.

We praise you, O incomparable, inspiring Source of hope,
   for opening new paths from where we are
   toward fresh horizons where peace is dawning.
   Hear now, O Holy One, our prayers of praise and thanks.

Petition and Intercession

Unending, loving Source of healing and forgiveness,
   we come into your holy presence today
   carrying pain and sorrow from the wounded places
   in our lives, our community, and the world.

This late spring day
   there seem to be so many places where a flood of unease
   has swept the gentle blossoms of hope
   into a muddy puddle by the roadside.

We know so many people
   whose lives are soiled by disgrace,
   or scarred by violence, betrayal, and illness,
   or buried in the chaos of grief.

Holy God,
   we know that often we cannot see the way
   to offer healing help;
   the logs that cloud our vision get in the way
   even as we try to remove
   much smaller specks that block the sight of others.

We turn to you, O bright Fountain of deliverance,
  for help in letting go of all that clouds our vision
  and sinks us to the bottom.
God of all creation, we pray for healing now,
  for those whose pain and grief wash over us,
  for those whose pain and grief
  are crashing waves on distant shores,
  and for ourselves as we struggle to catch our breath.
We offer prayers of petition and intercession,
  aloud and lifted up in the silence of our hearts.

SUNDAY BETWEEN MAY 29 AND JUNE 4 INCLUSIVE (IF AFTER TRINITY SUNDAY)

PROPER 4, ORDINARY 9

1 Kings 8:22–23, 41–43; Psalm 96:1–9; Galatians 1:1–12; Luke 7:1–10

Opening Prayer

O God, we are surrounded
  by the power of your love for all creation.
We gather to praise you for the richness of your imagination.
We gather to know the presence of your Holy Spirit,
  pouring through us in this time of summer celebration.
O God, how manifold are your works!
In wisdom you have made them all,
  and we give thanks that we are here among them.
Let heaven and earth be glad,
  the sea and sea creatures roar,
  the field and its beasts exult.
Let the trees of the forest sing as you draw near,
  coming to judge the nations,
  to set the earth aright,
  restoring the world to order.

Today we come to pray and sing and celebrate,
  for you have gathered us together
  in the name of Jesus, who is our hope and our salvation.
Amen.

▬▬▬ **Thanksgiving and Praise** ▬▬▬

O holy Mover of the green tops of the trees
  and the grasses leaping from the warm earth,
  we come together to sing to you, O Holy One,
  a new song, filled with hope and wonder.

We marvel at the mysteries of healing
  beyond our understanding.

We are amazed as forests, fields, and oceans spring to life,
  a testimony to your care.

Hear now, O holy Fire of creation,
  our prayers of praise and thanks
  as we share them aloud
  and whisper them in the silence of our hearts.

▬▬▬ **Petition and Intercession** ▬▬▬

Holy Healer of every affliction,
  we know that there are so many, many places
  where the pain of daily living
  feels strong enough to drown out hope.

In this land of plenty,
  we grieve that there are millions
  who do not have enough to eat.

We know that as the days grow warmer,
  and there is no school,
  the number of our children
  threatened by not having food enough grows larger.

And there are others whose lives are filled
  with pain and sickness, suffering, and uncertainty.

We would have the faith of that centurion
  who only needed to know
  that you had spoken a healing word.

Hear now our prayers for those in need,
  for those whose lives are burdened
  by hunger, illness, violence, and fear.
Receive our prayers of petition and intercession,
  as we share them aloud
  and speak them silently in our hearts.

SUNDAY BETWEEN JUNE 5 AND JUNE 11 INCLUSIVE (IF AFTER TRINITY SUNDAY)

PROPER 5, ORDINARY 10

1 Kings 17:8–16, (17–24); Psalm 146; Galatians 1:11–24;
Luke 7:11–17

Opening Prayer

Faithful God of sacred stories,
  bountiful God of all our dreams,
  compassionate God of new life,
  the ancient tales remind us
  of your care for widows and orphans,
  your passion for justice for those who have nothing,
  the good news that your love is stronger than death.

Today, we see you in small moments of mercy and grace:
  in the courtesy of a bus driver waiting,
  so that someone unable to run
  will not have to wait in the rain;
  in the sudden arrival of someone who opens a door,
  just when we are burdened with too many bags or boxes;
  in the astonishing splendor of a dogwood tree
  so covered with blossoms
  that it looks like a night filled with stars.

Today, you call us to bear witness to your life among us,
to pour out our lives just as you pour out yours,
filling the world with love as the Body of Christ,
joyfully bearing the burdens of the world. Amen.

Thanksgiving and Praise

Bountiful God of all our dreams,
you invite us into your community of love,
to share our burdens and our hopes,
to rejoice in each eternal moment of life in you.

We give you thanks for the wonders of creation:
for banks of glowing, orange daylilies,
nodding their heads in the steady rain;
for the red cardinal hopping along the sidewalk,
looking for breakfast in the first light of dawn;
for the first cherries of summer,
tart and sweet and dripping with juice.

We give you thanks for the wonders of human invention:
for airplanes and telephones and computers
that keep us connected to distant loved ones;
for handwoven fabrics that delight the eye
and protect the body;
for music and paintings and dance and poetry
that lighten our burdens and bring us to laughter and to tears.

Aloud and in silence, we give you thanks for all these gifts,
and for more than we can imagine or name.

Petition and Intercession

Compassionate God of new life,
you carry all our burdens,
and know all our secret hurts.

When our lives become too full of sorrow,
when the morning news speaks only of disaster
and every evening brings more stories filled with pain,
when death and destruction seem to spill out

of every river and cloud,
our cups of compassion overflow
with the anguish of the world,
and we cry out to you.

We pray that you will comfort
all who have lost homes and loved ones to flood and tornado,
send rain on all who suffer from drought and famine,
bring an end to war and violence and oppression.

We pray that you will give wisdom and courage
to those who must make hard decisions,
and patience and strength
to those who have few choices except to endure.

We pray for all who live in sickness or in pain,
for those who tend to their needs,
and for all who live in sadness and grief.

Aloud and in silence, we pray for our own needs,
for all who have asked for our prayers,
and for all whose burdens are hidden from us.
And for what else shall we pray this day?

SUNDAY BETWEEN JUNE 12 AND JUNE 18 INCLUSIVE (IF AFTER TRINITY SUNDAY)

PROPER 6, ORDINARY 11

1 Kings 21:1–10, (11–14), 15–21a; Psalm 5:1–8, Galatians 2:15–21,
Luke 7:36–8:3

Opening Prayer

God of justice and compassion,
God of love and wonder,
God of past and future and each eternal moment,
you reveal yourself
in the overwhelming abundance of the natural world,
in the stories of ancient rulers and prophets,
in the grace-filled actions of those who love you.

When the rain comes down so hard
  that we cannot see the road ahead,
  and rivers overflow their banks,
  you remind us of your wild, unknowable power.

When Ahab and Jezebel conspired against their neighbor,
  you sent your prophet Elijah to condemn their evil ways.
When an unnamed woman brought costly ointment,
  anointing the feet of Jesus and washing them with her tears,
  you forgave all her sins and sent her on in peace.

Teach us your ways, Holy One,
  so that it is no longer our selfish desires that live,
  but Christ who lives in us, and around us, and through us.
Amen.

Thanksgiving and Praise

God of love and wonder,
  like the woman who anointed your feet with oil,
  our hearts overflow with gratitude that our sins are forgiven,
  and for the good news of your life in us.

We give you thanks for the freedom to pray,
  for music and laughter and moments of joy.

We give you thanks for parents and children,
  for sisters and brothers and families of faith.

We give you thanks for rainstorms and rainbows,
  for rushing rivers and quiet streams,
  for sandy beaches and rock-strewn shores.

We give you thanks for the breath that sustains us,
  for the salty smell of the ocean
  and the sweet scent of jasmine growing on a backyard fence.

For all this, and for so much more,
  we give you thanks aloud and in the silence of our hearts.

Petition and Intercession

God of justice and compassion,
  when rivers overflow their banks,

when tornadoes and hurricanes turn whole towns into
    rubble,
when fields no longer yield their harvest
and children die of hunger,
    our hearts become heavy for the sake of all who suffer,
and we cry out to you
    for help that is beyond our means, beyond our reach.

We plead for an end to violence in homes and in the streets,
    for an end to oppression, war, and genocide,
    for an end to all the ways
    that governments betray their people.

We beg for an end to poverty and hunger,
    for an end to sickness, disease, and pain,
    for an end to all the anguish that fills too many lives.

Hear us, Holy One, as we pray aloud and in silence
    for the courage and patience to work with you
    for the healing of the world.
And for what else shall we pray this day?

SUNDAY BETWEEN JUNE 19 AND JUNE 25 INCLUSIVE (IF AFTER TRINITY SUNDAY)

PROPER 7, ORDINARY 12

1 Kings 19:1–4, (5–7), 8–15a; Psalms 42 and 43; Galatians 3:23–29;
Luke 8:26–39

Opening Prayer

Compassionate, loving, surprising God,
    you send us hard questions
    in the news that greets us over the breakfast table,
    in the people we pass as we walk down the street,
    in the echoing silence of our hearts.

As we listen for new ways to live in your presence,
    feed us with your holy Word,
    as you fed Elijah in the wilderness

with bread that sustained him
for forty days and nights of hard travel.

Help us to hear your call
in the voices of workers who rise before dawn,
carrying hard hats and tool belts
and the hopes of their families
in their strong, calloused hands.

Help us to see your face
in people who sleep in doorways,
and in people who sleep in comfortable beds,
to know that you are hidden
in those who have too much,
and in those who have too little.

Send out your light and your truth,
and show us how to be your holy people.
Lead us into your eternal realm,
in the strength and love and courage
of Jesus, who is the Christ. Amen.

Thanksgiving and Praise

Loving, compassionate, surprising God,
you welcome all who seek you
with open arms and an open heart,
and our hearts and arms open, too,
in grateful response.

We give you thanks for the sound of birds,
even when they waken us before the dawn.

We give you thanks for cool mornings and sunlit days,
for dark thunderclouds and torrents of rain,
for sandy beaches and the endless movement of the sea.

We give you thanks for starlight and moonlight
and candlelight and flashlights,
and for the true light of Christ,
in whom we become your people.

Like people who have been possessed by demons
  and now are healed, we give thanks, aloud and in silence,
  for all that you have done for us.

Petition and Intercession

Tender, surprising, compassionate God,
  we give you thanks for all that you have done,
  yet still we dare to ask for more.

Your broken, aching world is filled with violence and grief,
  with anger and desolation.

And so we pray for all who live in constant fear,
  whose lives are marked by war,
  for those who are wounded in body or soul,
  and for those whose hearts are broken
  by a life without hope.

We pray for all whose lives are marked
  by natural and industrial disasters,
  for people who have lost livelihoods
  and homes and loved ones,
  for livestock and pets that are frightened and hungry,
  and for all who work tirelessly to help.

We pray for those who live in sickness or pain,
  for those who love them and give them care,
  and for all the healers who bring them relief.

We pray for those in far-off places,
  and for those who are closest to us;
  we pray for our own needs,
  and for those who cannot pray for themselves.
And for what else shall we pray this day?

SUNDAY BETWEEN JUNE 26 AND JULY 2 INCLUSIVE
PROPER 8, ORDINARY 13

2 Kings 2:1–2, 6–14; Psalm 77:1–2, 11–20; Galatians 5:1, 13–25;
Luke 9:51–62

Opening Prayer

Holy, wonder-working God,
  you show your power in the wind and rain,
  the crash of your thunder,
  your lightning that lights up the world.

You sustain the universe with love,
  filling the earth with overflowing abundance,
  filling the night skies with more stars
  than anyone can count.

You parted the waters for Moses and the Israelites,
  allowing them to escape from slavery into freedom,
  and allowed Elisha a glimpse of your glory
  when his teacher, Elijah, disappeared in a whirlwind.

Pour out your grace on us as we gather here today.
  Fill us with your Holy Spirit
  so that we may become fruitful bearers
  of love, joy, peace, patience, kindness,
  generosity, faithfulness, gentleness, and self-control,
  as the living Body of Christ on earth. Amen.

Thanksgiving and Praise

Holy, generous God,
  your ways are beyond our understanding,
  your gifts more numerous than we can count or name.

We give you thanks for the flash of white feathers
  on the edge of a seagull's wing;
  for the sharp, salty tang of the ocean,
  spraying up from the rocks at water's edge;
  for the fragile, sparkling glint of dew,
  trembling on the edge of a rose petal at dawn.

We give you thanks for waking up each morning,
 for breathing in and breathing out,
 for opening our senses to the world you have created.

For all these things and all that is,
 aloud and in silence,
 we give you our thanks and praise.

══════ **Petition and Intercession** ══════

Holy, redeeming God,
 in times of trouble, we seek you.
 All night long, our hands reach out to you,
 our souls long to be comforted,
 we cry aloud, that you may hear us.

We cry for children, left abandoned and afraid
 because their parents fall victim to war, poverty, or disease.

We cry for those who are in prison,
 for the daily indignities that leave them without hope.

We cry for those who sleep in doorways,
 for the fear of violence that haunts their dreams.

We cry for all who live in sickness and pain,
 for all whose lives are worse than death.

For all that is broken, for all that is lost,
 we bring our prayers to you in spoken words
 and in the silence of our hearts.

Sunday between July 3 and July 9 inclusive
Proper 9, Ordinary 14

2 Kings 5:1–14; Psalm 30; Galatians 6:(1–6), 7–16; Luke 10:1–11, 16–20

══════ **Opening Prayer** ══════

God of healing and hope,
 God of shimmering heat and rushing rivers,
 God of ancient tales of warriors and new stories of peace,
 you call us to proclaim that your realm is coming near.

Just as Naaman saw your power
  when you healed him in the Jordan,
  we see your grace in a gentle breeze,
  lifting the heavy air of a sultry, summer afternoon;
  in miraculous moments
  when our mourning is turned into dancing,
  and our tears of despair into shouts and cheers of joy.

As we sing your praises and swim in the river of your love,
  teach us how to carry one another's burdens,
  to work for the good of all,
  to bear witness to the power of the risen Christ
  flowing in us and around us and through us. Amen.

Thanksgiving and Praise

God of shimmering heat and rushing rivers,
  we give you thanks for cheeky little sparrows
  begging for crumbs at an outdoor cafe;
  for the sweet smell of honeysuckle
  filling the air as we brush past its yellow blossoms;
  for the raucous call of a blackbird,
  its bright red shoulders flashing as it rushes by.

We give you thanks for ceiling fans and air conditioning;
  for pitchers filled with clear, cold water;
  for swimming pools filled with laughing children.

We give you thanks for sparklers and picnics,
  for families of birth and families of choice,
  for old, familiar tales that have shaped the past,
  and for new stories of hope and peace.

For all of these, and more than we can name,
  we bring our prayers of thanksgiving and praise
  aloud and in the silence of our hearts.

Petition and Intercession

God of healing and hope,
  you call us to bear one another's burdens,

to heal those who suffer,
and cast out demons in your name.

Knowing our own weakness and fear, we ask you to help us,
to give us the strength to swim against the current
of violence and oppression and disdain.

We pray for all whose minds are clouded by disease,
whose bodies are filled with pain,
whose spirits are deadened by hopelessness and despair.

We pray for all whose lives are hemmed in by war,
for those who see violence as the only choice they can make,
and for those who must live and die by their rules.

We pray for those who grieve, and for those who long for death;
we pray for all who have asked us to pray,
and for all who do not know they need our prayers;
we pray for the earth,
and for all of the creatures that you have made.

And for what else shall we pray this day?

SUNDAY BETWEEN JULY 10 AND JULY 16 INCLUSIVE
PROPER 10, ORDINARY 15

Amos 7:7–17; Psalm 82; Colossians 1:1–14; Luke 10:25–37

Opening Prayer

God of justice and compassion,
you have told us that if we love you
with all our heart and soul and strength,
and love our neighbors as ourselves,
we will inherit eternal life.

You give us gifts beyond our imagination,
filling our ears with the song of mockingbirds,
filling our eyes with the sight of falling stars,
filling our whole bodies
with the sweet, heady scent of new-mown grass
drifting on the gentle breeze of a summer morning.

You measure our lives with a plumb line,
   calling us to live with integrity and generosity.

Hold us in your love and guide our thoughts and actions
   so that we may serve the world as the Body of Christ,
   shining with the light of your eternal realm. Amen.

Thanksgiving and Praise

God of compassion and love,
   we give you thanks for neighbors,
   for those who need our support and comfort,
   and for those who help us when we are lost or in pain.

We give you thanks for all the wonders of the natural world:
   for badgers and porcupines,
   for elephants and whales,
   for peacocks and earthworms
   and honeybees and butterflies.

We give you thanks for mountain and seashore,
   for desert and forest,
   for fertile farmland and city gardens,
   for all the places that renew our connection
   to the earth that you have made.

And more than these, we give you thanks
   for the forgiveness you offer in every moment,
   bringing us ever closer to the measure of your love.

And for what else shall we give thanks this day?

Petition and Intercession

God of love and justice,
   you call us to help those who are weak and in need,
   to protect them from those who do harm,
   to remember that your gifts are not for us alone,
   but are meant for the nourishment of all of your children.

Therefore, with the psalmist who sings
   that all the nations belong to you,

we cry out: How long will you judge unjustly
and show partiality to the wicked?
Give justice to orphans, rescue all who are weak,
deliver them from the hand of the wicked.

We pray for an end to the anguish of war,
the fear of oppression,
the pain of violence.

We pray for just leaders in every country,
for peace among the nations, and among all people.

Aloud and in silence, we pray for the strength and courage
to do the work you have called us to do,
to love you with all our hearts and souls and strength,
and to love our neighbors as ourselves.

SUNDAY BETWEEN JULY 17 AND JULY 23 INCLUSIVE
PROPER 11, ORDINARY 16

Amos 8:1–12; Psalm 52; Colossians 1:15–28; Luke 10:38–42

Opening Prayer

O Holy Maker of this great green earth,
great source of all the energy of creation
that dances for an instant
in the stuff that is us and all we know;
wonderful God of fruitful orchards
and chirping choruses in the night,
we gather in your presence
to celebrate your gifts of life and community.

We come to pray and sing and celebrate,
to share our burdens and our joy.

We come because you have called us to be your people,
one small part of the Body of Christ.

We come to sit at your feet like Mary, learning from your love,
so we can leave refreshed and ready to serve.

Reveal yourself to us in the prayers
  and the stories
  and the songs we share,
   for we gather in the name of our Savior,
   who is Jesus the Messiah. Amen.

Thanksgiving and Praise

Holy God of fruit and flower,
  you give us overflowing gardens,
   you give us fireflies and katydids to liven up the night.

This is a world of rich variety you have created.
There is so much to delight our senses
  and bring us refreshment,
   if we can just step back and take the time to see.

You bless us with community;
  you guide us into close relationships;
  you heal our illness and our wounds;
  and you forgive us when we sin.

O God, we give you praise and thanks,
  for all the richness in this world you've made,
  and for making room for us here in your family of faith.

For what else should we give praise and thanks,
  O wonderful Wellspring of re-creation?

Petition and Intercession

Holy God of heat and storm,
  we know that there are so many places
  where the peace that you offer seems out of reach,
   where war and drought bring grief and hunger to millions
  we must search to learn about.

And close at hand, we know the pain of illness,
  the sadness of parting,
  the grief of death.

Our nation seems mired in feuding politicians,
  who sit in flocks, high in the trees

and crow out their warnings,
   then fly away to settle on another branch
   and take up the call again.

We pray for them, and for ourselves,
   for ears to hear,
   and the strength to be bold witnesses to your healing grace.

O holy Healer of the lame and broken,
   we raise our prayers to you,
   for all those whose pain outweighs their joy.

Hear now our prayers for those in need,
   and for ourselves, for we hunger for your healing love.

Sunday between July 24 and July 30 inclusive
Proper 12, Ordinary 17

Hosea 1:2–10; Psalm 85; Colossians 2:6–15, (16–19), Luke 11:1–13

Opening Prayer

Perpetual Fount of every blessing,
   faithful Creator of all that we know,
   holy Healer of the iniquity of humankind,
   we come together on this day of rest
   to worship with each other in your presence.

We bring our weariness,
   our longing for peace and justice,
   our hunger for a good night's sleep
   free from pain, or worry, or work.

We come because you have called us to be your people.
Carry us into the ocean of your love, O holy River of life,
   for we gather as one small band of pilgrims,
   on the way as part of the Body of Christ. Amen.

Thanksgiving and Praise

Holy Mystery of life and love,
   we come to share the word you speak to us,

the news of trial and triumph,
the pain of violence and isolation,
the gentle embrace of reunion and rest.

We come to share the words of peace that you have spoken to us,
the signs that your salvation is at hand,
the promises that your glory will dwell in the land.

We come to share the good news
that steadfast love and faithfulness are met,
that righteousness and peace
have kissed each other in our time.

Hear now our prayers of praise,
for the wonder of your creation,
our prayers of thanks for your forgiving love.

We lift them aloud, and in the silence of our hearts.

Petition and Intercession

Long-suffering Healer of nations,
we gather with hearts filled with anger and sorrow
for the violence that our brothers and sisters
feel compelled to bring.

An angry man strikes out and two or three are killed:
the story reverberates throughout the world.

But other angry, fearful people strike out
and many more are killed,
and yet no one seems to know or care.

On fretful nights,
when summer lays upon us like a wet wool blanket,
we wonder if you have heard us whisper in our hearts:
"There is no God," and you've decided to withdraw
and leave our nation and our world
to reap the harvest of tears,
the tares that grow up quickly,
overpowering the wheat of faith.

And yet we've come today
  because we know you are a mystery of love.

We come together, and bring our cares and pains
  to share with each other and with you.

We come because we know your promise
  to be with your people throughout the ages.

We ask, and claim your promise
  that when we ask in love we will receive.

Hear now, O God of healing love,
  our prayers for those in pain and need,
  our prayers for healing and reconciliation.

And for what else shall we pray,
  O perpetual Fount of every blessing?

SUNDAY BETWEEN JULY 31 AND AUGUST 6 INCLUSIVE
PROPER 13, ORDINARY 18

Hosea 11:1–11; Psalm 107:1–9, 43; Colossians 3:1–11; Luke 12:13–21

Opening Prayer

O holy God of this hot, wet time of growth,
  source of lazy days and sudden storms,
  maker of sharp-tongued cardinals
  and long-winded politicians,
  we've come together here this morning to remind ourselves
  that all of this reality is your creation.

The muggy heat, the quiet street,
  the novel calling to us late into the night,
  that little breeze at sunset reminding us
  that summer is a season rather than forever—
  O Holy One, you make them all.

Reveal yourself to us, O God of every thought and thing.
Send your Holy Spirit through us
  so that no leaf, no page,

no dark corner of our minds remains unturned,
for we are here to celebrate
the wonder of your bountiful creation,
gathered in the name of Jesus, who is the Christ. Amen.

Thanksgiving and Praise

God of new hope, holy, patient Lover of creation,
we come together as your people,
moved by your call to care for every part of this reality.

We thank you for the goodness of your steadfast love,
enduring even through the times
when we have turned away from you, O Holy One.

We give thanks for the different rhythm of these days,
with slower schedules and unexpected absences,
and time to step aside and take a longer view.

We celebrate the mysteries
of truth we do not yet understand,
for birth and death,
which although central to your vision of reality
seem so amazing to us when we stand in their presence.

We give thanks for the power of questions,
which call us into learning we might otherwise ignore,
and lead us to new truth.

Hear now our prayers of praise and thanks,
for all the richness of your beautiful creation.

Petition and Intercession

Holy Maker of miracles,
we know that there are so many places where, this year,
the heat of summer doesn't feel very much like good news.

Here, it seems we're looking
for new answers to old problems,
for peace in the face of loss,
for hope in the face of death and separation.

We hunt for ways to meet the needs of those
  who hunger and thirst for more than food can satisfy:
  for love and acceptance,
  for hope and healing;
  for peace and justice.

Close at home, we carry our concerns for those among us
  who are hurting and bereft,
  for others who are slowly healing
  and for those whose grief is bigger
  than they can acknowledge.

Holy God of summer growth and summer rest,
  we bring our prayers to you with thanks and gratitude,
  trusting that you know, and care, and act in our best interests,
  even when we cannot recognize
  your presence in the moment.

O Holy God of rampant gardens and a coming harvest,
  hear now our prayers for those in pain and need.

SUNDAY BETWEEN AUGUST 7 AND AUGUST 13 INCLUSIVE
PROPER 14, ORDINARY 19

Isaiah 1:1, 10–20; Psalm 50:1–8, 22–23; Hebrews 11:1–3, 8–16;
Luke 12:32–40

Opening Prayer

Holy God of life, Artist of these sultry afternoons
  and tumbling storm clouds of relief,
  we've come together here today
  to worship, sing, and celebrate your holy transcendent power.

Fill us full to overflowing with your gifts
  of faith and hope and love
  for we are here to learn anew how to be a people full of faith,
  a people sharing hope,
  a loving little part of the body of the risen Christ

in whose name we've come together here.

Come, Holy Spirit, come. Amen.

Thanksgiving and Praise

Holy, loving God,
  creator of the rich, moist heat
  that brings the little things to life,
  this week has been a festival for katydids and lightning bugs,
  an open season for mosquitoes, mold, and black-eyed Susans,
  a festival of life.

Amazing Builder of this rich, diverse creation,
  by faith we understand that this world
  was created by your word, and we give thanks.

We've come in faith,
  in the assurance of things hoped for,
  the conviction of things not seen.

We give you thanks for what we know,
  O God of every thought and thing,
  and praise for all the unknown that is yet to come.

We know that healing is a gift from you
  to those who long for resolution, reconciliation and relief,
  and we give thanks.

We know that this life, so rich and full and complicated,
  is all a gift from you,
  and we give thanks for all the wonder and revelation.

Hear now our prayers of praise and thanks,
  O wonderful Architect of all experience.

Petition and Intercession

Holy God, we try to be as ready as those
  who wait for their leader to return
  from the wedding feast:
  bags packed, tanks full, just waiting for the word to move.

But you have given us a call to be here now,

to live and give ourselves away,
and follow Christ here in this Babylon,
even as we wait to follow you
into some already-present, future realm.

But, Holy One, there are needs here
that we just can't seem to carry by ourselves.

We watch the anger flare in distant lands.
And here we watch as friends and colleagues lose their jobs,
and others struggle with despair, disease, and death.

Holy God, artist of these sultry, torpid days
we lift our prayers
and ask your loving, reconciling presence in our midst.

Hear now our prayers
for those in need of comfort, hope, and healing,
and for ourselves,
for we, too, hunger for the coming of your loving grace.

Sunday between August 14 and August 20 inclusive

Proper 15, Ordinary 20

Isaiah 5:1–7; Psalm 80:1–2, 8–19; Hebrews 11:29–12:2; Luke 12:49–56

Opening Prayer

Holy Fountain of rest and healing, we are a scattered people,
a few who come to celebrate the joy of being called by you,
a tiny band in the midst of a nation busy with its own affairs.

Be with us as we listen to your voice
welling up in unexpected places.

We gather in the memory of witnesses of old,
who, through faith,
conquered kingdoms,
administered justice,
obtained promises,
won strength out of weakness.

We come to run with perseverance
  the race that is set before us,
  looking to Jesus as our guide.

Be here among us, deep within us,
  as we gather in the name of the Holy One
  who is our Savior, Jesus the Christ. Amen.

Thanksgiving and Praise

Great burning Mystery of ripening harvest,
  we gather once again to contemplate this heavy cross,
  big enough to hold any one of us
  outside in the merciless heat
  until we die from dehydration and exposure.

We want to rest, but still we labor on,
  and rest comes fitfully,
  squeezed into quiet moments
  surrounded by our work and worry.

But this time in each week is time to breathe,
  a time to listen to your voice within,
  a time to notice just how much good news we really know.

We read of Esther, Daniel, Naomi, and Gideon,
  whose faith led them to mighty acts
  and often to a cross like this empty one before us.

But there are other faith-full people in our day
  whose servant leadership is opening the doors to peace,
  even though the risk of crucifixion is never far away.

For when the people turn to you
  they find a path between their anger and their fear,
  a path of faith and hope and love.

We offer prayers of thanks for them.

And as we pray,
  we know that you are stirring visions deep within us,
  calling us to faithful service here and now.

Hear now, O Holy One, our prayers of praise and thanks
for all the bounty of this time in our unfolding story.

Petition and Intercession

Revolutionary Maker of this harsh reality,
we feel the tension of our house divided,
our nation pulled from left and right
by such divergent visions
of life and liberty and happiness,
and what it should take from each of us
to make your holy vision a reality.

This week the psalmist offers us the vision of a vineyard
planted carefully and nurtured into productivity,
then left alone, and opened to the ravages of storm and beast.

O God of all creation, do not abandon us, we pray,
to random acts of greed and violence.

Turn toward us, holy Maker of the future,
look out and see our little efforts to bring healing, justice, love.

We hear the fear and anger,
the mounting frustration caused by heat and boredom,
the growing feelings of uselessness among so many,
old and young.

And there are those who suffer, whose pain has grown
beyond the level where they are learning from experience.

Hear now our prayers for those who suffer,
for those who follow where you call them
even in the face of pain and doubt,
and for ourselves,
for we are hungry to hear your call,
and follow where you lead.

O holy Fountain of rest and healing,
receive us as a living prayer for peace and justice in this time.

Sunday between August 21 and August 27 inclusive
Proper 16, Ordinary 21

Jeremiah 1:4–10; Psalm 71:1–6; Hebrews 12:18–29; Luke 13:10–17

Opening Prayer

O Holy One, we gather in your presence here.
We gather to take refuge from a stormy world,
 to find here the hope we need to live.

Come, wild, consuming Fire of empowerment,
 come show us what it means to be your people,
 gathered to praise you,
 bound together in the presence of Jesus the Messiah. Amen.

Thanksgiving and Praise

Holy, enlivening Guide to all reality,
 we marvel at the richness of these times,
 the hint of changing seasons in the air,
 new possibilities for peace in war-torn lands,
 and words of wonder from the young.

We give you praise and thanks
 that Jesus mediates for us the new covenant,
 a promise that although your presence is like consuming fire,
 you offer us a realm of love that will not be consumed.

We bring our praise for all that you create
 and for each moment of our lives.

For you, O Holy One, are our hope,
 our trust from long ago,
 our source of healing.

We raise our prayers of thanks
 for the good news of Christ among us,
 the signs of reconciliation and hope.
Hear now our prayers of praise and thanks.

▰▰▰ **Petition and Intercession** ▰▰▰

Great mystery of growth and healing,
  we know that in so many ways
  the world seems always to run downhill,
  grow older and less strong,
  degenerate to anger, war, and violence.

But we have seen your healing presence
  in the lives of those we know and love,
  and in the world beyond:
  signs of the end of violence,
  decisions to build together,
  real efforts to care for all of your creation.

We know that we are part of that creation,
  called to be good stewards of the healing you bring.

O holy Healer of the broken and despairing,
  we pray for those who suffer,
  those who are afraid,
  and those whose anger drives them to destruction.

We bring our prayers to you
  knowing that, through the presence of the Holy Spirit,
  your healing love is present in the world.

Hear now our prayers for those in need
  as we share them in this sacred space,
  and ponder them in the silence of our hearts.

SUNDAY BETWEEN AUGUST 28 AND SEPTEMBER 3 INCLUSIVE
PROPER 17, ORDINARY 22

Jeremiah 2:4–13; Psalm 81:1, 10–16; Hebrews 13:1–8, 15–16; Luke 14:1, 7–14

Opening Prayer

O holy Maker of all creation,
  we gather here today to celebrate the good news
  that you are our God and we are your people.

We gather to celebrate
  the gift of your loving presence in our daily lives,
  offering each of us a path of freedom and reconciliation.

We come together with humility,
  without the need to fight for recognition,
  knowing that you have saved for us
  the right place at your banquet table.

Be present in us at this celebration, we pray,
  for we gather in the name of our Savior,
  the Holy One who is your child, this Jesus,
  the Messiah, who delivers us from sin. Amen.

Thanksgiving and Praise

O holy Mystery, we give you thanks that in your wisdom
  you keep us connected while we are apart,
  and bring us back together
  to celebrate the evidence
  that you are present throughout this time.

We give you thanks that in your love
  you teach us how to show hospitality to strangers.

We give you thanks that in your compassion
  you help us learn to be content with what we have
  and share it ever more freely with others.

We give you thanks that you make our world so complex
  that we are never at a loss

for opportunities to follow Christ,
to discover ever new ways to serve the whole human family,
and act as loving stewards of the rest of your creation.

Hear now our prayers of praise and thanks
for all you have created and set before us
as an opportunity for loving and doing your will.

Petition and Intercession

All-knowing God, although your light shines everywhere,
we know so many places
where darkness seems to have the upper hand.

We know so many people who are in pain,
with bruised relationships, and fractured health,
and sick communities.

We carry our own pain,
and that of others,
and sometimes the burden seems almost too much to bear.

O holy Giver of life and love,
help us learn to let your love flow through us
to those in greater need.

We bring our prayers to you
knowing that you give yourself in love
to nurture deep communion with all of your creation.

We long for healing, and pray for the humility
to follow where you lead,
to choose to serve,
to let your healing overflow through us,
to let you strengthen us so we can help.

Hear now our prayers for those in sickness, pain, and need,
and for ourselves, for we would be your servant people.

SUNDAY BETWEEN SEPTEMBER 4 AND SEPTEMBER 10 INCLUSIVE

PROPER 18, ORDINARY 23

Jeremiah 18:1–11; Psalm 139:1–6, 13–18; Philemon 1–21;
Luke 14:25–33

Opening Prayer

Holy God of growth and learning,
  we have come here
  as Jeremiah came down to the house of the potter,
  to see that you can start again to reshape us,
  no matter how out of balance we have become;
  to be reminded that just as a potter reworks the clay,
  you are constantly remaking your people.

We come to be remade,
  to learn how we are part of your creating process
  and how to let your loving spirit shape us
  into something new.

We come to learn
  how to remake what has been spoiled in this world.

Teach us how to build again with love,
  for we gather in the name of the master builder,
  your child, Jesus the chosen one, the Christ. Amen.

Thanksgiving and Praise

God of crisp new mornings
  with just a hint of crimson in the dense, green canopy;
  holy Maker of the universe
  tapping on the roof with seeds of hope
  loosed in the oak high overhead,
  you bring us promises of food for winter
  and new growth in spring.

Creator and re-creator of community;
  you have known us
  since we were being knit together in the womb.

You've given us the power to learn, to grow,
  to change the universe,
  and be the instruments of peace and justice in our time.

We also raise our thanks for showing us the way,
  the path into the wilderness,
  where we have never been, but know you go before us.

Hear now our prayers of praise and thanks,
  for all the richness of your bountiful creation.

Petition and Intercession

Persistent, life-giving Potter of peace,
  we know that you have brought us
  to a place of new beginnings,
  but we are fearful of the path ahead.

Like yellowing oaks, we long for quiet, and chance to rest.
We think we're hungry for earlier times,
  misremembered as simple because we were less aware.

We see so much that seems to need remolding.
This nation is torn by growing anger,
  anger fueled in turn by fear
  that there will never be enough to satisfy
  the growing hunger for toys, diversions, and desserts.

This nation needs your healing touch.
This earth, where war is born of pride and greed,
  needs your healing hands as well.

Holy Pioneer of mercy and justice,
  we stand at the edge of what we know.

We want to be on the journey with you,
  and yet we're burdened by the pain around us and within us.

Help us make ready for the journey;
  receive our prayers for those who suffer,
  and for ourselves,
  that we may have the courage
  to stay with you in the wilderness.

Sunday between September 11 and September 17 inclusive

Proper 19, Ordinary 24

Jeremiah 4:11–12, 22–28; Psalm 14; 1 Timothy 1:12–17; Luke 15:1–10

Opening Prayer

O God, holy Source of healing and renewal,
  we gather today to claim a place in your creation,
  to rekindle in our hearts the gift of your love.

You are our God, and we are your people.
You have given us your one true child, Jesus the Christ,
  who frees and reconciles to you the whole creation.

Show us your presence in us and among us we pray,
  for we gather in the name of our Savior,
  who is Jesus the Messiah. Amen.

Thanksgiving and Praise

O God, holy Mystery,
  we thank you that we know your presence with us,
  even during fearful times.

We give you thanks that your love and compassion
  reach through our unfaithful behavior
  to welcome us as soon as we turn again to you.

Good Shepherd,
  you call each of us to shepherd some small flock
  of family or workplace or community—
  to walk with them as we follow you,
  to help them get the nourishment and rest and shelter
  that they need to live and thrive.

And when they wander off,
  you lead us out to find the lost sheep,
  and help them return and reconnect.

Thanks and praise to you, O holy Shepherd,
  for leading us along the way.

Hear now our prayers of praise and thanks
   for all you have created and set before us
   as opportunities for loving and doing your will.

And for what else shall we offer prayers of praise and thanks?

▬▬ **Petition and Intercession** ▬▬

All-knowing God,
   you send a fierce wind across our land,
   a wind of judgment and correction.

Help us, we pray, to understand
   that your love endures beyond that burning wind,
   that your call is to give our lives
   to help you restore peace with justice.

But there is so much work to do, O holy Healer.

We see around us so many people whose lives are scorched
   by lack of work and food, and shelter,
   by isolation and lack of community.

The needs are so great,
   O holy Shepherd, and our efforts seem so small.

Give us the strength to step up
   when you call us to leave the flock
   and set out to find one who is lost,
   the strength and faith to trust
   that you will be there with us as we search.

We lift our prayers for those in pain and need,
   and for ourselves, for we would be your servant people.

Receive the prayers we offer aloud,
   and those we whisper in the silence of our hearts.

SUNDAY BETWEEN SEPTEMBER 18 AND SEPTEMBER 24 INCLUSIVE

PROPER 20, ORDINARY 25

Jeremiah 8:18–9:1; Psalm 79:1–9; 1 Timothy 2:1–7; Luke 16:1–13

Opening Prayer

Loving, mysterious Maker of new realities,
  we stand today with Jeremiah, crying out,
    "My joy is gone, grief is upon me, my heart is sick."

Holy Source of life and light and love,
  we've gathered here this morning,
  just a tiny band of faithful folk
  hungry for a clear sense of your presence.

We gather in this sacred space
  to pray for rulers and those in high positions
  so we may lead quiet, peaceful lives
  in godliness and dignity.

We want to celebrate the mystery of life;
  we hope to comfort one another;
  we pray that you will fill us with your holy love,
  for we gather in the name of Jesus of Nazareth,
  who is the Christ. Amen.

Thanksgiving and Praise

O God of mystery, holy Source of healing love,
  we thank you for your presence with us
  as we get ready for the winter that we know will come.

The squirrels who claim their turf above the yard,
  so high up in the oaks that we can hardly see them,
  are busy renovating old squirrel-houses,
  tearing out the dry, brown leaves,
  getting rid of rot born of neglect,
  reinforcing what remains
  to make a snug home for themselves,

a place to rest and nurture offspring,
  and wait with patience for the fresh, new year.

It is a time of healing in the yard,
  and there are subtle signs of healing in the wider world.

When we are in the depths of our distress,
  we find you there.

When we must share the pain of loss and grief,
  we find you there.

When sudden sunshine bursts the sultry grey,
  we find you there.

And when we think about the years to come,
  we know we'll find you there as well.

We thank you for a chance to make ready
  for the rest of winter,
  and the fresh new life of spring to come.

We thank you for the courage we have received from you
  to go on living in the face of all the terrors that beset us.

O holy Source of healing love,
  hear now our prayers of praise and thanks
  as we offer them aloud in the safety of this sanctuary,
  and lift them in the silence of our hearts.

Petition and Intercession

O holy Healer of a hurting world,
  you give us room when we are in distress;
  you hold us close and wipe away our tears;
  you help us see that there are paths into the future
  that we have never known about before.

You call us to be healers in a hurting world,
  and so we bring the pain we bear, the grief, the fear,
  the emptiness when hope has fled.

Holy Healer, we've had our hands so full
  that more than once we've let some pain

slip through our fingers
and fall on those around us,
like those little branches from the oak trees,
only heavier and sharper, sharp enough to hurt.

So now, we bring the pain we've still got hold of,
and offer it to you,
our prayers for those whose souls and bodies
cry out for comfort, hope, and healing.

O holy Mystery of healing love,
we celebrate the hard reality of life.

We pray that you will fill us with your holy love
until the only choice we have
is where to spread it in the week to come.

Sunday between September 25 and October 1 inclusive

Proper 21, Ordinary 26

Jeremiah 32:1–3a, 6–15; Psalm 91:1–6, 14–16; 1 Timothy 6:6–19;
Luke 16:19–31

Opening Prayer

Holy Lover, our refuge and our strength,
as our ancestors in faith faced exile in the days of Jeremiah,
you promised to be with them in their trouble,
that one day houses and fields and vineyards
would again be bought and sold in their land.

Like those people long ago,
we long to know your loving presence,
to trust that you are with us no matter what our struggles,
no matter what our fears.

Help us to find you in the white moon flowers
that open their broad petals in the gathering dusk;
in the sweet scent of honeysuckle that envelops us

as we walk along the path at evening;
in the bright, blue sky of an autumn dawn.

Show us the true riches of life in you,
in the songs and stories that we hear this day,
in your call to open our hearts,
to live in kindness, generosity, and gentleness,
as the Body of Christ on earth. Amen.

Thanksgiving and Praise

Bold, creating Lover of life,
we bring nothing into the world,
and take nothing out of it.
Everything we touch,
every breath we take,
every moment of our lives
is a gift from you.

We give you thanks for the first hints of autumn,
for crisp, cool mornings and warm afternoons,
for the sweetness of berries and melons,
for the full moon sailing in a sea of stars.

We give you thanks for the simple comforts
of hot tea and cold water,
for the shy smile of a toddler just learning to wave hello,
for the exuberant energy of a group of teenagers
waiting for the bus.

We give you thanks for this day and every day,
for the love that creates us and sustains us
and fills us with hope and joy.
And for what else shall we give thanks?

Petition and Intercession

Merciful, saving Lover of rich and poor alike,
you have promised to be with your people in times of trouble.

With open, breaking hearts, we cry out to you,
asking not for worldly riches and privilege,

but that everyone might have enough to eat,
a place to live that is comfortable and safe,
and someone to take care of them
when they are unable to care for themselves.

We pray for those who have too little of life's goods,
and for those who have more than they can ever use;
we pray for those whose lives feel empty,
and for those whose lives are too full;
we pray for those who long for death,
and for those who fear it.

We pray for those who make our laws,
that they will govern with wisdom and compassion.

We pray for those who wage war,
that they will come to know your ways of peace and justice.

We pray for all who suffer,
we pray for all who grieve,
we pray for all who have asked for our prayers.

Holy Lover, we ask you to comfort and protect
all who are in need.
Aloud and in silence, we pray for our own needs,
and for the healing of the world.

SUNDAY BETWEEN OCTOBER 2 AND OCTOBER 8 INCLUSIVE

PROPER 22, ORDINARY 27

Lamentations 1:1–6; Lamentations 3:19–26 or Psalm 137;
1 Timothy 2:8–15; Luke 17:11–19

Opening Prayer

Holy Creator of the universe,
we come as your people,
gathered here before your altar of blessing to celebrate!

We come to celebrate your presence in this time and place.
We come to celebrate the power of your creating love.

We come to celebrate the good news
  that you have made all things new in Christ.

Reveal yourself to us,
  O relentless, forgiving Spinner of good news,
  for we gather to celebrate the way you came among us
  as friend to sinners and redeemer of the world,
  your good news incarnate in Jesus,
  who is the chosen one, the Christ. Amen.

Thanksgiving and Praise

Creator of the universe, holy nurturing River of life,
  we come to think again about what it means
  to claim our place as one small body of your people.

We come with deep gratitude
  for all the blessings that you have brought to those we love
  and those we do not even know.

This harvest season,
  we remember those who have taken your call to heart:
  saints like Eunice the mother of Timothy,
  and Francis who loved the animals.

This harvest season, we remember how it is
  to live among strangers while carrying your law of love,
  and we give thanks.

Hear now our prayers of praise and thanks
  for those who summon this world to praise
  and true thanksgiving,
  for all the rich, creative love you pour forth in our time.

Petition and Intercession

O loving Lord of life,
  so often we would stand with the apostles,
  and call to you: "Increase our faith!"
  as though by simply asking
  the answer will come down like lightning,
  in a flash of faith that lays bare the truth of reconciliation,

and brings the world to harmony,
shalom, some kind of heaven here and now.
We hunger for the satisfaction
of being part of your good news.
We want the lame to walk, the sick to heal, the blind to see.
We want the prisoners freed
to take their rightful place in community.
We want to be a part of your loving and creating body,
part of your good news for the world.
We hunger for your call on us
as individuals and as a family of faith.
And though we want the easy answer,
we understand that truth comes slowly,
rising like the sun,
chasing imperceptibly the dark of doubt away.
Because we care, we carry with us
burdens of the needs of others
and the weight of our own needs.
O holy Sunrise of new beginnings,
hear us as we lift our prayers
for those who need your healing, loving presence
in their lives.
Be present with us as we listen deeply for your guidance.
Enfold us in your healing embrace as we listen for your call.
Hear now our prayers for those in need
as we share them in this sacred space
and lift them in the silence of our hearts.

SUNDAY BETWEEN OCTOBER 9 AND OCTOBER 15 INCLUSIVE

PROPER 23, ORDINARY 28

Jeremiah 29:1, 4–7; Psalm 66:1–12; 2 Timothy 2:8–15; Luke 17:11–19

Opening Prayer

Holy God of healing,
  we gather once again
  as one small part of your living body in this time and place.

We gather to worship and sing praises to you,
  O mighty, surprising Maker of reality.

The prophet Jeremiah reminds us of your call
  to serve those to whom you send us:
  build homes, raise families
  and seek the welfare those we live among,
  for in their welfare we shall find our own.

God of the open future,
  show us your ways of caring and compassion,
  this morning and in the days to come,
  for we gather as a people committed to your way,
  the way of Christ, who is our Savior. Amen.

Thanksgiving and Praise

O God of all generations,
  God of all creatures,
  God of every leaf and grain of sand,
  we bring our praise for your whole creation.

God of birth, and death, and resurrection,
  we are bound together
  by the knowledge of your love for us.

We praise the complex beauty of your lands and seas.

We stand in awe before the power of storms and tides.

We delight in the rich variety of creatures you have made.

We cherish the love of friends and family,
  knowing that it comes from you.

Magnificent Lover of justice and compassion,
  hear now the prayers of praise and thanks we lift to you,
  for all the power of your presence in the world.

▰▰▰ **Petition and Intercession** ▰▰▰

God of love and hope,
  today we know how much it means to us
  to have a home, a home in faith,
  a place where we can celebrate
  the good news of your presence in our lives.

And yet, we know so many places
  that seem cut off from the joy of that good news.

God of mystery beyond our understanding,
  your world seems filled with pain and suffering.

So many times we don't know what to do;
  there are so many people who need healing,
  and the help we have to offer
  seems too small to make a difference.

Where are you calling us to be your hands and feet?
What are you asking us to do
  to bring your healing love
  to those who are in pain and need?

We cry out for the plight of those who are not rich enough
  to buy themselves the safety, opportunity, and justice
  that should be the right of all.

O God who dwells within us,
  we raise our prayers for those in need,
  for those who grieve the loss of loved ones,
  for those who suffer sickness and pain,
  for those who have no homes, no food.

Hear our prayers for those in need.

SUNDAY BETWEEN OCTOBER 16 AND OCTOBER 22 INCLUSIVE

PROPER 24, ORDINARY 29

Jeremiah 31:27–34; Psalm 119:97–104; 2 Timothy 3:14–4:5; Luke 18:1–8

Opening Prayer

Astonishing God of justice and kindness,
  God of patience and promises,
  God of sunlight and moonlight and starlight,
  you have held and preserved us for many years
  as one small part of your holy Church,
  filling us with the fire of your Holy Spirit
  so that we can do your work in the world.

You have called us to make commitments
  to those who depend on us
  and to those on whom we depend,
  to the whole of your creation,
  and most especially to you, to whom we owe our very lives.

As we gather to remember the past
  and look forward towards a future that only you can know,
  help us to remember that you are always with us,
  to feel your presence in our songs and stories,
  in our laughter and in our tears,
  in the brilliant sunshine of a bright fall day,
  and in the darkest night.

Show us the astonishing light of your being,
  shining among us and through us and around us,
  as members of the risen Body of Christ, alive in the world.
Amen.

Thanksgiving and Praise

Astonishing God of memory and promise,
  we give you thanks for this day of commitments,

for the covenant you made with our ancestors in faith
that you would be our God, and we would be your people.

We give you thanks for all who work for the good of others,
for those who work in homeless shelters and soup kitchens,
for social workers and therapists and teachers,
for healers and childcare workers and first responders,
for all who give their time and care to those who are in need.

We give you thanks for each new day,
for homes and for families and for friends,
for the work of our hands
and the work of our hearts,
for the strength and courage to carry out our commitments,
and the forgiveness and understanding
that sometimes our strength and courage fail.

Aloud and in silence,
we give our thanks for all that we can name,
and all that remains hidden in our hearts.

Petition and Intercession

Astonishing God of healing and hope,
in the light of your compassion,
we cannot hide our eyes from the broken, hurting places
of the world around us.

We pray for an end to war and to violence,
that you will lead every person and nation
along the path of peace.

We pray for those who are sick in body, in heart, in spirit,
that you will hold them in your loving arms
and give them comfort.

We pray for those who mourn
and for those who are close to death;
we pray for loved ones and strangers and for our own needs;
we pray for those for whom we have promised to pray,
and for those who cannot pray for themselves.

And for what else shall we pray this day?

SUNDAY BETWEEN OCTOBER 23 AND OCTOBER 29 INCLUSIVE

PROPER 25, ORDINARY 30

Joel 2:23–32; Psalm 65; 2 Timothy 4:6–8, 16–18; Luke 18:9–14

Opening Prayer

God of rain and sunshine,
  God of seed time and harvest,
  God of dreams and visions,
  you have promised to be our God,
  and that we shall be your people.

You call us to notice the wonders of the world around us:
  to rejoice in the way the sky brightens at dawn;
  to delight in the trees that seem to be filled
  with more singing birds than leaves;
  to celebrate the first cold bite of the changing seasons.

You call us to fight the good fight for justice and for peace,
  to keep faith with those who are oppressed,
  to be poured out as a libation for the healing of the world.

Pour out your Spirit on us gathered here,
  teach us to pray with open hearts and open hands,
  and form us into your holy Body,
  your loving presence in a world that longs for joy. Amen.

Thanksgiving and Praise

Be glad and rejoice in the Holy One, our God!
We praise you and thank you, Creator of all that is
  and all that ever shall be.
  You answer prayer,
  you forgive our sins,
  you are the hope of all who look to you.

We give you thanks for water,
  for salty oceans and fresh-flowing streams;
  for lakes and ponds and rainstorms,
  and the clean, clear water that flows from our taps.

We give you thanks for the air that we breathe,
   for the blood that courses through our veins,
   for the miracle that changes food into energy
   and thought into movement.

We give you thanks for forming us into your Body,
   so that we may support one another
   for the healing of the world.

And for what else shall we give thanks this day?

Petition and Intercession

God of rain and sunshine,
   God of seed-time and harvest,
   God of dreams and visions,
   like the tax collector who prayed for mercy
   we stand in awe of your presence,
   pleading for you to remember your promises
   to deliver all of your creatures from all hurt and harm.

Restore the years that the locust has eaten
   to those who have lost homes and possessions
   to fire and flood;
   restore the health
   of those who are broken in body and spirit;
   restore hope to the hopeless,
   and give strength to all who are weary.

Pour out your Spirit on all who yearn for your guidance,
   give clear vision to all who must make decisions,
   and courage to all who wait for justice.

We pray for those who are near to us,
   and for those who are far away.
   We pray for those for whom we have promised to pray,
   and we pray for ourselves,
   that you will guide us and teach us,
   and help us do your will.

Aloud and in silence, we bring our prayers to you.

SUNDAY BETWEEN OCTOBER 30 AND NOVEMBER 5 INCLUSIVE

PROPER 26, ORDINARY 31

Habakkuk 1:1–4, 2:1–4; Psalm 119:137–144;
2 Thessalonians 1:1–4, 11–12; Luke 19:1–10

Opening Prayer

Holy God of all creation,
  we gather here in this familiar place,
  hungry for the good news of your presence.

We gather to share what we are learning
  of your vision for this time,
  so we can clarify it in a way
  that even those who hurry past may recognize
  the love you have for all of your creation.

We pray that you will quicken our awareness
  as we share this time with you,
  that you will stay to hear the news we bring,
  and offer us your blessing.

Come, Holy Spirit, come. Amen.

Thanksgiving and Praise

Holy Jeweler of that crystal sky held up just out of reach
  by rusty oaks and bright copper maples,
  these caramel days melt slowly, sweetly in our minds
  as we let the late, gold sun fill us to the brim.

We know that life is changing … fast!

The sun is gone before the day is done:
  we've changed our clocks to chase it!

The geese are leaving,
  and the leaves are piling up beneath our feet,
  opening a window on that crystal sky.

Like Zacchaeus, we scramble to catch sight of you
  coming into town,

and marvel at the way our lives are changed
  by having you sojourn with us.
Some things will never be the same.

The pain and violence of war
  have beat our consciousness and our conscience
  into something new;
    there are opportunities to serve
  in places where we've never thought to look.

Golden Harvest of the heart
  we thank you that you show us extraordinary wonders
  in the midst of ordinary days,
    and that you give us strength and skill
  to serve you in so many places.

Hear now our prayers of praise and thanks,
  O holy God of all creation,
  as we offer them aloud and in the silence of our hearts.

▬▬ **Petition and Intercession** ▬▬

Loving Healer of the sick and needy,
  when we came in to worship we set our burdens at the door,
  and there's a pile out there tall enough to cover up the sun.

We see how many lives are imprisoned
  by power, hate and greed,
  and there are painful joints and throbbing heads
  and overwhelming tiredness,
  enough to send us all to bed.

We passed a stack of grudges, waiting to be held again,
  and there's a mound of righteous indignation
  big enough to fuel a fight for justice.
And here, with all those burdens just beyond our reach,
  you call us to a place where sacrificial service holds the key
  as we remember saints whose gifts of love and life
  have given hope to others.
You offer us a time to know
  that we are called to love each other,

and love the world you've brought us to,
while you take care of vengeance.

Help us, O holy God of rebirth and renewal,
help us to claim your promises of healing, justice, mercy.

Help us leave our burdens in that pile by the door,
and listen with fresh ears for the good news of your presence,
and your call to serve in fresh, new ways.

Hear now our prayers for those in need,
including all of us.

SUNDAY BETWEEN NOVEMBER 6 AND NOVEMBER 12 INCLUSIVE

PROPER 27, ORDINARY 32

Haggai 1:15b–2:9; Psalm 145:1–5, 17–21;
2 Thessalonians 2:1–5, 13–17; Luke 20:27–38

Opening Prayer

Holy God of new beginnings, we come as a people
who long for clearer understanding
of your presence in our time.

We have seen signs and heard suggestions
about what your fuller coming may mean,
but we know that fuller coming will happen
only when you know the time is right.

And so we gather here to celebrate the presence we already know
even as we wait and pray to know the fuller presence
of the one who came from you,
that child of yours who is the salvation of all the earth,
whose family we claim and in whose name we gather,
our Savior, who is Jesus the Christ. Amen.

Thanksgiving and Praise

Holy, loving Mystery, we come to bless your holy name.
Today we celebrate
the promise of your presence in the depths of tribulation,

the power of salvation, new life, new opportunity,
the chance to start again.

Compassionate, forgiving Friend of justice,
it is the traditional time of harvest,
and we gather to give thanks,
even though the produce section of the market
still has asparagus and leaf lettuce.

We know that fall has come, and it is time to rest,
even though the world around us
never seems to slow its pace.

We know that there are seasons when it is better
to gather in and set aside,
rather than plant or start, or risk a new adventure.

This is the time for looking back
to see how far we have been led by your grace,
and giving thanks for life, and love, and family.

Gracious, healing Maker of the earth,
we pause to give you thanks for bringing us to life
in this time and place.

Hear now our prayers of praise and thanks,
for all that you have given us, as we lift them up,
in silence and aloud.

Petition and Intercession

God of every moment, Creator of all history,
we celebrate your call to us to serve,
to love and care for all the world around us,
to find food for the hungry, warm garments for the naked,
a place of safety for all who are threatened,
and justice for those who are oppressed
by individuals and the systems they create.

Compassionate, healing Fountain of love,
we know that we are small and our horizons are limited.

Most of the time we cannot see
  the destination you have in mind for every journey.

Most of the time we see the stones and potholes in the road,
  and lose sight of where the road is heading.

Most of the time we do not know how much you care,
  and how you watch with love while we struggle
  to do what is so natural for you.

O gentle, forgiving Friend of the forgotten,
  help us to remember
  how closely we are connected to each other;
  help us see past those differences that we think divide us;
  help us reach out in love to those who seem so different.

Help us to be your hands and feet, your heart and soul
  in every place where we are called to serve;
  and help us lift the burdens of the pain we know
  to you, O holy Maker of the universe.

Hear now our prayers for those in need,
  for those in pain, for those who grieve,
  for those who think that they have been forgotten
  by us and by you.
We lift the prayers of our hearts in silence and aloud.

SUNDAY BETWEEN NOVEMBER 13 AND NOVEMBER 19 INCLUSIVE

PROPER 28, ORDINARY 33

Isaiah 65:17–25; Isaiah 12; 2 Thessalonians 3:6–13; Luke 21:5–19

Opening Prayer

God of celebration and promise,
  you have called us to live in hope
  even when the world around us
  seems to be filled with terror and sorrow.

When we wonder how we can go on another day
  you give us the gift of a blazing, red maple,

backlit against a crystalline blue sky,
a burning bush lighting our way into the future.

When our minds shut down at the news of yet another
flood or earthquake or volcano,
you break open our hearts with a story
about a cold, hungry, little mouse,
or wolves and lambs who feed together,
showing us how to share your glorious feast
with all who are hungry or thirsty or in need.

When the world around us seems too full
of anger and violence and discord,
you call us to be glad and rejoice
that we are the holy, risen Body of Christ,
a beacon of hope and promise
of a time in which none shall hurt or destroy
in all your holy creation. Amen.

Thanksgiving and Praise

The psalmist says,
"Surely God is my salvation; I will trust, and will not be afraid,
for the Holy One is my strength and my might;
God has become my salvation."

And so with joy we draw water from the wells of salvation,
giving thanks to the Holy One and singing praises
for the astonishing gift of each new day.

We give thanks for the bright colors of autumn,
for the red and gold and orange leaves
that shimmer on branches and crunch under our feet
and float through the air like improbable angels,
announcing the coming winter in the crisp, morning wind.

We give thanks for the members of this church
for the life that has led them to this place,
and that they have answered your call
to be members of the Body of Christ to the world.

We give thanks for the generosity of friends and of strangers
who share their resources with generous hearts,
giving us the opportunity to consider what we can do
towards the healing of the world.

For all these things, and for more than we can think or name,
we bring, now, our thanks and praise,
aloud or in the silence of our hearts.

Petition and Intercession

God of hope and new life,
you have promised a day in which none shall hurt or destroy
in all your holy creation.

And yet, all around us, we see violence and destruction,
we see people in pain because they have no food,
no shelter, no place of safety from the cruelty of others
or the illness that fills their bodies or their minds.

And we, ourselves, are filled with anguish
when the world around us makes no sense;
when people lie and cheat and steal, and yet go unpunished;
when those we love make decisions
that will lead to ongoing pain and sorrow.

Holy Bringer of healing and wholeness,
we pray for an end to suffering and grief
in all the broken places of the world.

Aloud and in silence, let us now pray for those we love,
and for those we do not know,
for our own needs,
and for those who cannot pray for themselves.

THE REIGN OF CHRIST

SUNDAY BETWEEN NOVEMBER 20 AND NOVEMBER 26 INCLUSIVE

PROPER 29, ORDINARY 34

Jeremiah 23:1–6; Luke 1:68–79; Colossians 1:11–20; Luke 23:33–43

Opening Prayer

Blessed be you, Holy One, our God,
  for you have looked on your people with grace
  and promised to gather the remnant of your flock,
  to raise up a shepherd from the root of David,
  to remember your holy covenant of peace and wholeness.

Blessed be you, Holy Spirit of God,
  for you blow among us and through us and around us,
  turning the last leaves from red to brown
  as the bare tips of branches scratch the clouds
  and the sun rises and sets
  amid fast-moving pennants of pink and gold.

Blessed be you, Holy Child of God,
  for you reign in our hearts
  as the image of the invisible One,
  the firstborn of all creation,
  for in you the fullness of God was pleased to dwell,
  in you we live and breathe and have our being.

Blessed be you, Holy One, Holy Three.
  Make yourself known in us gathered here,

so that we may learn to be your blessed Body,
broken and whole for the healing of the world. Amen.

═══ Thanksgiving and Praise ═══

Blessed are you, Holy One, our God,
as the seasons tumble into one another,
we celebrate the eternal reign of Christ,
and look for signs of new beginnings
in the dark night of the year.

We give you thanks for each morning as a bright, new gift:
our breath like smoke in the crisp morning air;
the frost sparkling like jewels on brown, fallen leaves;
the bright blue sky that makes us squint as we walk along.

We give you thanks for friendship that lasts for decades,
and for conversations that turn strangers into friends.

We give you thanks for students and for teachers,
for librarians and scholars and theologians and preachers,
and all who remember what has gone before;
for astronomers and botanists and gardeners and farmers,
and all whose days bring them to wonder
in the light of your creation;
for sales clerks and short-order cooks
and cleaners and menders,
and all whose work is invisible and hard and poorly-paid.

Most of all, we give you thanks for your Holy Child, Jesus,
who lives among us
as the image of your own, invisible reality,
teaching us to live in love with one another,
spreading your grace and mercy to all of your creation.
And for what else shall we give thanks this day?

═══ Petition and Intercession ═══

Blessed be you, Holy One, Holy Three,
for all the gifts that we have named,
and all the gifts that we never even notice.

As we give thanks for your gifts to us,
  we dare to ask for even more:
  we pray that in your coming reign,
  you will bring an end to all suffering and pain.

We pray for those who shiver in the cold,
  for those who have no homes,
  for those who have no hope.

We pray for those who greet each day with sorrow,
  for those who have lost their dignity,
  for those who have lost their dreams.

We pray for those whose bodies ache and sigh,
  for those who long for the release of death,
  and for those who fear the end of their days.

We pray for justice and for peace in every country
  in every home and in every heart.
  Aloud and in silence, we bring our prayers to you.

Acknowledgments

It has become a commonplace observation that no one writes a book alone. This is particularly true for a book of prayers composed for the public worship of a community of faith. Without Seekers Church, this book would simply not exist. And Seekers Church would not exist except for the vision of Fred Taylor and Sonya Dyer, who called it into being in 1976 out of the New Lands process of the Church of the Saviour of Washington, DC. This is not the place to recount that history, but it is only right for me to give thanks, first and foremost, to Sonya, who baptized me in 1990, and later welcomed me into Celebration Circle and taught me how to write for worship. Other members of Celebration Circle who helped me hone my writing and who shaped my theology have included, at various times, Sherri Alms, Kate Amoss, Billy Amoss, Julie Arms, Sheri Bergen, Sandra Miller, Jesse Palidofsky, Dan Phillips, and the late Kate Cudlipp, as well as the Circle's two current members besides Peter and myself, Ken Burton and Elizabeth Gelfeld. I also would like to thank Gail Ramshaw, whose liturgical writing has so permeated my own that to address God as "Holy One, Holy Three," seems as natural as breathing. I am grateful to Janet Walton, Heather Murray Elkins, Susan Roll, Martha Ann Kirk, Carol Cook Moore, Marcia McFee, Silvia Sweeney, Hae Ran Kim-Cragg, and the other members of the Feminist Studies in Liturgy Seminar of the North American Academy of Liturgy who have taught me what it means to be a feminist Christian and encouraged me to publish my prayers; and to Laurence Hull Stookey, who introduced me to liturgical studies and whose prayers and thoughts in *This Day* continue to shape my devotional life. Finally, I give thanks to Marjory Zoet Bankson, for introducing me to SkyLight Paths; to our editors, Emily Wichland, who kept asking me when I would be ready to bring this book to SkyLight Paths, and Rachel Shields, who has helped us make this a better book;

to Peter, who has been my writing partner and my friend for over twenty years; and to my husband, Glen Yakushiji, who supports me in my passion for liturgy, writing, and art.

Deborah Sokolove

When I joined the Celebration Circle mission group in the fall of 1982, Sonya Dyer was our regular worship leader. On most Sundays in those early years, our two cofounders led worship. Fred Taylor preached and Sonya Dyer presided, leading us in prayer and song. Their combined presence modeled gender balance in leadership in a day when that was still a new concept for many churches. Sonya's prayers were fresh, inclusive, and inviting. As our vision of shared leadership deepened and we began to include preaching by many members of the congregation, we maintained the commitment to embodying a balance of female and male leadership in worship by having a man preside whenever a woman brought the Word. As the only man in Celebration Circle at the time, I began to preside whenever a woman was preaching. I followed Sonya's lead, crafting prayers that rose out of the weekly lections, the life of our community and the season of the year. Sonya was a mentor for presiding at worship. Her commitment to inclusive language and creative prayers was an inspiration to me. I am grateful for her patient support as my on-the-job training in leading worship began to take hold. As I began to find my place at the lectern, my wife, Marjory Zoet Bankson, suggested that it might help if I wrote down my prayers, to help me stay focused in the moment and avoid repetitious language. It was one of those well-crafted suggestions that went in easily and took root. Thank you, Marjory! So when Deborah Sokolove invited me to bring my collection of prayers to this project, I had almost 30 years' worth of files to draw on. Working with Deborah has been an exciting opportunity to look again at how we have been calling on God in Seekers Church since we began in 1976. Thank you, Deborah. And finally, thanks to all who have been part of Seekers Church, the family of faith that has given me the opportunity to help us stay on the road, together with Christ, and all the members of Celebration Circle, whom Deborah has mentioned above. Thank God we've been on this journey together.

Peter Bankson

About the Lectionary

In general, the church year is shaped by the festal cycles of Advent-Christmas-Epiphany and Lent-Easter-Pentecost. The weeks between Epiphany and Ash Wednesday are considered the Season of Epiphany, and the long Ordinary Time season from Pentecost to Advent is broken into four thematic sections suggested by the life of the community. In order to maintain some consistency in the preaching—a difficult task with an "open pulpit" policy—as well as to maintain a connection with other churches worldwide, Seekers Church follows the Revised Common Lectionary for its weekly readings from Scripture. The entire congregation is encouraged to study the lectionary scriptures each week in order to be fully prepared for Sunday worship. Preachers are asked to work with at least one of the lectionary scriptures, as well as the theme for the season, as they prepare to share the Word as they understand it.

A lectionary is a list of Scripture readings to be read in Christian worship in accordance with the annual flow of the church's year. At least since the fourth century, various churches created such lists, and over the centuries certain readings have come to be associated with certain Sundays and holy days. However, aside from the major holy day readings, these lists differed between traditions and sometimes even between local congregations.

In the exciting days of liturgical renewal surrounding the Second Vatican Council, an ecumenical group called the Consultation on Common Texts (CCT) began to harmonize the various lists, attempting to create a single, common pattern—a common lectionary—that would serve as a sign of unity in the fragmented Christian world. The hope was that, regardless of denomination or liturgical tradition or geographical location, on any given Sunday the same readings from Scripture would be read in every Christian church all over the world.

In 1983 the CCT published its first Common Lectionary. As the member churches worked with it and made comments, various changes were suggested. In 1992 a new version incorporating many of those suggestions was published as The Revised Common Lectionary (RCL). Today, the CCT includes representatives from more than twenty denominations and agencies, from Baptists to Lutherans, from Mennonites to Roman Catholics, from the Reformed Church in America to the Unitarian Universalist Christian Fellowship. You can find more information about the CCT and its work at its website (www.commontexts.org).

Although the dream was that every church everywhere would proclaim the same scriptures every Sunday, it hasn't quite worked out like that. One reason is that some denominations use lectionaries that agree generally with the RCL, but differ somewhat on particular Sundays or feast days of importance to their own tradition. Another reason that readings may differ from church to church is found in the current version of the RCL itself, which provides two sets of readings for half the year. As the CCT website explains:

> The basic, weekly pattern of the Revised Common Lectionary is to provide an Old Testament reading, a psalmody response to that reading, a New Testament reading from an epistle or Revelation, and a gospel reading.
>
> From the First Sunday of Advent to Trinity Sunday of each year, the Old Testament reading is closely related to the gospel reading for the day. From the first Sunday after Trinity Sunday to the last Sunday of the church year, provision has been made for two patterns of reading the Old Testament: a complementary series in which the Old Testament reading is closely related to the gospel reading, and a semicontinuous series in which large portions of the Old Testament are read sequentially week to week. (www.commontexts.org/rcl/usingrcl.html)

Our custom at Seekers is to use the semicontinuous readings, so the prayers in this volume are crafted with those in mind. However, most of the prayers can be adapted for use with the complementary, or thematic, series with relatively small changes in references to the scriptural themes.

We have followed the RCL in identifying when each set of readings should occur. The numbering system for Ordinary Time can be confusing, as it gives options for various denominational traditions. Some churches begin counting Ordinary Time with the first Sunday after Epiphany. Others start counting what they call "propers" on the sixth Sunday after Epiphany. In years in which Easter comes early, readings that are designated for the later weeks in the season after Epiphany appear instead in the first few weeks after Trinity Sunday. For this reason, a few identical sets of readings are referenced in this volume, with the prayers adjusted for events in the natural world that differ according to whether the readings might occur before Lent or after Pentecost. Finally, the Sundays of Ordinary Time that fall between Trinity Sunday and the Feast of the Reign of Christ are not only numbered but also tied to specific ranges of dates, such as "Sunday between July 24 and July 30 inclusive." While this may seem a little redundant, the word inclusive is meant to avoid any ambiguity, as both the starting and ending dates are included along with the days between them. In case all of this is too complicated to keep in mind, the Revised Common Lectionary website at http://lectionary.library. vanderbilt.edu always shows the actual dates of all the readings for the current year, as well as the next two years of the three-year cycle.

Resources

About Designing and Leading Worship

Bell, John, and Wild Goose Worship Group. *Cloth for the Cradle: Worship Resources and Readings for Advent, Christmas and Epiphany.* Chicago: GIA Publications, 2000.

Long, Kimberly Bracken. *The Worshiping Body: The Art of Leading Worship.* Louisville, KY: Westminster John Knox Press, 2009.

Morley, Barry. "Beyond Consensus: Salvaging Sense of the Meeting," Pendle Hill Pamphlet 307. Wallingford, PA: Pendle Hill Publications, 1993.

Neu, Diann L. *Return Blessings: Ecofeminist Liturgies Renewing the Earth.* Cleveland, OH: Pilgrim Press, 2002.

Saliers, Don E. *Worship Come to Its Senses.* Nashville: Abingdon Press, 1996.

———. *Worship as Theology: Foretaste of Glory Divine.* Nashville: Abingdon Press, 1994.

Seekers Church. "Word and Music in Worship." Accessed, May 28, 2014, www.seekerschurch.org/life-together/core-documents/19-life-together/core-documents/181-word-and-music-in-worship.

Stookey, Laurence Jull. *Let the Whole Church Say Amen!: A Guide for Those Who Pray in Public.* Nashville: Abingdon Press, 2001.

About Inclusive Language

Duck, Ruth C. *Finding Words for Worship: A Guide for Leaders.* Louisville KY: Westminster John Knox Press, 1995.

Hays, Edward. *Prayers for the Domestic Church: A Handbook for Worship in the Home.* Notre Dame, IN: Forest of Peace, 1979.

———. *Pray All Ways: A Book for Daily Worship Using All Your Senses.* Notre Dame, IN: Forest of Peace, 2007.

Ramshaw, Gail. *God beyond Gender: Feminist Christian God-Language.* Minneapolis, MN: Fortress Press, 1995.

Wren, Brian A. *What Language Shall I Borrow?: God-Talk in Worship: A Male Response to Feminist Theology.* Eugene, OR: Wipf & Stock, 2009.

Sources for Reflection Paragraphs

Berry, Wendell. *A Timbered Choir: The Sabbath Poems 1979–1997.* Washington, DC: Counterpoint, 1998.

———. *Collected Poems 1957–1982.* San Francisco: North Point Press, 1984.

Bly, Robert. *Selected Poems.* New York: Harper & Row, 1986.

De Waal, Esther. *To Pause at the Threshold: Reflections on Living on the Border.* Harrisburg, PA: Morehouse, 2001.

Falk, Marcia. *The Book of Blessings: New Jewish Prayers for Daily Life, the Sabbath, and the New Moon Festival.* San Francisco: HarperSanFrancisco, 1996.

Frost, Robert. *The Poetry of Robert Frost: The Collected Poems, Complete and Unabridged.* Edited by Edward Connery Lathem. New York: Henry Holt and Company, 1969.

Hays, Edward. *Prayers for a Planetary Pilgrim: A Personal Manual for Prayer and Ritual.* Notre Dame, IN: Ave Maria, 2008.

———. *Prayer Notes to a Friend.* Notre Dame, IN: Forest of Peace Books, 2002.

Huck, Gabe, ed. *A Sourcebook about Liturgy.* Chicago: Liturgy Training Publications, 1994.

Intrator, Sam M., and Megan Scribner, eds. *Leading from Within: Poetry That Sustains the Courage to Lead.* San Francisco: Jossey-Bass, 2007.

Merrill, Nan C. *Psalms for Praying: An Invitation to Wholeness.* New York: Continuum, 2006.

Oliver, Mary. *New and Selected Poems.* Boston: Beacon Press, 1992.

———. *Winter Hours: Prose, Prose Poems, and Poems.* Boston: Houghton Mifflin Company, 1999.

Piercy, Marge. *Circles on the Water.* New York: Alfred A. Knopf, Inc., 1982.

Rilke, Rainer Maria. *Selected Poems of Rainer Maria Rilke.* Translated by Robert Bly. New York: Harper & Row, 1981.

Rumi, Jalal al-Din. *The Essential Rumi.* Translated by Coleman Barks. San Francisco: HarperOne, 2004.

———. *The Soul of Rumi: A New Collection of Ecstatic Poems.* Translated by Coleman Barks. San Francisco: HarperOne, 2001.

Whyte, David. *Everything Is Waiting for You.* Langley, WA: Many Rivers Press, 2003.

———. *Fire in the Earth.* Langley, WA: Many Rivers Press, 1999.

———. *The House of Belonging.* Langley, WA: Many Rivers Press, 1996.

———. *Songs for Coming Home.* Langley, WA: Many Rivers Press, 1999.

———. *Where Many Rivers Meet.* Langley, WA: Many Rivers Press, 1993.

Inspiration

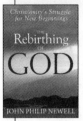

The Rebirthing of God
Christianity's Struggle for New Beginnings
By John Philip Newell
Drawing on modern prophets from East and West, and using the holy island of Iona as an icon of new beginnings, Celtic poet, peacemaker and scholar John Philip Newell dares us to imagine a new birth from deep within Christianity, a fresh stirring of the Spirit.
6 x 9, 160 pp, HC, 978-1-59473-542-4 **$19.99**

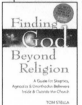

Finding God Beyond Religion: A Guide for Skeptics, Agnostics & Unorthodox Believers Inside & Outside the Church
By Tom Stella; Foreword by The Rev. Canon Marianne Wells Borg
Reinterprets traditional religious teachings central to the Christian faith for people who have outgrown the beliefs and devotional practices that once made sense to them.
6 x 9, 160 pp, Quality PB, 978-1-59473-485-4 **$16.99**

Fully Awake and Truly Alive: Spiritual Practices to Nurture Your Soul
By Rev. Jane E. Vennard; Foreword by Rami Shapiro
Illustrates the joys and frustrations of spiritual practice, offers insights from various religious traditions and provides exercises and meditations to help us become more fully alive.
6 x 9, 208 pp, Quality PB, 978-1-59473-473-1 **$16.99**

Journeys of Simplicity: Traveling Light with Thomas Merton, Bashō, Edward Abbey, Annie Dillard & Others   *By Philip Harnden*
Invites you to consider a more graceful way of traveling through life. PB includes journal pages to help you get started on your own spiritual journey.
5½ x 7¼, 144 pp, Quality PB, 978-1-59473-181-5 **$12.99**
5½ x 7¼, 128 pp, HC, 978-1-893361-76-8 **$16.95**

Perennial Wisdom for the Spiritually Independent
Sacred Teachings—Annotated & Explained
Annotation by Rami Shapiro; Foreword by Richard Rohr
Weaves sacred texts and teachings from the world's major religions into a coherent exploration of the five core questions at the heart of every religion's search.
5½ x 8½, 336 pp, Quality PB Original, 978-1-59473-515-8 **$16.99**

Saving Civility: 52 Ways to Tame Rude, Crude & Attitude for a Polite Planet
By Sara Hacala
Provides fifty-two practical ways you can reverse the course of incivility and make the world a more enriching, pleasant place to live.
6 x 9, 240 pp, Quality PB, 978-1-59473-314-7 **$16.99**

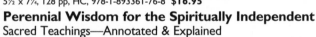
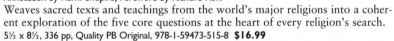

Spiritually Healthy Divorce: Navigating Disruption with Insight & Hope
By Carolyne Call
A spiritual map to help you move through the twists and turns of divorce.
6 x 9, 224 pp, Quality PB, 978-1-59473-288-1 **$16.99**

Or phone, fax, mail or email to: SKYLIGHT PATHS Publishing
Sunset Farm Offices, Route 4 • P.O. Box 237 • Woodstock, Vermont 05091
Tel: (802) 457-4000 • Fax: (802) 457-4004 • www.skylightpaths.com
Credit card orders: (800) 962-4544 (8:30AM–5:30PM EST Monday–Friday)
Generous discounts on quantity orders. SATISFACTION GUARANTEED. Prices subject to change.

Prayer / Meditation

Calling on God
Inclusive Christian Prayers for Three Years of Sundays
By Peter Bankson and Deborah Sokolove
Prayers for today's world, vividly written for Christians who long for a way to talk to and about God that feels fresh yet still connected to tradition.
6 x 9, 400 pp, Quality PB, 978-1-59473-568-4 **$18.99**

Openings, 2nd Edition
A Daybook of Saints, Sages, Psalms and Prayer Practices
By Rev. Larry J. Peacock
For anyone hungry for a richer prayer life, this prayer book offers daily inspiration to help you move closer to God. Draws on a wide variety of resources—lives of saints and sages from every age, psalms, and suggestions for personal reflection and practice. 6 x 9, 448 pp, Quality PB, 978-1-59473-545-5 **$18.99**

Men Pray: Voices of Strength, Faith, Healing, Hope and Courage
Created by the Editors at SkyLight Paths
Celebrates the rich variety of ways men around the world have called out to the Divine—with words of joy, praise, gratitude, wonder, petition and even anger—from the ancient world up to our own day.
5 x 7¼, 192 pp, HC, 978-1-59473-395-6 **$16.99**

Honest to God Prayer: Spirituality as Awareness, Empowerment,
Relinquishment and Paradox
By Kent Ira Groff
6 x 9, 192 pp, Quality PB, 978-1-59473-433-5 **$16.99**

Praying with Our Hands: 21 Practices of Embodied Prayer from the World's
Spiritual Traditions *By Jon M. Sweeney; Photos by Jennifer J. Wilson; Foreword by Mother Tessa Bielecki; Afterword by Taitetsu Unno, PhD*
8 x 8, 96 pp, 22 duotone photos, Quality PB, 978-1-893361-16-4 **$16.95**

Sacred Attention: A Spiritual Practice for Finding God in the Moment
By Margaret D. McGee
6 x 9, 144 pp, Quality PB, 978-1-59473-291-1 **$16.99**

Secrets of Prayer: A Multifaith Guide to Creating Personal Prayer in Your Life
By Nancy Corcoran, CSJ
6 x 9, 160 pp, Quality PB, 978-1-59473-215-7 **$16.99**

Women of Color Pray: Voices of Strength, Faith, Healing, Hope and Courage
Edited and with Introductions by Christal M. Jackson
5 x 7¼, 208 pp, Quality PB, 978-1-59473-077-1 **$15.99**

Prayer / M. Basil Pennington, OCSO

Finding Grace at the Center, 3rd Edition: The Beginning of
Centering Prayer *With Thomas Keating, OCSO, and Thomas E. Clarke, SJ; Foreword by Rev. Cynthia Bourgeault, PhD* A practical guide to a simple and beautiful form of meditative prayer. 5 x 7¼, 128 pp, Quality PB, 978-1-59473-182-2 **$12.99**

The Monks of Mount Athos: A Western Monk's Extraordinary
Spiritual Journey on Eastern Holy Ground *Foreword by Archimandrite Dionysios*
Explores the landscape, monastic communities and food of Athos.
6 x 9, 352 pp, Quality PB, 978-1-893361-78-2 **$18.95**

Psalms: A Spiritual Commentary *Illus. by Phillip Ratner*
Reflections on some of the most beloved passages from the Bible's most widely read book. 6 x 9, 176 pp, 24 full-page b/w illus., Quality PB, 978-1-59473-234-8 **$16.99**

The Song of Songs: A Spiritual Commentary *Illus. by Phillip Ratner*
Explore the Bible's most challenging mystical text.
6 x 9, 160 pp, 14 full-page b/w illus., Quality PB, 978-1-59473-235-5 **$16.99**
HC, 978-1-59473-004-7 **$19.99**

Sacred Texts—SkyLight Illuminations Series

Offers today's spiritual seeker an enjoyable entry into the great classic texts of the world's spiritual traditions. Each classic is presented in an accessible translation, with facing pages of guided commentary from experts, giving you the keys you need to understand the history, context and meaning of the text.

CHRISTIANITY

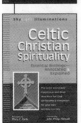

The Book of Common Prayer: A Spiritual Treasure Chest— Selections Annotated & Explained
Annotation by The Rev. Canon C. K. Robertson, PhD; Foreword by The Most Rev. Katharine Jefferts Schori; Preface by Archbishop Desmond Tutu
Makes available the riches of this spiritual treasure chest for all who are interested in deepening their life of prayer, building stronger relationships and making a difference in their world.   5½ x 8½. 208 pp, Quality PB Original, 978-1-59473-524-0 **$16.99**

Celtic Christian Spirituality: Essential Writings—Annotated & Explained
Annotation by Mary C. Earle; Foreword by John Philip Newell
Explores how the writings of this lively tradition embody the gospel.
5½ x 8½, 176 pp, Quality PB, 978-1-59473-302-4 **$16.99**

Desert Fathers and Mothers: Early Christian Wisdom Sayings— Annotated & Explained   *Annotation by Christine Valters Paintner, PhD*
Opens up wisdom of the desert fathers and mothers for readers with no previous knowledge of Western monasticism and early Christianity.
5½ x 8½, 192 pp, Quality PB, 978-1-59473-373-4 **$16.99**

The End of Days: Essential Selections from Apocalyptic Texts— Annotated & Explained   *Annotation by Robert G. Clouse, PhD*
Helps you understand the complex Christian visions of the end of the world.
5½ x 8½, 224 pp, Quality PB, 978-1-59473-170-9 **$16.99**

The Hidden Gospel of Matthew: Annotated & Explained
Translation & Annotation by Ron Miller
Discover the words and events that have the strongest connection to the historical Jesus.
5½ x 8½, 272 pp, Quality PB, 978-1-59473-038-2 **$16.99**

The Imitation of Christ: Selections Annotated & Explained
Annotation by Paul Wesley Chilcote, PhD; By Thomas à Kempis; Adapted from John Wesley's The Christian's Pattern
Let Jesus's example of holiness, humility and purity of heart be a companion on your own spiritual journey.
5½ x 8½, 224 pp, Quality PB, 978-1-59473-434-2 **$16.99**

The Infancy Gospels of Jesus: Apocryphal Tales from the Childhoods of Mary and Jesus—Annotated & Explained
Translation & Annotation by Stevan Davies; Foreword by A. Edward Siecienski, PhD
A startling presentation of the early lives of Mary, Jesus and other biblical figures that will amuse and surprise you.   5½ x 8½, 176 pp, Quality PB, 978-1-59473-258-4 **$16.99**

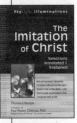

John & Charles Wesley: Selections from Their Writings and Hymns— Annotated & Explained   *Annotation by Paul W. Chilcote, PhD*
A unique presentation of the writings of these two inspiring brothers brings together some of the most essential material from their large corpus of work.
5½ x 8½, 288 pp, Quality PB, 978-1-59473-309-3 **$16.99**

Julian of Norwich: Selections from *Revelations of Divine Love*—Annotated & Explained   *Annotation by Mary C. Earle*
Addresses topics including the infinite nature of God, the life of prayer, God's suffering with us, the eternal and undying life of the soul, the motherhood of Jesus and the motherhood of God and more.
5½ x 8½, 224 pp, Quality PB Original, 978-1-59473-513-4 **$16.99**

Sacred Texts—continued

CHRISTIANITY—continued

The Lost Sayings of Jesus: Teachings from Ancient Christian, Jewish, Gnostic and Islamic Sources—Annotated & Explained
Translation & Annotation by Andrew Phillip Smith; Foreword by Stephan A. Hoeller
Depicts Jesus as a Wisdom teacher who speaks to people of all faiths as a mystic and spiritual master. 5½ x 8½, 240 pp, Quality PB, 978-1-59473-172-3 **$16.99**

Philokalia: The Eastern Christian Spiritual Texts—Selections
Annotated & Explained *Annotation by Allyne Smith; Translation by G. E. H. Palmer, Phillip Sherrard and Bishop Kallistos Ware* The first approachable introduction to the wisdom of the Philokalia. 5½ x 8½, 240 pp, Quality PB, 978-1-59473-103-7 **$16.99**

The Sacred Writings of Paul: Selections Annotated & Explained
Translation & Annotation by Ron Miller Leads you into the exciting immediacy of Paul's teachings. 5½ x 8½, 224 pp, Quality PB, 978-1-59473-213-3 **$16.99**

Saint Augustine of Hippo: Selections from *Confessions* and Other Essential Writings—Annotated & Explained
Annotation by Joseph T. Kelley, PhD; Translation by the Augustinian Heritage Institute
Provides insight into the mind and heart of this foundational Christian figure.
5½ x 8½, 272 pp, Quality PB, 978-1-59473-282-9 **$16.99**

Saint Ignatius Loyola—The Spiritual Writings: Selections
Annotated & Explained *Annotation by Mark Mossa, SJ* Focuses on the practical mysticism of Ignatius of Loyola. 5½ x 8½, 288 pp, Quality PB, 978-1-59473-301-7 **$18.99**

Sex Texts from the Bible: Selections Annotated & Explained
Translation & Annotation by Teresa J. Hornsby; Foreword by Amy-Jill Levine
Demystifies the Bible's ideas on gender roles, marriage, sexual orientation, virginity, lust and sexual pleasure. 5½ x 8½, 208 pp, Quality PB, 978-1-59473-217-1 **$16.99**

Spiritual Writings on Mary: Annotated & Explained
Annotation by Mary Ford-Grabowsky; Foreword by Andrew Harvey
Examines the role of Mary, the mother of Jesus, as a source of inspiration in history and in life today. 5½ x 8½, 272 pp, Quality PB, 978-1-59473-001-6 **$16.99**

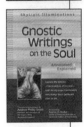

The Way of a Pilgrim: The Jesus Prayer Journey—Annotated & Explained
Translation & Annotation by Gleb Pokrovsky; Foreword by Andrew Harvey A classic of Russian Orthodox spirituality. 5½ x 8½, 160 pp, Illus., Quality PB, 978-1-893361-31-7 **$15.99**

GNOSTICISM

Gnostic Writings on the Soul: Annotated & Explained
Translation & Annotation by Andrew Phillip Smith; Foreword by Stephan A. Hoeller
Reveals the inspiring ways your soul can remember and return to its unique, divine purpose. 5½ x 8½, 144 pp, Quality PB, 978-1-59473-220-1 **$16.99**

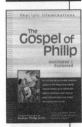

The Gospel of Philip: Annotated & Explained
Translation & Annotation by Andrew Phillip Smith; Foreword by Stevan Davies
Reveals otherwise unrecorded sayings of Jesus and fragments of Gnostic mythology.
5½ x 8½, 160 pp, Quality PB, 978-1-59473-111-2 **$16.99**

The Gospel of Thomas: Annotated & Explained
Translation & Annotation by Stevan Davies; Foreword by Andrew Harvey
Sheds new light on the origins of Christianity and portrays Jesus as a wisdom-loving sage.
5½ x 8½, 192 pp, Quality PB, 978-1-893361-45-4 **$16.99**

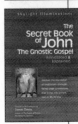

The Secret Book of John: The Gnostic Gospel—Annotated & Explained
Translation & Annotation by Stevan Davies The most significant and influential text of the ancient Gnostic religion. 5½ x 8½, 208 pp, Quality PB, 978-1-59473-082-5 **$16.99**

See Inspiration for *Perennial Wisdom for the Spiritually Independent: Sacred Teachings—Annotated & Explained*

Women's Interest

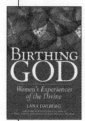

Birthing God: Women's Experiences of the Divine
By Lana Dalberg; Foreword by Kathe Schaaf
Powerful narratives of suffering, love and hope that inspire both personal and collective transformation. 6 x 9, 304 pp, Quality PB, 978-1-59473-480-9 **$18.99**

On the Chocolate Trail: A Delicious Adventure Connecting Jews, Religions, History, Travel, Rituals and Recipes to the Magic of Cacao
By Rabbi Deborah R. Prinz
Take a delectable journey through the religious history of chocolate—a real treat!
6 x 9, 272 pp, 20+ b/w photographs, Quality PB, 978-1-58023-487-0 **$18.99***

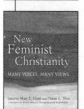

Women, Spirituality and Transformative Leadership
Where Grace Meets Power
Edited by Kathe Schaaf, Kay Lindahl, Kathleen S. Hurty, PhD, and Reverend Guo Cheen
A dynamic conversation on the power of women's spiritual leadership and its emerging patterns of transformation.
6 x 9, 288 pp, Quality PB, 978-1-59473-548-6 **$18.99**; HC, 978-1-59473-313-0 **$24.99**

Spiritually Healthy Divorce: Navigating Disruption with Insight & Hope
By Carolyne Call A spiritual map to help you move through the twists and turns of divorce. 6 x 9, 224 pp, Quality PB, 978-1-59473-288-1 **$16.99**

New Feminist Christianity: Many Voices, Many Views
Edited by Mary E. Hunt and Diann L. Neu
Insights from ministers and theologians, activists and leaders, artists and liturgists offer a starting point for building new models of religious life and worship.
6 x 9, 384 pp, Quality PB, 978-1-59473-435-9 **$19.99**; HC, 978-1-59473-285-0 **$24.99**

Bread, Body, Spirit: Finding the Sacred in Food
Edited and with Introductions by Alice Peck 6 x 9, 224 pp, Quality PB, 978-1-59473-242-3 **$19.99**

Dance—The Sacred Art: The Joy of Movement as a Spiritual Practice
By Cynthia Winton-Henry 5½ x 8½, 224 pp, Quality PB, 978-1-59473-268-3 **$16.99**

Daughters of the Desert: Stories of Remarkable Women from Christian, Jewish and Muslim Traditions
By Claire Rudolf Murphy, Meghan Nuttall Sayres, Mary Cronk Farrell, Sarah Conover and Betsy Wharton
5½ x 8½, 192 pp, Illus., Quality PB, 978-1-59473-106-8 **$14.99** Inc. reader's discussion guide

The Divine Feminine in Biblical Wisdom Literature
Selections Annotated & Explained
Translation & Annotation by Rabbi Rami Shapiro; Foreword by Rev. Cynthia Bourgeault, PhD
5½ x 8½, 240 pp, Quality PB, 978-1-59473-109-9 **$16.99**

Divining the Body: Reclaim the Holiness of Your Physical Self
By Jan Phillips 8 x 8, 256 pp, Quality PB, 978-1-59473-080-1 **$18.99**

Honoring Motherhood: Prayers, Ceremonies & Blessings
Edited and with Introductions by Lynn L. Caruso
5 x 7¼, 272 pp, Quality PB, 978-1-58473-384-0 **$9.99**; HC, 978-1-59473-239-3 **$19.99**

Next to Godliness: Finding the Sacred in Housekeeping
Edited by Alice Peck 6 x 9, 224 pp, Quality PB, 978-1-59473-214-0 **$19.99**

ReVisions: Seeing Torah through a Feminist Lens
By Rabbi Elyse Goldstein 5½ x 8½, 224 pp, Quality PB, 978-1-58023-117-6 **$16.95***

The Triumph of Eve & Other Subversive Bible Tales
By Matt Biers-Ariel 5½ x 8½, 192 pp, Quality PB, 978-1-59473-176-1 **$14.99**

White Fire: A Portrait of Women Spiritual Leaders in America
By Malka Drucker; Photos by Gay Block 7 x 10, 320 pp, b/w photos, HC, 978-1-893361-64-5 **$24.95**

Woman Spirit Awakening in Nature: Growing Into the Fullness of Who You Are
By Nancy Barrett Chickerneo, PhD; Foreword by Eileen Fisher
8 x 8, 224 pp, b/w illus., Quality PB, 978-1-59473-250-8 **$16.99**

Women of Color Pray: Voices of Strength, Faith, Healing, Hope and Courage
Edited and with Introductions by Christal M. Jackson
5 x 7¼, 208 pp, Quality PB, 978-1-59473-077-1 **$15.99**

* A book from Jewish Lights, SkyLight Paths' sister imprint

Spirituality

Like a Child
Restoring the Awe, Wonder, Joy and Resiliency of the Human Spirit
By Rev. Timothy J. Mooney

By breaking free from our misperceptions about what it means to be an adult, we can reshape our world and become harbingers of grace. This unique spiritual resource explores Jesus's counsel to become like children in order to enter the kingdom of God.   6 x 9, 160 pp, Quality PB, 978-1-59473-543-1 **$16.99**

The Passionate Jesus: What We Can Learn from Jesus about Love, Fear, Grief, Joy and Living Authentically
By The Rev. Peter Wallace

Reveals Jesus as a passionate figure who was involved, present, connected, honest and direct with others and encourages you to build personal authenticity in every area of your own life. 6 x 9, 208 pp, Quality PB, 978-1-59473-393-2 **$18.99**

Gathering at God's Table: The Meaning of Mission in the Feast of Faith
By Katharine Jefferts Schori

A profound reminder of our role in the larger frame of God's dream for a restored and reconciled world.   6 x 9, 256 pp, HC, 978-1-59473-316-1 **$21.99**

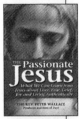

The Heartbeat of God: Finding the Sacred in the Middle of Everything
By Katharine Jefferts Schori; Foreword by Joan Chittister, OSB

Explores our connections to other people, to other nations and with the environment through the lens of faith.
6 x 9, 240 pp, HC, 978-1-59473-292-8 **$21.99**

A Dangerous Dozen: Twelve Christians Who Threatened the Status Quo but Taught Us to Live Like Jesus
By the Rev. Canon C. K. Robertson, PhD; Foreword by Archbishop Desmond Tutu

Profiles twelve visionary men and women who challenged society and showed the world a different way of living.
6 x 9, 208 pp, Quality PB, 978-1-59473-298-0 **$16.99**

Laugh Your Way to Grace: Reclaiming the Spiritual Power of Humor
By Rev. Susan Sparks

A powerful, humorous case for laughter as a spiritual, healing path.
6 x 9, 176 pp, Quality PB, 978-1-59473-280-5 **$16.99**

Claiming Earth as Common Ground: The Ecological Crisis through the Lens of Faith
By Andrea Cohen-Kiener; Foreword by Rev. Sally Bingham
6 x 9, 192 pp, Quality PB, 978-1-59473-261-4 **$16.99**

Living into Hope: A Call to Spiritual Action for Such a Time as This
By Rev. Dr. Joan Brown Campbell; Foreword by Karen Armstrong
6 x 9, 208 pp, Quality PB, 978-1-59473-436-6 $18.99; HC, 978-1-59473-283-6 **$21.99**

Renewal in the Wilderness
A Spiritual Guide to Connecting with God in the Natural World
By John Lionberger 6 x 9, 176 pp, b/w photos, Quality PB, 978-1-59473-219-5 **$16.99**

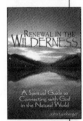

Spiritual Adventures in the Snow
Skiing & Snowboarding as Renewal for Your Soul
By Dr. Marcia McFee and Rev. Karen Foster; Foreword by Paul Arthur
5½ x 8½, 208 pp, Quality PB, 978-1-59473-270-6 **$16.99**

A Walk with Four Spiritual Guides: Krishna, Buddha, Jesus, and Ramakrishna
By Andrew Harvey 5½ x 8½ 192 pp, b/w photos & illus., Quality PB, 978-1-59473-138-9 **$15.99**

Who Is My God? 2nd Edition: An Innovative Guide to Finding Your Spiritual Identity
By the Editors at SkyLight Paths

Provides the Spiritual Identity Self-Test™ to uncover the components of your unique spirituality.
6 x 9, 160 pp, Quality PB, 978-1-59473-014-6 **$15.99**

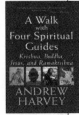

About SKYLIGHT PATHS Publishing

SkyLight Paths Publishing is creating a place where people of different spiritual traditions come together for challenge and inspiration, a place where we can help each other understand the mystery that lies at the heart of our existence.

Through spirituality, our religious beliefs are increasingly becoming a part of our lives—rather than *apart* from our lives. While many of us may be more interested than ever in spiritual growth, we may be less firmly planted in traditional religion. Yet, we do want to deepen our relationship to the sacred, to learn from our own as well as from other faith traditions, and to practice in new ways.

SkyLight Paths sees both believers and seekers as a community that increasingly transcends traditional boundaries of religion and denomination—people wanting to learn from each other, *walking together, finding the way.*

For your information and convenience, at the back of this book we have provided a list of other SkyLight Paths books you might find interesting and useful. They cover the following subjects:

Buddhism / Zen	Gnosticism	Poetry
Catholicism	Hinduism / Vedanta	Prayer
Chaplaincy		Religious Etiquette
Children's Books	Inspiration	Retirement & Later-Life Spirituality
Christianity	Islam / Sufism	
Comparative Religion	Judaism	Spiritual Biography
	Meditation	Spiritual Direction
Earth-Based Spirituality	Mindfulness	Spirituality
	Monasticism	Women's Interest
Enneagram	Mysticism	Worship
Global Spiritual Perspectives	Personal Growth	

Or phone, fax, mail or email to: SKYLIGHT PATHS Publishing
Sunset Farm Offices, Route 4 • P.O. Box 237 • Woodstock, Vermont 05091
Tel: (802) 457-4000 • Fax: (802) 457-4004 • www.skylightpaths.com
Credit card orders: (800) 962-4544 (8:30AM–5:30PM EST Monday–Friday)
Generous discounts on quantity orders. SATISFACTION GUARANTEED. Prices subject to change.